MW00938247

"*Unlocking the Invisible Child* is a riveting a̶c̶c̶o̶u̶n̶t̶ ̶o̶f̶ ̶w̶h̶a̶t̶ ̶h̶e̶a̶l̶i̶n̶g̶ about. It is must-reading for all who seek wholeness."

—CHRISTIANE NORTHRUP, M.D., author of the New York Times bestsellers *Women's Bodies, Women's Wisdom and The Wisdom of Menopause*

"There are as many paths toward healing as there are individuals in need of healing. This means there is no formula, no sure-fire, cookie-cutter method that applies to everyone. *Unlocking the Invisible Child* is the amazing account of Laura Mayer's remarkable journey. She reveals to us a truth—that healing is and has always been the unique journey of the soul. Mayer writes from the heart. Her courageous account will inspire and encourage anyone who wants to be more than they are at present."

—LARRY DOSSEY, M.D., author of *The Power of Premonitions, Healing Words,* and *Reinventing Medicine*

"Laura Mayer has written a gentle and engaging guide to inner and outer healing. She displays a deep understanding of how relinquishment of the past is accomplished and the essential role it plays in transformation. The reader feels lifted into arms of understanding and love and carried down a path of enlightenment. Perhaps most importantly, as a parent and spiritual teacher, her insights into how to see through the eyes of children are revolutionary."

—HUGH PRATHER, author of *Notes to Myself* and *The Little Book of Letting Go*

"I have known Laura Mayer for many years and have witnessed her transformation into an inspiring teacher with an amazing life story. She is dedicated to helping others discover the healing powers that reside in each of us and is a living example of someone who has successfully challenged predictions of western medicine which, had they been correct, would have buried this remarkable woman many years ago. Her own story is important for many to experience, and I would encourage anyone to take a few minutes and find out why."

—DAVID COOPER, author of *God Is a Verb*

Unlocking the Invisible Child will not only touch your heart but also give you the courage to heal absolutely anything about your life. Through the lens of her own life experiences, Laura Mayer shows the reader how she healed herself from a genetically degenerative disease. *Unlocking the Invisible Child* is a must-read for anyone who doubts the power of the human spirit to heal and transform, and for every parent to learn how to best nurture a sensitive child."

—CAROL LYNN FITZPATRICK, author of
A Call to Remember and *Fear Not My Child*

"Laura Mayer's journey to mental, physical and spiritual healing will give hope and motivation to many on a similar path. Revealed within her personal story is the profound connection between our precious thoughts and their astonishing effect on our mental and physical condition. Her transformation from victim of circumstance bearing the feeling of unworthiness to the creator of circumstance sustaining the feeling of love and self-worth is inspiring. It is a great testament to the power of the will within each of us for peace."

—HOWARD FALCO, author of
I AM: The Power of Discovering Who You Really Are

"Laura Mayer is a brave, courageous woman, who refused to let the adversity of severe physical pain ruin her life. With deep soul-searching and abiding faith in the world of Spirit, she came to understand her suffering and — with the help of many — bring about her own healing. Her story is an inspiration to every human being who seeks the hope and promise of recovery, and the grace of God's love and blessing.

—RABBI WAYNE DOSICK, PH.D & ELLEN KAUFMAN DOSICK, MSW authors,
Empowering Your Indigo Child and 20 Minute Kabbalah

"Laura's thoughtful and detailed analysis of the influences in her life that made her a beautiful woman is shared in easily readable prose. [Her] journey, made possible by her intense curiosity and courage, captivates the reader and provides a metaphor for all of us to try to understand why we are who we are and what we can do to improve the quality of our lives. Read this book and be prepared to challenge yourself to a life worth living."

—MARK BELSKY, M.D., Chief of Hand Surgery
Newton-Wellesley Hospital Tufts-New England Medical Center

UNLOCKING
THE INVISIBLE CHILD

A Journey from Heartbreak to Bliss

Sarah — Open your heart to who you are and not what you believe to be. Be open to you. Blessing

Laura Mayer

BALBOA
PRESS

A DIVISION OF HAY HOUSE

Copyright © 2012 Laura Mayer

All rights reserved. No part of this book may be used or reproduced by any means, graphic, electronic, or mechanical, including photocopying, recording, taping or by any information storage retrieval system without the written permission of the publisher except in the case of brief quotations embodied in critical articles and reviews.

Balboa Press books may be ordered through booksellers or by contacting:

Balboa Press
A Division of Hay House
1663 Liberty Drive
Bloomington, IN 47403
www.balboapress.com
1-(877) 407-4847

ISBN: 978-1-4525-4190-7 (sc)
ISBN: 978-1-4525-4192-1 (hc)
ISBN: 978-1-4525-4191-4 (e)

Library of Congress Control Number: 2011919523

Because of the dynamic nature of the Internet, any web addresses or links contained in this book may have changed since publication and may no longer be valid. The views expressed in this work are solely those of the author and do not necessarily reflect the views of the publisher, and the publisher hereby disclaims any responsibility for them.

The author of this book does not dispense medical advice or prescribe the use of any technique as a form of treatment for physical, emotional, or medical problems without the advice of a physician, either directly or indirectly. The intent of the author is only to offer information of a general nature to help you in your quest for emotional and spiritual well-being. In the event you use any of the information in this book for yourself, which is your constitutional right, the author and the publisher assume no responsibility for your actions.

Author photo and front cover photo by Carole Hodges

Printed in the United States of America

Balboa Press rev. date: 1/27/2011

Author's Note

Everything in this book is true. I have
changed some names out of respect
for privacy.

To my parents,
and
in memory
of
Buddy

CONTENTS

PART III. HERE I AM: STEPPING UP TO THE PLATE

There once was a bird that was let out of a cage.
Are you the bird or the cage?

Tell us a story about freedom,
and how you make choice.
—Carol Fitzpatrick

INTRODUCTION

Having the courage to love yourself enough . . .

THIS BOOK, *UNLOCKING THE INVISIBLE Child: A Journey from Heartbreak to Bliss* is about my personal transformation to wholeness, and what it may mean for others yearning to be healed. My original story no longer defines me. I have written a new and unabridged version of my story in which I healed my soul and my body.

Throughout most of my life, I suffered from Anterior Horn Cell disease, a progressive, degenerative neurological condition originating in the gray matter of the spinal cord, which doctors told me would leave me crippled by age twenty-five and would end my life by forty. Physically, this meant I was locked inside a body slowly collapsing inward, losing muscle mass in my arms and pulling the tendons of my hands into the shape of claws. Despite this prognosis, I never gave up on improving my life. I attended both college and graduate school, and then pursued a career in occupational therapy. I married and gave birth to two healthy children. After numerous operations on my hands, and, more importantly, traveling into and through the heart of my darkness, I have reversed the course of this "incurable" malady and emerged as a victorious representative of faith over fear and of will over weakness and powerlessness.

As you read my story of transformation, acceptance, empowerment, and grace, I hope that you will connect with your own healing energy.

For you, too, have a right to be healthy and fully present in your life as a co-creator of your destiny. No matter what type of disease or discomfort you face, my story is here to inspire you, so you can develop the courage to believe you can achieve the life you want. You can let go of fear and control and replace it with the willingness to trust in something larger than yourself. And you can cultivate the determination to move forward and disentangle yourself from whatever ails you or disturbs your peace.

Disease comes from spiritual uneasiness embedded deep within our cellular makeup. The name of any "dis-ease" is merely a medical term used to classify a particular set of symptoms so they can be managed; it does not reveal the *root cause* of those symptoms, which is invisible to the eye. My life experiences demonstrate that healing begins on unseen levels of the soul, beliefs, and emotions before manifesting at the level of the physical body. As you read on, you'll become acquainted with a woman who struggled to find herself since her childhood, and who ultimately was able to appear in the radiant and loving way she chose to be seen. This book is about her invisible child becoming visible.

Fortunately, at age twenty-six, while employed at Tufts–New England Medical Center as an occupational therapist, I met a courageous hand surgeon who suggested we perform a series of reconstructive tendon transfers to restore some semblance of functioning to my nearly paralyzed hands. Most other specialists in his field wouldn't have taken on such a task, because the disease I had was based in my spine, not in my hands. He saw beyond the disease and witnessed a tenacious yet scared young woman who was losing the battle of performing the simplest tasks of daily living. The surgeries helped for a while, but through the years my hands continued to deteriorate. Eventually, I had to stop working and accept the reality that I was disabled.

At my rock bottom, feeling there was nowhere to go but up, I became deeply involved in a spiritual healing path that combined teachings from the mystical traditions of Kabbalah and Eastern philosophies. That's when the real miracle began. There were moments of pure ecstasy interspersed with moments of pure grief, as I placed myself within a community of like-minded individuals dedicated to spiritual awakening. My eyes were being opened to the parallel patterns of my inner life and my illness. If the gray matter of the spine is connected to movement, where had I felt emotionally constricted? If I felt alone and deprived of love, how could I demonstrate loving-kindness to myself? As I explored these patterns through the metaphor of Jacob's ladder reaching toward God, I began to view my illness as a tremendous opportunity for understanding.

In December of 2002, I asked, "What is this sadness that permeates my being? Why are my body, mind and soul filled with such unbearable pain, and how can I let go of it?" To find answers, I threw myself even more wholeheartedly into my spiritual quest, entering a deepening process in which I began questioning aspects of my life that I had never investigated before. I immersed myself in the metaphysical world of soul readings, energetic healing and vibrational medicine. And I made a total commitment to become healed, knowing with certainty that this had to occur on a cellular level. There would be no shortcuts, no magical cures.

My belief was pure and my vision was guided. Nothing was going to stop me on my path. I began to focus on developing my intuitive and healing abilities. I studied various modalities and attended many spiritual workshops and retreats. Through activations and clearings on the soul level, I was eventually able to shift my body matrix and redefine "me." Gradually, my body responded and became stronger. The tendons in my hands began to open and relax of their own accord. My ability to function and manage daily activities improved. The more I healed, the more I was encouraged to act as an open channel to guide others in their healing.

Thus, over a period of several years, I developed a sense of greater inner knowing, from which has arisen a profound shift in my consciousness. This led to the restoration of my health. Most importantly, I witnessed the miracle of my heart healing. I'm no longer the person I was before. My "new" story is about never losing faith, no matter what threatens to erode my spiritual core.

Sitting down to write this book, I began stepping back into the "old" story again while bringing to the surface detailed memories of my early life. During this emotional excavation, I witnessed the tremendous energy that my memories evoked within me. Feelings of anger, sadness, regret and loneliness bubbled up as my fingers danced on the keyboard. As new connections emerged between various events and my feelings about them, I was provided with a constant wellspring of insights to contemplate. I contacted the sadness and pain I endured throughout my life, as well as the joy and gratitude I felt upon realizing the universe had always been benevolently guiding me. I also recognized the inner strength I had always possessed that enabled me to continue in my quest to understand the "me nobody knew."

Writing this book enabled me to relive feelings I repressed long ago. It helped me release pain long-buried in my body and psyche, and breathed new life into my soul. In this final part of my grieving, I had a powerful moment of realization, when I finally understood why I had suffered from such a debilitating disease.

Today, I have love and compassion for others who struggle with similar soul confusion. I hold out my arms to the children and adults in our world who feel they have never been seen or heard. May this story reach into your heart if you are afflicted with any form of dis-ease— emotional, physical or spiritual—and provide you with comfort and motivation. May it empower you to trust in yourself and the universe, to overcome your dis-ease with honor and grace, and to be fully seen, fully heard and fully present in your life from this day forward.

PART I

THE ORIGINAL STORY

"Life can't give to you if your hands are closed."
—Louise Hay

CHAPTER 1

My Story

*I wanted to find the truth even if it killed me—
and it almost did.*

JOYFUL AT AGE FIFTY-FIVE, I witness how my life has completely turned around. Unable to handle the world I lived in as a young child, I had shut down. At the time, I wasn't aware of doing this, but today it is obvious that my cells heard my cry and reacted to the emotional little girl struggling to be noticed and loved. I became the product of an environment in which the message was: Children should be seen and not heard. But I was also not meant to be seen—a belief locking into place a series of traumas that eventually imprisoned me emotionally and physically.

The Lesser Child

She was the child born of hope; I was born of despair. She was my older sister. When I was conceived, my seventeen-year-old mother felt disillusioned in her marriage to my father, whose outlook on life was based on fear and defeat. At the young age of twenty, Buddy was living out a death sentence battling Hodgkin's disease. He had been in the Air Force, stationed at the nuclear testing sight in the Nevada desert, surviving in the only way he knew how: by fighting the world.

It is no wonder my birth was traumatic—two months premature and necessitating my reliance on incubator support for three weeks. I'll never know if Buddy came to hold me or reached his hands through the plastic draping around the incubator to touch me. I longed for his presence throughout my young life.

While he apparently spent most of his time in and out of veteran's hospitals, battling his terminal illness, my mother traveled between Maine, where his family resided, and Manhattan, where her mother lived. My mother, sister, and I soon moved into my grandmother's apartment in Manhattan. Nana, as I called her, was divorced and lived with her teenage son Carl, who now shared his apartment with his older sister and her two young babies. Nana Ruth, who played the role of mother, guided us through this tumultuous period in our lives, while my grandpa lived a short distance away.

My mother divorced Buddy when I was two years old and soon afterward met Saul, a dentist in the Air Force, and married him. Six months later, my mother left my sister and me behind and joined Saul in Newfoundland to set up our home. During this time, we lived with Nana until my mother returned four months later to take us to our new home on the Air Force Base in Stevensville, Newfoundland, far away from Nana and Grandpa.

Buddy died at age twenty-five, shortly after my third birthday. I have no memories of him, although I do have photographs.

My inner story was all about suffering. It came from feeling disconnected from my parents and older sister—from not being loved—a sense of isolation that later manifested itself in the form of a physical dis-ease. In addition, I suffered from the loss of my biological father, and used my bereavement to keep my sadness and emptiness alive.

The Suffering Child

Throughout my childhood and early teen years, emotional traumas took up residence in my cellular makeup, and my personality responded. At age three, for example, I announced one evening during dinner that I wanted to be a dog, and I started barking as I moved away from the table and onto the floor. My new father, finding my antics neither funny nor cute, proceeded to walk me out to our front porch. "You'll have to stay here because this is where dogs belong," he said. Years later I wondered why my mother or sister didn't come to my rescue, and why I lacked the courage to go inside, scream, or fight. Why did I just stand outside the door watching my family carry on as usual at the dinner table?

When I did start to cry, because I had to go to the bathroom, my new father said, "Dogs go to the bathroom outside." Intense fear coursed through me as I refused to suffer further embarrassment by peeing in my pants. When I was later let back into the house, my father said, "I guess you'll never want to be a dog again."

That day I lost a piece of myself to a world of grief, shame and despair. The resulting sense of separation, alienation and annihilation soon became part of my personality. Over time this primordial scene of humiliating abandonment crystallized into a feeling of being a perpetual outsider looking in. My mother, still a child herself, together with my sister and my new father, were unable to stir a sense of self-awareness within me. As such, the truth of who I was beneath the facade of my story was not revealed.

It took forty years of battling the effects of a crippling disease before I decided not to suffer anymore. "Either I heal or I'm out of here," I stated emphatically to the universe, fully believing that healing was a physical event. Very soon I realized that real healing was soul deep, cellular in nature, and that healing the wounds of my heart would eventually heal every other piece of my being and reveal my true nature.

To Tell the Truth

I have always honored truth. But I was taught when I was very young that truth wasn't always necessary. That set up a conflict in my core beliefs. For example, soon after my stepfather legally adopted both my sister and me, I told a friend that my biological father had died when I was three. My mother scolded me for revealing the truth, and told me not to tell anyone again, stating, "Sometimes it's best not to tell the truth." I left it alone. We never discussed it again. But even though I heard my mother's words, I knew this sentiment could never apply to the girl who came into this world seeking truth. This scenario repeated itself throughout my life.

"Love Me Do"

Invisible to my real self at age nine, I hid away from life, without any clue that I was the perpetrator of my own disembodiment. I felt so lost that I came to believe the only way I could be loved was to be in the hospital. I had learned from watching television that everyone in the hospital gets attended to. So it came as no surprise that one night while trying to fall asleep, I cried out to God, "Maybe if I were in the hospital, the Beatles would come and visit me and then I would be loved by someone." Four years later I ended up in the hospital, but the Beatles never came.

Of course, the Beatles were just the first plea, the outcry of my anguished heart. I reached out to anyone who had the potential to take this inner pain away. Some relief arrived with the birth of a baby brother when I was just shy of my tenth birthday. Andrew, a sweet addition to the family, was the only member who was touchable and who desired my hugs and kisses. Otherwise, feeling unloved myself, I remained wedded to my sense of victimhood, and put out a powerful message that I would accept anything as long as it brought me some attention.

As time passed, I made an effort to gain visibility by becoming a cheerleader, part of the pack of popular girls who were noticed and seen. Cheerleading became the focal point of my social life, making me feel powerful and important. It gave me the confirmation I needed to believe I had a right to belong. But I did not yet realize the necessity of being fully visible to myself before becoming visible to anyone else.

Then at thirteen, I met Michael, who came as a blessing into my emotionally starved life. Michael was by far the best thing that had ever happened to me, giving me what my parents could not—attention, affection, and the freedom to be myself. But so entrenched was I in my suffering, I couldn't fathom that someone could really love me. I often feared that Michael would leave me—and that I wouldn't survive without him. How easy it was for the fear of abandonment to rear its ugly head. And because of my insecurity, I became very needy, an unappealing trait even to a fifteen-year-old boy.

Michael was my first experience in truly giving and receiving the gentleness of love. My psychiatrist explained many years later that Michael wasn't just a first boyfriend, but in fact the first person in my life who was loving. Most people experience the first union of love with their mother, but this was never available to me, because my mother was struggling with her own sense of self and couldn't be emotionally present for me. But Michael could be, and therefore became my prototype for all relationships that followed. I compared everyone to this gold standard in lovability.

Michael carried his own brand of wound, especially a lot of grief and sadness over losses in his own life. But I set aside these observations and focused on the Michael whom I loved and felt safe with. Unfortunately, the tendency to be present to another **when it undermined me** caused me great anguish in every relationship that followed, until I had the courage to love myself enough.

Despite cheerleading and my attachment to Michael, by age thirteen the hole in my soul was so deep no one could fill it. My fear of reliving my relationship with my parents had given birth to another motif— that something—even crumbs of affection—was better than nothing.

Becoming My Story

Everything changed during my freshman year of high school. I was in the kitchen mixing ingredients with an electric eggbeater and accidentally got my left pinky caught in the rotating blades. It was no big deal; it didn't even hurt. I would have forgotten about the incident, except that months later I noticed I couldn't straighten that finger. My mother thought the problem might be connected with the eggbeater incident. My father speculated that a doctor might have to make a small incision on the left side of my hand to repair the damage. He spoke those words while tracing a line down the outside of my hand just below the pinky finger.

Within a few months, I began to feel some numbness and tingling in the area. My parents and I started to wonder. Little did we know that my hands were about to become the physical manifestation of my tormented heart.

CHAPTER 2

The Medical World
Through the Eyes
of a Teenager

I was diagnosed with a disease that was supposed to get worse as I got older, but against all odds, I got better.

To UNRAVEL THE MYSTERY OF my contracted pinky finger with as little trouble as possible, my father suggested we make an appointment with his longtime friend Shelley, a radiologist at the Mount Sinai Medical Center in New York City. Whatever is wrong, he said, would show up in an X-ray. So we traveled the forty minutes to see someone he trusted. From that day forward, nothing would ever be the same.

Batteries of Tests

I liked Shelley. His office felt friendly, and I felt a sense of importance being there because Shelley let me go inside the viewing room to see the results of the films, a privilege most patients did not have. Shelley explained to us that the X-rays indicated no damage to the finger; the source of the problem lay higher up in my arm. He recommended that we seek a second opinion, and referred us to a radiologist who ran his own series of X-rays. The radiologist agreed with Shelley, and referred us to a neurologist. By this time, similar symptoms were manifesting in the fingers of my right hand. Clearly, my symptoms were not related to the eggbeater incident. We continued making our way from one doctor's office to the next, unaware that the contraction in my little finger was just the tip of the iceberg.

In the months following my first set of X-rays, my father and I made many trips to the Mount Sinai Medical Center, meeting with New York City's finest physicians, all of whom diligently tried to find the source of my problem. I soon noticed that the fingers in my right hand were starting to contract, accompanied by numbness and tingling sensations. As months passed, there was clear evidence that I was losing muscle bulk in my fingers and in the palm of my hand. My fingers were starting to claw and hyperextend at the joints, and I couldn't open them fully.

By my freshman year in high school, the disease was already deeply embedded in my cellular makeup. The progression was slow but dramatic. My entire life had altered in the course of several years, and I was constantly plagued with anxiety and stress, never knowing or trusting whether I would be able to perform certain tasks. Always in the back of my mind lurked the biggest fear of all: that someone would notice I was not normal.

My disease soon affected both sides of my body. On December 24, 1969, my dad and I drove into New York City for an appointment with Dr. Seymour Gendelman, a neurologist at the Mount Sinai Medical Center. Although it was Christmas Eve, he was working late and had agreed to see me in his private office on 88th Street, just blocks from the medical center. I instantly took a liking to this kind and gentle man whose desk contained pictures of his three young boys and his wife. A colleague of Shelley's, he did a routine neurological workup and then sent us home.

When we left Dr. Gendelman's office, my dad and I noticed an old-fashioned ice cream parlor on the corner of 88th Street. On the spur of the moment, he suggested that we go inside and have an ice cream. What a treat! My dad rarely made spontaneous offerings, so I seized the occasion to connect with him. Sharing an ice cream gave him the opportunity to express his concern and to show that he understood what I was going through. This extra dose of attention became a ritual I looked forward to whenever we went to see Dr. Gendelman. As much as I enjoyed my visits with him, however, they brought me much anxiety and fear, because I never knew whether the news would be good or bad.

Shortly after our initial visit to Dr. Gendelman, we were referred to Dr. K, the director of rehabilitation medicine at Mount Sinai. When we arrived at our initial visit with her, Dr. K, a pleasant woman in her mid-fifties, came out to greet us and usher us into her office. As she prepared to administer a test called an electromylograph (EMG), a diagnostic tool to measure the electrical activity of muscles at rest and during contraction, she explained the procedure. In conjunction with this test, she also administered a nerve conduction velocity test (NCV) used to measure how well and how fast the nerves send electrical impulses, which make the muscles react in specific ways. Together, the diagnostic tests help evaluate the health of the muscle and the nerves that supply them. Dr. K stuck needles into my muscles, first in my hands, then my arms, shoulders, neck, and chest. This procedure was extremely painful, because after inserting each needle she would wiggle it until some measurable sign registered on the machine. I sat as still as I could while she performed this procedure, one needle at a time. From time to time over the years, Dr. K would have me lie down on the examining table and check my lower extremities as well. Occasionally, she would place needles down my spine.

Disillusionment

One time my mother accompanied me on a follow-up outpatient visit with Dr. K, which was a rarity for her. I was sitting across from Dr. K, with the machine to my left; and my mother was seated behind me, watching. As usual, Dr. K inserted the needles into my hands, arms, chest, and neck, after which she placed them in my spine. It was so painful I wanted to cry, but I fought back my tears. My mother, instead of supporting me in my discomfort, got up and left the room. I was stunned. I remember thinking, "Where is she going? Is she sick?" I never forgot how alone I felt following her departure.

After this battery of tests, my mother and I went to get something to eat at the corner coffee shop. While we were sitting there, I asked her why she had left the office. She replied, "I couldn't sit there and watch what the doctor was doing to you." I replied, "How do you think it felt being *me*? I couldn't get up and walk away." I wanted to say: "I had no one to share my grief and sadness with, no one to help me deal with the excruciating pain. I wanted a loving presence to stand by me on this painful journey."

We never discussed the episode again.

As an adult, I understand how difficult it must have been for her to witness the pain and suffering her daughter had to endure; but had she at least expressed her feelings to me, I would not have felt alone. I was simply looking to my mother for connection and validation.

Another disillusioning moment had occurred earlier, during an appointment with Dr. J., chief of vascular surgery at the Mount Sinai Medical Center. My father and I had spent more than two hours in the waiting room before being called into his office. Dr. J. was a tall man with a strong presence, whose cold, distant demeanor made him seem more like a businessman than a doctor. After a brief physical exam, he concluded that the problem stemmed from the brachial plexus area (spinal nerves C5, C6, C7, C8, and T1 from the roots of the brachial plexus). An impingement on the brachial nerve, he said, caused my symptoms of weakness, tingling, and muscular atrophy. He also noticed that I would lose my pulse when my arms were above my head, a symptom of nerve entrapment.

Dr. J, after confirming this diagnosis with Dr. Gendelman, decided to surgically remove the scalene muscle, which lies just above the clavicle bone on the right side. He hoped the procedure would reverse the process that had been set in motion. The surgery was scheduled for early February, about four weeks away. At the time, the doctors felt positive about the outcome, which was reassuring to both my parents and me. I would miss one week of school, and then life would return to normal.

My parents and I arrived at the hospital. We went through the admissions ordeal, and I was placed in the adult vascular surgical unit rather than the pediatric unit. Because I was fourteen years old, the decision could have gone either way.

Initially, I was relieved when I heard I wouldn't be in the pediatric unit, because I didn't want to listen to the children crying. Here I would have to act like an adult and thus withhold my tears. Later I changed my mind and wished many times that I had been placed in the pediatric unit, where I would have allowed myself to cry with the other children, who were experiencing confusion and fear, just like me. The pediatric unit would also have offered me the opportunity to be loving and available to the younger children in pain. I would have held them and helped them emotionally and spiritually.

First Hopes

I had entered the hospital with a relatively uncomplicated diagnosis: brachial plexus injury. The removal of the scalene muscle was expected to be an easy surgery, and the doctors agreed that the procedure would alleviate pressure on the nerve that was causing the tingling, numbness, and muscular atrophy. The operation, to be performed by Dr. J, would be quick and straightforward, and I would be out of the hospital in a week.

I was escorted to a room with four beds in the vascular surgical unit. The patient next to me, a sixteen-year-old girl who had just undergone back surgery to correct scoliosis, lay flat on her back all day while friends and family visited her. I felt fortunate to have someone young like me in the room; most patients on the floor were older and much more severely ill than I was.

The second day of my hospital stay, a physician came into the room, walked over to the woman diagonally across from me, stood at the foot of her bed, announced that they would be amputating her leg the following morning, and then walked out of the room. I was horrified. I couldn't believe what I had just heard. Who can make such an announcement without showing empathy? How callous and crude these people were! I was grateful that he was not my surgeon. The day of my surgery came. I remember how painful it was. After the operation, just the act of breathing caused me pain. I had to vomit, which I knew was a side effect of the anesthesia. My mother held the bean-shaped "puking" bowl, and I felt grateful that she was there. I also felt ashamed, however, because the sixteen-year-old girl in the bed next to me was now in a total body cast. I had no right to complain about a thing.

As I tried to sleep that first night, I wept quietly, unable to withstand the pain. More than anything I wanted to go home to Michael **and** my friends. A week later, I finally returned home, with a scar just above my collarbone. Michael sent me a loving get-well card with a boy and girl on the front. He had drawn a scar just above the clavicle bone on the right side of the girl so she looked just like me, a sensitive touch that I thought was cute at the time. I believed I was cured, that I would never again set foot in a hospital. The problem persisted, however, and after a few months it became clear that the surgery had not been unsuccessful. The removal of the scalene muscle had done nothing to alter the course of this yet-to-be-defined disease.

I don't remember my family sharing thoughts, feelings, or concerns with me, nor do I remember sharing mine with them. I just wanted the problem to be "fixed." In order to survive as a normal teenager,

I blocked my emotional response, because it would have been too overwhelming.

What I do remember is giving my precious guitar to Michael; I no longer could pluck the strings or place my fingers properly to make the chords. I loved playing the guitar, which brought me joy and solace. Soon I would have to surrender other activities that had been integral to my young life. It became increasingly necessary to learn the subtle art of determining what I could and couldn't do anymore.

Fortunately, the degeneration was slow. The loss of muscle bulk amounted to one millimeter a month. This enabled me to learn compensatory skills—to use other parts of my body and still feel normal. To compensate for the weakness in my fingers, I often used my teeth to open bottles and packages. As a babysitter, I was required to change diapers, so I figured out how to use my teeth to open diaper pins as well.

Because of my weakened, clawed fingers, I had to give up cheerleading, because I could no longer do cartwheels, backward bends or the acrobatics at which I had previously excelled. I was giving up what made me feel special and whole. I watched as my once strong, flexible body slowly disappeared. The doctors advised me not to engage in physical activity, for fear that I would fall on my hands and cause even more damage. Thus, I was exempt from physical education class and prohibited from after-school activities such as tennis and skiing. Nor was I allowed to use the diving board at the town swim club. Swimming, in fact, became arduous, because I had difficulty cupping my hands.

Inwardly, what arose in me was deeper than fear: it was a grief never before externalized. I never grieved for the loss of my physical expression. I'm not even sure I knew what I was feeling at the time. My parents never explored my emotions with me, or guided me in adjusting to my new physical limitations. In fact, no one addressed my physical disease. I just continued living as normally as possible, with only a few people noticing that I was incapable of functioning at my usual level.

As a teenager, I had achieved success by being part of a group that engaged in physical sports. My only sense of belonging was about to end. I would no longer take part in sporting events, cheerleading spectaculars, swim races, or diving competitions with my group of fun-loving friends. I would no longer join my friends for ski trips or for tennis, volleyball, or softball games. With all these losses, I smothered myself in my relationship with Michael, who unfortunately became my magnificent but unhealthy obsession. Since I could still dance, Michael and I would go to dances all the time, allowing me to hold on to a piece of my former life.

As for school, it didn't matter to me anymore, even though Michael would encourage me to do well so we could go to college together. While Michael was an excellent student, all I wanted was to be accepted by my peers. My priorities clearly were wrapped around my relationships, which meant being loved and being important to someone. My happiest moments were in Michael's arms, where I felt safe and never wanted to ever let go.

I spent countless hours on my bedroom floor, listening to my collection of 45s and crying—over other people's heartache, losses, grief, and sadness. Listening to music enabled me to cry freely and to release some of my deepest sorrow.

Socially, I didn't know how to fit in except as Michael's girlfriend and part of a group. I didn't play a musical instrument, I was no longer involved in extracurricular activities. This engendered feelings of tremendous inadequacy. So I sat back and watched the world revolve around me, jumping in when it was safe or when I was invited. I spent most of my time either cheering Michael on in sports or championing my friends.

I did have one passion, art, and I would spend all my free time in my school's art room. I established a wonderful relationship with the art teacher, who understood that I was not involved in gym or sports and who allowed me to "hang out" in the art room whenever I wished. He encouraged me and understood my situation. Sometimes feelings of inadequacy would show up there as well, but mostly it felt like a safe place for me to explore my creativity. I found a way, albeit limited, to engage in art projects throughout my four years of high school.

Second Time Around

On Christmas Eve of 1970, ten months after my first hospitalization, I returned for a five-week stay as doctors ran multiple diagnostic tests to determine the etiology of my disease, now defined as a progressive degenerative muscular atrophy. Again, I was placed in an adult unit, this time with three other patients. I was terrified witnessing the enormity of disease around me and encountering many I never knew existed, such as brain cancer. Once, when I was sitting in the dayroom, a woman asked me what was wrong with me. I replied that the doctors didn't know, but I was having difficulty straightening my fingers, accompanied by muscle weakness and tingling. Then I asked her about herself. "How did it happen?" I asked. "What did you do to get this disease?" I'll never forget her response to my question. She did not tell me her diagnosis. She simply replied, "I don't know. It can happen to anyone!"

My fifteen-year-old mind believed her, and from that day on I prayed to God not to let me fall prey to these awful diseases. I was relieved to soon be moved to the neurological unit, where doctors treated adults with diseases of unknown etiology, which of course proved to be no better. I was placed in an L-shaped room with three roommates, all women suffering from various stages of brain cancer. My bed was in the back of the room in the small end of the L, so I had my own little alcove that I called home. I was glad to have a window by my bed, and when I drew the curtain I could actually drown out the hospital noises for a while. My dad brought my small phonograph from home, so I could play my 45s, and I decorated my walls with cards and pictures. I brought with me a stuffed Snoopy animal Michael had given me as a reminder of our love. I actually had what my friends would call a "cool space," exuding a homelike feeling.

I received cards from Michael almost every day, which I taped up on the wall behind me. I lived for those cards. I would call him every day from the pay phone down the hall, an activity that was by far the best part of my day. No matter how I felt, I would always take my daily stroll to the hall telephone. Once or twice my mother brought Michael and my best friends to visit. My sister never came to see me, nor did my brother. I never understood why, and I never asked. Thankfully, my Nana and Grandpa were there almost every day.

Over the next five weeks, I had an angiogram, myelogram, spinal taps, and EMGs— everything that could possibly address the malady wreaking havoc in my young body. I remember an especially painful myelogram, in which dye was injected into my spinal column to check for blockage. I was then placed on a tilt board as the dye ran through my spinal column. The procedure left me with a severe headache for hours afterward. Outside, waiting in the crowded hallway with my head exploding, I begged for someone to wheel me back to my room. Thank God my Nana was there that day to take some of the emotional and physical pain away. She stayed with me well into the night, long after visiting hours were over. Only after she left did I cry.

The next morning I felt better, so I got out of bed to use the bathroom. When I was standing by the sink, everything started to spin. I tried to call for help, but the words didn't come out, and I fell to the floor. The next thing I knew, a staff person was putting me back into my bed and I heard him say, "She doesn't have a pulse." When I came to, I couldn't see a thing. The world around me was black. I could hear people but couldn't see them or use my voice to speak to them, and I thought I might be dead. I am not sure how long I remained in that state, but when I next opened my eyes, I was relieved to see doctors and nurses hovering over me. Thank God I was alive! This time I listened to their instruction and did not get up again until I received their permission. Years later I learned that this bizarre experience is called a near-death experience. It occurs when a person is clinically dead but then survives, often emerging with new spiritual awareness and a changed attitude. In my case, the experience simply left me perplexed and fatigued.

By now I was tired of the ceaseless pain caused by the needles and probing. My Nana empathized with my suffering and showed up every day to be with me and help me feel better in her kind, compassionate way. The nursing staff was also helpful and kind, for the most part. All the nurses on the unit would visit my stuffed Snoopy animal and me, and our exchanges were playful and fun. The rest of the experiences were not. I never understood why my primary doctor didn't put me on the pediatric floor, which would have been less frightening. On the adult neurological floor, I soon learned that patients had no privacy but instead were subjected to daily doses of humiliation.

My three roommates with terminal brain cancer lay almost lifeless in their beds, totally covered up and attended by the staff. They were motionless bodies whose names I did not know. I never would have known of their existence except that I had to pass their beds to get to mine. The woman directly across from me would leave her bed occasionally to go to the bathroom or take a short walk with her private nurse. Once in a while I would help her by cranking her bed up or down to make her comfortable. Imagine how ironic it was for me, a patient with hand issues, helping others with my hands! In this isolating, frightening place, I desperately needed to connect with my roommate, to be there for her, and to help combat her loneliness and my own. Like all the other patients, I experienced the hospital's unwavering rhythms: waiting for visitors, hoping doctors would come in with some important news, eating hospital food, looking forward to the joy of night, so I could finally go to sleep and feel relieved, knowing I had made it through another day. The days I had my diagnostic tests were trying. I would be picked up in my room, told to sit in a wheelchair, and then taken by elevator to the basement, where all the major diagnostic tests were administered. On the day I was scheduled to have an angiogram, which was a tough procedure, I had to lie on the examining table as the doctor injected a contrast dye into my arteries. He hoped to get a visual picture of where the blockage originated, thereby explaining the source of my upper extremity weakness. He first placed the needle in my armpit, so I couldn't use my hands to grip the side rails. I gripped my feet under the bar at the bottom of the bed to help me bear the immense pain. My parents stood at the side of the table and witnessed the event, so I heroically held back my tears. The doctors first did the test on my right side, and then repeated the procedure on the left, trying to find the source of the problem. I prayed fervently that this agony would be over soon. Unfortunately, despite the doctors' efforts and the pain I endured, the results of the angiogram proved inconclusive.

In general, the diagnostic tests provided no clear evidence of the underlying cause of my baffling illness, but the doctors continued administering them in the hopes of solving the mystery. For my part, I just wanted the doctors to "fix" my body. The only diagnostic tests that offered any conclusive evidence of pathology were the EMG and NCV. Dr Steven Horowitz, Dr. Gendelman's chief resident, administered these tests while I was an in-patient. Because of my lengthy stay, I saw Dr. Horowitz often, and he soon became someone with whom I felt safe and comfortable. Younger than most of the other doctors, and gentler, he was different from his peers. He even wore desert boots, which to a fifteen-year-old girl was definitely cool. I never felt like just another patient with him, and in a way I fell in love with this sympathetic man.

Dr. Horowitz performed the neurological exams, including the EMGs. I already knew what to expect during this test because I already had it done once prior to my hospitalization. He placed the customary needles into my hands, arms, neck, and shoulders. Then he placed them in my chest and back. I lay on the table and fought back a flood of tears. He inserted needles into the back of my neck and down my spine, one at a time, into the belly of each muscle as he wiggled it around, hoping to receive feedback from the machine that indicated healthy electrical impulses in the muscle. Reasonably soon, I reached my pain threshold and wanted to explode with the torrent of tears I had been holding in as proof of my strength and bravery. I didn't want to be brave anymore. But I didn't cry. I bit my upper lip and held it in, so that Dr. Horowitz wouldn't see me cry. Always considerate and thoughtful, Dr. Horowitz asked if I was all right, as he placed the needles into my neck and spine. Even though I was in excruciating pain, I forced out, "Yes, I'm fine."

"How brave you are!" he said with glowing admiration, making me feel amply rewarded for keeping the expression of pain to myself. I learned to grin and bear it while remaining silent. I couldn't see what the doctor was doing. When he was pushing the needles into my chest and arms, I could see them going in and could brace myself against the pain. But when he was working on my back, every insertion came as a surprise for which I was unprepared. Would Dr. Horowitz have understood why I needed to appear so strong—that I couldn't risk exposing the insecure, frightened, unacceptable child I thought I was? I resolved never to share my tears with anyone.

After three weeks of tests, the doctors finally diagnosed me with Anterior Horn Cell Disease, a lower motor neuron ailment located in the gray matter of the spinal column. The disease was bilateral, affecting both sides of the body. A progressive degenerative condition, it spreads throughout the spinal cord. I could look forward to experiencing muscle wasting, involuntary movements called fasciculations, abnormal reflexes, and contractions, along with peripheral numbness and tingling.

A Monumental Moment

I was lying in my hospital bed busily engaged in a needlepoint project when the chief of neurology, the top neurologist in the country, along with his neurology residents, entered my room. With the residents circling around me, the chief stood at the foot of my bed and announced his medical take on my condition. Thankfully, Dr. Horowitz was standing closest to the head of the bed, right next to me, and his presence comforted me.

The chief told the residents and me, in no uncertain terms, that there was nothing anyone could do to stop the progression of the disease, which would continue without relief throughout my spinal cord, affecting my entire body. He described to the residents the etiology of the disease, and stated that if the other attending physicians chose to remove the first rib in hopes of alleviating the clinical symptoms, it would make absolutely no difference at all. There was nothing anyone could do to prevent the progression. He made a polite comment about my needlepoint, remarking how wonderful it was that I could do the activity, and then he and his residents filed out of the room. Speechless and hardly knowing what to think, I exchanged glances with Dr. Horowitz, who had stayed behind.

I was grateful that Dr. Horowitz had shared this devastating experience with me. He broke the silence by saying, "I can't believe what he just told you. He shouldn't have said the things he did. It was just awful."

I was in shock, and had to agree that this was far too much for a fifteen-year-old to comprehend. Where are my parents? Why do I have this disease? Did I do something to cause it? Was I being punished by God? Couldn't that doctor have been more discreet in delivering this information? Did it have to be in front of a bunch of strangers? What does it mean? Is there any chance for a cure, no matter how experimental? I took my fear and anger and directed it at the great neurologist. I couldn't care less about his reputation. He was mean to me. I hated him for his lack of compassion, for his cool, rational detachment, for his inability to communicate sympathetically with a kid. How dare he be so aloof and so cold! How dare he treat *anyone* like that! As a doctor, he was supposed to take care of people, not hurt them. His words resounded in my head: "If they intervene, it won't matter anyway. *There's nothing anyone can do.*" When he uttered these words of doom, I wish I could have held that little girl in my arms to comfort and console her. I believe a part of me really didn't hear those life-negating, life-depriving words. Had I taken them in and accepted them, I wouldn't have had the courage to go on living, because he had just delivered a death sentence to me. The wound this world-famous doctor caused that day was unnecessary. No medical authority should ever issue a proclamation that destroys a person's faith and hope in healing.

Despite this setback, however, I just kept going. I somehow believed that everything would turn out okay. Because Dr. Horowitz had witnessed this traumatic experience, and, more importantly, had shared his feelings about it, I had the courage and support necessary to persevere.

The next morning during rounds, when Dr. Gendelman came to see me, I asked him whether he was aware of what the chief of neurology had said. He acknowledged that he was and that he and Dr. J decided to proceed with the surgery anyway. Dr. Gendelman felt that doing something was better than doing nothing. He said they would try anything in hopes of alleviating the symptoms and stopping the progression. I was so relieved. I had to believe that the terrible prediction was wrong and that these other doctors would be able to help me. Despite the frequent arrogance of the medical world, I was blessed to have outstanding, humane doctors like Dr. Gendelman and Dr. Horowitz, whose respect and graciousness nurtured me through some of the most difficult events in my life.

A brilliant surgeon but not a friendly man, Dr. J visited me each day, checked me out, and left. He was going to perform the surgery, which involved removing the first rib on my right side, in hopes that it would alleviate the pressure on the brachial plexus, and thus the tingling and numbness I was experiencing. The surgery was scheduled for early in the morning. Various physicians came in one by one to explain what would be taking place. The anesthesiologist then explained his procedure and warned me that I might be nauseous after the surgery. Next, an aide came in wheeling a bed and asked me to slide onto the gurney so he could transport me to the surgical suite. I lay there with an ugly blue cap on my head, which I hated, in an area with other patients waiting to be called in to the operating room. As time ticked on, I waited and waited, struggling with my fears. I just wanted to be drugged enough so that I could sleep and forget where I was. Finally, the aides wheeled me into the surgical suite, where I cheerfully greeted the surgical team led by Dr. J, until a mask was placed over my mouth and nose, and I was gone.

Hours later, I awoke on the operating table feeling disoriented. I fell back asleep, only to wake soon afterward in the recovery room with a tube down my throat. I was uncomfortable, feeling pain at the site of the surgery and very drowsy. After nurses removed the tube, I vomited, as the anesthesiologist had predicted, and I just wanted to die. Hours later, I was wheeled back to my hospital room, where my mother was waiting for me. The pain was excruciating, as this surgery was far more invasive than the first. Worse still, I knew they would have to repeat the surgery on the other side of my body at another time. I had to be the hero, the tough one who could withstand anything, a teenage Wonder Girl who was brave, who accepted adversity, who didn't make a fuss, and who didn't do anything out of line. I was creating a "me" that would be victorious no matter what life threw my way. I tried being a cooperative patient, asking for very little and always apologizing for bothering the nurses with my needs. I welcomed their presence, except for the ones who were curt and businesslike, and tried to exhibit kindness to them all, something I really wanted to receive from them. My need for isolation alternated with wanting to be surrounded by people, but they needed to be loving and caring.

Immediately after the surgery, I experienced a decrease in the numbness and tingling for a few months. But as the chief of neurology had predicted, the disease continued to progress. Five months later, the doctors repeated the same surgery on the left side. As I turned sixteen, I was left with three embarrassing scars on my body and a loss of hope for a permanent medical cure. Then reality set in: *I was wasting away.* As I watched my body deteriorate without being able to control it, I wondered how I was going to survive. I stared at my hands for hours at a time.

This period was a blur of torturous sensations. The doctor had removed the first rib by making an incision below the armpit, so the whole side of my body was affected, making it difficult to take deep breaths. To keep my lungs and chest clear of fluid, they put me on a breathing machine. But even with morphine injections every four hours, my body was fraught with pain from all the intrusive preoperative tests, while the surgery left me with raw, inflamed wounds from my neck down to my chest and arm. Nonetheless, the nurses forced me to get out of bed and walk down the hall, dragging my IV pole, to get to the shower room to bathe. I hated everything around me, including my own life. I just wanted to be home, living like a normal teenager, sleeping in my own bed, without constantly having to deal with the unknown. Somehow I endured, and a week later I returned home to a huge bouquet of balloons from my friends, and to my boyfriend, who was waiting for me when I arrived. It was wonderful to be home and to resume my life. Due to all the time I missed at school, I had a math tutor, Mr. Donofrio a benevolent, mild-mannered, high school teacher, who came to my home in the evenings to help me catch up with the missed work. Mr. Donofrio was also Michael's teacher and wrestling coach, which allowed me to bathe in the light of Michael's wonderful reputation. My connection to Michael in this way made me feel special once again.

Now that I had been returned to my life, I cheerfully attended Christian Youth Organization dances, practiced roller-skating at a nearby rink, which didn't please the doctors, and reestablished my social life. I acknowledged that I had a limiting physical condition, but I refused to let it keep me from enjoying my life. I adopted a strong, stoic persona to keep the hole in my soul concealed, ignoring the hideous drama I had been undergoing.

I didn't want to experience the disquieting reality that my parents never physically held me or tried to encourage me to release my feelings or deal emotionally with my illness. That would require me to feel that pain again, weakening the image of strength I was projecting. But although I appeared strong, I never felt that way.

It was clear now that this journey was mine to do alone, on a spiritual and emotional level. I'm grateful for the medical care my parents provided; indeed, I had the best medical care that was available. It would take almost forty years before I would realize that their lack of presence and validation unwittingly would send me on a spiritual journey that would explain the reasons for all of these life experiences and return me to my true self.

When I returned from the hospital, we had new neighbors, a young couple with a daughter. Within the first few weeks of my return home, they asked me whether I would babysit their year-old daughter, Tanya. I jumped at the prospect. Carole, who was twenty-three years old, and her husband, Robby, made me feel at ease, and became significant people in my life throughout my teenage years and beyond. Nurturing and supportive, Carole treated me like a member of her own loving family. I could always count on her to stand by me when things at home got too rough. I dropped by their house every day for one reason or another, although I knew I'd be welcomed without one. Carole and Robby would help me in any way possible, offering genuine support or a gentle hug. Often I would just cry, sharing my pain and allowing myself to grieve. They never once sent me away or stifled my emotions, for which I am eternally grateful. Today my relationship with Carole has evolved into a friendship of peers. She continues to be a tremendous support to me in every way. Now I can give back to her everything she so graciously gave me as a young woman seeking a safe haven.

Final Round

Five months later, in June 1971, I entered the Mount Sinai Medical Center for the third and last time, to have the first rib on my left side removed. The procedure was short and simple, and I was out of the hospital in a week. When I left, I heard the same old story—there was nothing else the medical establishment could do for me. As I turned sixteen, I could only wait to see what would happen next.

When I returned home, Michael was not at the door. I was devastated. It turned out that he had started dating my best friend. On my part, I had bonded with him at the level of heart and soul, but the relationship had become too much of a burden for him, and he wanted to feel lighthearted and free.

My parents recommended a change of pace, and thought I should go away for the summer to help my aunt and uncle who lived in Georgetown, near Washington, D.C. My relatives wanted me to take care of my cousins, a four-year-old and one-year-old. I loved the idea and needed a break from hospitals, doctors, my town, and Michael. I handed back Michael's high school ring, and as soon as school was out I boarded a bus for Washington. I was sixteen and at least momentarily free of everything that had caused pain in my life.

Living with my aunt and uncle was an expansive and rewarding experience. It allowed me complete freedom to go anywhere and do anything I wanted when I wasn't working. I spent a lot of time in Georgetown meeting interesting people. I would go to outdoor concerts in the park and to hippie festivals. What a different world it was from my small hometown in northern New Jersey! Although reveling in my new autonomy, I spoke with Michael every day. Despite his continued dating of my best friend, I could not let go of him, nor could he let go of me. Our connection was soul deep—as deep as my fear of abandonment.

My summer experience was of great benefit to me. I was on my own, away from my family, with the opportunity to spread my wings. Because I had few rules and lots of freedom, I took risks and explored my new environment. I felt freed from the medical world, with which I had become all too familiar. Most of all, I felt accepted and loved by my aunt and uncle.

One night at their house in Rehobeth Beach, I cried out to my absent biological father, "Please love me, and then I will know everything will be all right." I always felt that if he were alive, I would be loved. I would pray to him *and* ask God about him, as a plea to be heard and to be recognized. I thought my father was handsome, and I had carried his picture in my wallet for years. Actually, I even looked like him: I had his chin, his smirk, and the depth of his eyes. I secretly loved my real father very much. I had to hold on to something, and because he was no longer alive it was safe to hold on to him.

Home Alone

At the end of the summer, I returned home to begin my junior year of high school. Michael and I remained friends and continued seeing each other, though he was still dating my now ex-best friend. Yet my heart remained beyond repair, because nothing mattered but Michael. I lived for the next opportunity to be held and loved by him, even as just a friend. I truly had suffered an irreparable loss. It was easy to understand why he left me for my best friend.

Without the demands of a romantic relationship, I became more conscientious about my studies. I wanted to *be* somebody. As a little girl, I always wanted to become a nurse and marry a doctor. For some reason, my desire to work in a hospital didn't wane as a result of my experiences. For the next two years, I focused on my studies, but didn't get accepted into nursing school. Neither my physical strength nor my academics were up to par.

During the summer between my third and fourth years of high school, I was an infirmary assistant at the summer camp I had attended as a child. It was a rewarding experience working alongside the nurses and the doctor. I also met a young man named Larry, who soon became my boyfriend. He was four years older than me and was going into his fourth year of college in pre-med. I knew he was everything my parents would look for in a boyfriend, and I concurred. We spent the summer together, and when I returned home, we continued seeing each other as often as possible. Once again, I had a real boyfriend, which made my senior year of high school quite pleasant.

By this time, Michael had left for college, so I could avoid the awkwardness of running into him at school. My sister had also left for college, so my younger brother and I had the house to ourselves, and I was now the only daughter there. Without the competition between my sister and me, my parents were a bit more available, for which I was deeply appreciative.

I applied to a state university in New Jersey and was accepted. I decided to major in special education. I wouldn't need the same dexterity to be a teacher as I would have needed to be a nurse. I accepted my physical limitations; I had no other option. I was simply grateful for the opportunity to go to college and begin a new life, while Larry graduated from college and started medical school.

The Disease Gave Me the Courage to Survive

It was clear to my parents, the medical establishment, and me, that the chief neurologist's prediction was correct. The three surgeries had no impact on the slow but steady progression of the disease that was ravaging me from within. Surgery had exhausted its promises. The medical world could now offer me only yearly exams and a record of my body's degeneration process. My dad and I continued making our annual trips to Dr. Gendelman's office for routine neurological exams and for sporadic EMG updates by either Dr. K or Dr. Horowitz.

The disease was now starting to cause significant atrophy in my lower arms, and I was losing strength in both of my hands. I prided myself on knowing exactly what was happening before my doctor could tell me. I would announce to him that I had lost a bit more flexibility and had less control of my fingers. Thankfully, there was no sign that the disease was progressing to other parts of my body. My legs were not involved, a fact for which I was extremely thankful.

One time, my father told me that the disease was all in my head. I didn't understand how he could say such a terrible thing to me. Why would I inflict such a debilitating disease on myself? How would I ever come up with such a thing? The whole concept was foreign to me. At my next visit with Dr. Gendelman, I told him what my father had said. He replied, "You did not cause this disease. Your father is just scared." I was grateful for Dr. Gendelman, whose wise counsel relieved me of that guilt. He also told me to keep my chin up, and so I did.

In retrospect, I realize that much of the emotional pain I endured throughout my childhood and teen years was a reappearance of the pain endured by my parents in their childhoods—wounds carried from living with *their* parents. As a result, my parents couldn't give me the attention or the unconditional love that I needed so badly, and their emotional wounds became my own. We externalize love to our children by being tender, comforting them, and being emotionally available to them. Intellectualizing our love isn't enough; we have to radiate it from our hearts and embody it through our soulful presence.

We can't receive love on an intellectual level—it's not enough to know or even believe that we're loved. Love must be felt and experienced in a tactile and heartfelt way. We can feel the sensations of love through a gentle hug, a kind touch, a smile, a whisper, a word of reassurance. We must feel the love energetically or our cells will not open to receive it. This lack of soulful loving presence creates disease, which can be felt emotionally, physically, or spiritually. The energy of love is actually absorbed into the body's matrix, its DNA, which can change and heal the body's cellular structures.

I believe that on some level my disease became my badge of courage, and I became my disease. I was noticed for it. It was who I was. I received attention because of my hands, my prognosis, my trials and tribulations as a result of having this disease, and was recognized for my adaptation to it. While I never made this decision consciously, my entire identity nonetheless became wrapped up in my illness.

My life became what I couldn't do, not what I could. I was always waiting for the other shoe to drop, for more bad news to come. I never once believed that I would hear good news, and I completely stopped wishing for a cure to save me. Instead, I focused on getting through high school, going to college, and getting a job. Once I had a job, I would receive social security benefits so I would be taken care of when I no longer could support myself. My father actually shared this practical advice with me when I was a senior in high school.

Even though we had formulated this plan, my future was far from predictable. As I faced the prospect of going forward in my life, I was consumed with fear, loss, and uncertainty. Somehow I found the courage to keep fighting the disease that was wreaking havoc on me both internally and externally. As time went on, my fears and frustrations turned to anger, amplified by all the physical obstacles that kept blocking my way forward. My body was controlling my life. Little did I know that these same roadblocks were guiding the course of my life in a positive direction. A higher power was guiding my life, although at the time I was unaware of its presence, because I was so overcome with fright.

CHAPTER 3

The Journey

Can't go under it, can't go over it, got to go through it
—Eric Carle

A Turning Point

SOMEWHERE DEEP INSIDE OF ME I knew I deserved a better life. I also knew I would have to keep seeking until I found what I was looking for.

I left for college in the fall of 1973. I loved college: I loved being away from home, I made friends quickly and easily, and I was excited about the courses I was taking. Among the many science courses I took, my favorites were anatomy, physiology, biology, psychology, and even chemistry. I'm not sure why I chose those classes, since I wasn't pursuing a career in the medical field, but for some reason I took them. I minored in art history because my passion for art never subsided. I was blessed with wonderful teachers who were kind and accepting, and I never felt compromised or inadequate in any way.

It was an emotionally healing time, even though I wasn't healing physically. I felt included, smart, accepted, and involved in all that was happening around me. I was alive and handled my newfound freedom well. I was becoming someone I only dreamed of becoming. I worked hard and was rewarded with being on the high honor roll and having great academic success.

Nonetheless, I had daily reminders of my disease, which always lurked in the background. My incurable disease constantly haunted me; there was no answer, no cure, no hope. Even though I had a boyfriend at college, I was still mourning the loss of Michael. I felt this most acutely on weekends, when most of my friends went home to work, and I often remained alone. Sometimes I would listen to music in the dark, an experience that enabled me to feel the pain I desperately needed to release and to feel the depth of my terror and sorrow. What a gift I received from the music! After I left the hospital, I continued to needlepoint, and I carried it on at college where it became my pride and joy. I was artistic enough to create my own needlepoint from scratch and watch it come to life. I was proud of my ability to sustain such passion for an activity where hands were the tool of choice. I decided that come what may, I would never give up this soul-healing activity.

During this time I would travel to New York City to visit my boyfriend where he was living while in medical school. In the winter of 1974, Larry and I became engaged. We decided to wait and get married in two years when he would finish medical school. He wanted me bad hands and all! The relationship offered safety and security, which, I felt at the time, were the most important things in life. Unbeknownst to me, my soul was about to guide me on a whole new path.

Decoding the Messages

It's so important to be fully awake, because you never know when the universe will present you with a gift that could change your life forever.

During my second year of college, students who were declaring a major in special education were required to do volunteer hours in a special education program of their choice. The A. Harry Moore

School for the Multiple Handicapped was conveniently located across the street from Jersey State College. It was the student's responsibility to make an appointment with the administration, to set up an interview, and to schedule volunteer hours. I set up a schedule for myself in the spring of 1975. The administration placed me in the occupational therapy department rather than in a classroom, and I began to volunteer one morning a week. What I loved about occupational therapy is that it incorporated all my interests in one profession: the medical, psychological, and creative.

It was truly by chance that I was placed in this department and not in a classroom. What a gift that was! I felt instant rapport with Lois, who became my supervisor. I liked the large, sunlit room with large windows and a friendly atmosphere. The room, which was filled with gym-like equipment (big balls, toys, trampolines, blocks) had small, round tables instead of individual desks. The physically handicapped children who came to OT entered the room in braces, splints, walkers and wheelchairs. Some of the children were ambulatory, others were not. Initially, I was a bit frightened by them, but that feeling quickly turned into a desire to help these struggling children. I soon noticed that some of the children appeared absolutely normal but had difficulty with their sensory environment, an observation that definitely brought to the surface my own deep issues.

Lois, my supervisor, was a therapist whose skills and demeanor, as well as her expert instruction, made me fall in love with the profession. Lois explained to me that OT focuses on the rehabilitation of children with physical disabilities or sensory motor involvement (soft-sign neurological disorders). It has nothing to do with the term *occupation* per se when defined as an activity. Occupational therapy uses purposeful activity to facilitate the functioning of the child (or adult in other settings). I was thrilled to watch Lois as she provided services to these children, helping them increase their ability to function independently. I watched her do screenings, evaluations, and create individualized treatment programs. Because occupational therapy was touching the core of my own diseased body, I had more then just professional interest in the subject. And because Lois was kind and gentle with all the children, the child within me felt comfortable with her. She truly loved the children and her work, and she never judged people or committed any unkind actions.

On a personal level, I felt comfortable with Lois, who always found time to talk to me and encourage me. I didn't hesitate to let her into my life and to share the challenge of my disease and my professional aspirations. By now, at age 19, I was extremely motivated to work in the helping professions. Even with the uncertainty I had to face, I was excited about my life, and my future. With all the time I spent volunteering at the school, I decided to look into occupational therapy as my profession.

With Lois's encouragement, I applied as a third-year transfer student to New York University and three other schools offering occupational therapy as a college major. Something shifted in me as a result of this: I became motivated in a whole new way. I know I could have stayed at Jersey State with my friends and graduated with a degree in special education. Although I would have been a great teacher, something about the field of OT reached deep into my soul. I felt connected to being a healer in the medical field, especially connected to the children with their braces, splints, walkers, and wheelchairs. Something bigger than me had seized me, and I jumped at the chance of exploring it further.

My life was expanding in other ways, as well. I met someone at the college whom I became interested in. Born in Jersey City, Bob was studying for his master's degree to become a reading specialist. His family wasn't education-oriented, as my family and my fiancé's family were, and the fact that he was pursuing his heart's desire without anything being handed to him impressed me deeply. I admired him for pursuing a path that was "out of the box" from his upbringing. His independent way of thinking challenged me to revisit my own values.

I knew that if I married Larry, he would always take care of me, provide for me, and make my life easy. I didn't need to become anything in my own right but could be secure in being a wife and mother. Larry often told me not to worry about my career, since one doctor in the family would be enough. This attitude didn't sit well with me, even though my burden would be lightened and my welfare would be secure. I knew that marrying Larry would also alleviate my parent's fears about caring for me as they aged and my disease progressed.

However, I no longer felt the need to be safe; in fact, I felt excited about life and was willing to take risks on my own. So I broke off my engagement to Larry and started dating Bob. A month later I had a to go for an interview at New York University, with a man named Tony. Suddenly my whole life shifted. In my excitement I couldn't believe what was happening to me. Still I had one worry: Even though I had great grades, I wondered whether my hands would interfere with my getting accepted. I took the PATH train across the Hudson River and walked toward the building where I was to be interviewed, feeling like a million bucks. I loved NYU, the school where my father had graduated; if I were accepted, my father and I would have that in common, making the experience even more special. I felt great in my fisherman knit sweater, my homemade jean skirt, my tights, and my clogs—the standard apparel I wore when I wanted to feel wonderful. Nervous yet hopeful, I had worked hard in the past two years, and I wanted with all my heart to be accepted into the program, which would be a dream come true.

Choices

The OT department was located in the Barney Building, a cute four-story building on a short block of buildings close to the corner of 2nd Avenue and 9th Street. Tony, my interviewer, was a kind, affable man whose demeanor let me relax and be entirely present to his insightful comments and questions. In explaining the OT program, he asked me a fascinating question: "What percentage of you is *science* and what percentage is *art?*" I thought the question was intriguing, since I had such a deep connection to both. I answered 60% science, 40% art. Finally, he asked me about my hands. I looked him squarely in the eyes, and with complete frankness I told him everything, hiding nothing.

I told Tony about my disease as well as my deep desire to become an occupational therapist. Honestly, openly, and with complete calmness, I shared my truth, my history, my goals, and my desires. Never had I felt so guided from within and so confident in myself. I wanted to make sure that if I were accepted into this clinical program, it would be on the basis of my authentic truth, and thus for the right reason. Already I could sense that the interview at NYU would become an important marker for the rest of my life.

After I was done speaking, Tony looked at me and said, "You can make this disease an asset or a liability. The choice is yours." I had just received one of the most profound messages of my life, and I knew he was right. On that glorious day, Tony acknowledged me for who I was, and I knew in my heart that I had come to the right place. I left his office floating above the earth on cloud nine, knowing I had spoken my truth with integrity.

After I left the interview, I decided to telephone my parents to tell them how great the interview had gone. When I finished my story, my father said, "I hope you didn't tell them about your hands."

I was crushed, but replied, "Of course I did."

"Then," he said, "you probably won't be accepted."

Summoning up all my courage and determination, I said, "If they don't take me because of my hands, it's better I know now, and not when I'm in a clinical situation that I couldn't handle, and which would embarrass me because I wasn't honest from the beginning."

I knew that I had nothing to hide. And because I trusted myself as never before, I wouldn't allow myself to hide. Once again I heard the dictum from a parent, "Do not tell the truth!"

"Wasn't I brought up to tell the truth?" I thought. "Isn't that what all children are told?" The statement from my father left me confused, bewildered, and disappointed that his fears took precedence over the values I was brought up with. Now, on reflection, I have said many times to my own children, "Speaking the truth is critically important, and far exceeds anything else."

Acceptance and Faith

Three weeks later I received my acceptance letter from NYU, and in my joy I realized that all my hard work and perseverance had paid off. I had been accepted into this prestigious university even with my disease. During this exceptional moment of celebration and gratitude, I knew that Tony was right: I had to choose to make this disease an asset or a liability. That day I chose to make it an asset. What I realized many years later was that Tony was an angel sent to guide me along my path. Choosing to go into occupational therapy was especially significant to me because it's about helping people function at their highest level, using the practitioner's hands. Since OT focuses on purposeful activity, mastery of needs, and positive self-esteem, it was no coincidence that I was led to that field of study.

I finished my semester at Jersey State and entered NYU in the fall of 1975 as a junior transfer student. I loved the school and the vibrancy of living in Greenwich Village. I got along well with my roommate Robin, with whom I had quite a bit in common. When Robin was in high school, she became ill and ended up in Rusk Institute with Guillain Barre Disease, which attacks the neurological system and paralyzes the person from head to toe. She not only survived but regained her strength and physical health. One day Robin told me a story that I'll never forget. She once mentioned to her mother how afraid she was that her boyfriend would touch her leg, realize that she had a brace on, and no longer like her. Her mother replied, "If he doesn't like you because you have a brace, then he's not good enough for you." When I heard this, I cried. "How I wished my parents had said that to me just once in my life," I said. I envied Robin's experience and her parents' ability to support their daughter with her disability. I saw clearly that there was no coincidence in our being together, and we stayed roommates for the next two years.

As I had made lots of friends within and outside my academic program, I became a leader in my class. I was determined to do well and become a top professional in my field. The occupational therapy curriculum was rigorous and demanding, and schoolwork became my number one focus. Because the course of study was physically challenging, my decreased muscle strength and dexterity got in the way during some of the clinical lab experiences. At these times, I had to gratefully and honestly acknowledge my weaknesses as well my strengths. I never deceived my professors about my capacity to do something I couldn't handle.

For example, sometimes in a lab or in a class, I lacked sufficient muscle strength to complete a task adequately. This happened in my splinting course and my hands-on practical classes. These experiences, which made me feel embarrassed and incompetent, always reminded me that I was not like everyone else. Still, I managed to accomplish my required tasks, sometimes with the grace of a compassionate and understanding professor. Usually, the professors would allow my peers to assist me when necessary to manage some of the finer details, especially in splinting class.

I did have one experience in which a professor failed me during a clinical lab test, and I became angry and scared. During this lab, each student had to take turns physically manipulating the muscle belly in the arm as part of facilitation techniques we were to learning. I couldn't exert enough muscle strength because of the weakness in my hands. I said to the professor, "I can't do this because of my hands," and she replied, "That's not an excuse." Terrified that I would fail to make it to the next level because of my shortcomings, I went downstairs to Tony's office in tears and explained what had happened. I reminded him I had fully disclosed my situation during my interview with him, and her attitude was unfair. He and the other professors were supportive, although they couldn't do very much. I felt trapped and discouraged because I couldn't do better on the physical exam, no matter how hard I tried. If, however, I did exceptionally well on the written portion of the neurological exam, getting a 94 or above, I would pass the course; otherwise, I would have to repeat it the following semester. With that information motivating me, I spent the next few days in the library, studying around the clock with the determination to get though this challenge. There was no way I was going to repeat the class and not continue studying with my friends.

Happily, I aced the written portion of the test and passed the course. With my life on the line, I found the courage and determination to rise to the occasion and excel on the written test. But it took me years to forgive the professor who made me feel so little that day.

In My Face

I always excelled in my clinical endeavors, so I was excited about starting my first clinical affiliation at Roosevelt Hospital in New York City in the summer between my junior and senior years of college. The other student affiliate that summer, Leah, who had a history of polio and who walked with a limp, was another courageous soul learning to live with a handicap. My supervisor, Wendy, was encouraging and thoughtful. She became my mentor and friend. An amazing therapist, Wendy believed in me and knew that I had the makings of an excellent therapist. She and I spoke openly about the disease process, and she honored my fortitude and courage.

During the first month of my summer affiliation, Wendy suggested that I see the director of rehabilitation medicine. She felt I might benefit from wearing a hand splint that would stabilize my joints, thus giving me more dexterity in my fingers. Because I respected and admired her, I agreed to make an appointment with the doctor. Wendy brought me to the office and introduced me as her OT student. This meeting wasn't easy for me, having had my fill of physicians and their fearful pronouncements. The doctor, a nice man, suggested that I have a lumbrical bar splint made for me. The device, which looks like a cuff, slides onto the hand and rests on the large knuckles or joints. The pressure the splint places on the joints automatically bring the fingers into extension, thus keeping them from staying in a fist position. By opening my fingers, I could hold more in the palm of my hand.

While this was good news, it actually felt like defeat wrapped in acceptance. The defeat was that I really was damaged and now required external support to assist me. In my mind, the lumbrical splint announced to the world that I was handicapped. The acceptance was that Wendy, whom I admired, believed in me just as I was. Weighing both the defeat and the acceptance, I left the doctor's office with the decision to have the splint made. Although I was not happy, I had to follow through, mainly because I wanted Wendy to know I trusted her judgment. I didn't want to let her down. As a compromise, I wore the splint occasionally, especially when it didn't matter who was looking. I wore it mostly in the sanctuary of my dorm room and during a few of my classes. As uncomfortable as it was, I continued to remind myself that I was an occupational therapist who was practicing what I preached. Despite everything, I just wanted to be normal.

Survival of the Fittest

Seven years had gone by since my disease first presented itself, and the progression continued as predicted. Now, because of muscle wasting, I had difficulty holding my eating utensils, which caused me great anguish. I was embarrassed to eat in public, fearing that people in the dorm cafeteria would see me unable to hold my knife and fork. I started using my teeth to open bottles and containers that I couldn't manipulate with my fingers. I also made a conscious decision to eat sandwiches that didn't require me to struggle with a knife. Often throughout this period I wanted to hide away and not be seen.

I would do everything in my power to avoid the embarrassment of not being physically able to do something. I didn't have an issue with people I knew well. I was mainly concerned about acquaintances and strangers, who would require an explanation for my unusual behavior. I was embarrassed and damaged, a fact that I didn't want to share with anyone. When I went out to restaurants, I would order food that didn't require the use of a knife. Since I had to maintain a state of heightened alertness, I had to exert a lot of energy to protect my secret. It was emotionally hard work to always be "on," to be aware, to be in hiding.

Another Trip Around the Block

When reality slaps you in the face it takes an enormous amount of energy to make lemonade out of lemons. Every year I continued to visit Dr. Gendelman, who would do a neurological exam and take new measurements of muscle loss, after which we would make an appointment for the following year. When I was a college senior, I told him that I was finding it difficult at times to keep my right shoe on my foot. Because of his concern, Dr. Gendelman recommended a consultation with a physician at the University of Philadelphia Medical Center who specialized in Anterior Horn Cell Disease.

My father and I drove two and a half hours to Philadelphia for the appointment. Located right next to the college and its beautiful campus, the medical center was much prettier than Mount Sinai Medical Center, which was in the heart of Manhattan. I was anxious but also excited that maybe this specialist would have an answer and give me something new to hope for. When we found the neurology department, I felt the usual pang of disgust and hatred I felt in hospitals, tired of the whole medical game and doctors. I thought, "Here we go again." This doctor was a specialist in Anterior Horn Cell Disease. He exuded confidence as he took me into his examining room while my father waited outside. He did a neurological exam, checking my legs as well for any signs of progression. I had not experienced any difficulty with my legs, except to notice that sometimes I had difficulty keeping my clog on my right foot. My right big toe couldn't grip down inside my shoe to hold it on. In those days I wore clogs a lot, and I didn't want to give them up for anything, including neurological dysfunction. Not so secretly, I feared the disease was spreading, and I braced myself against this possibility. Fortunately, he found only slight neurological involvement in my right big toe, certainly not anything to worry about at this point. He finished his exam, and we both went outside to meet my father in the waiting room.

With great solemnity, this doctor issued a pronouncement that even today amazes me with its incredible arrogance and insensitivity. He said to my father and me, "The disease will continue to progress throughout Laura's body. She'll be in a wheelchair by 25, and die by age 40, because her respiratory muscles will become compromised."

Heartache/Heartbreak

Our heart, our cells, can hold only so much pain and grief. It is remarkable how much we can endure when we have to.

We were standing in a hallway in the neurological wing of the hospital as the doctor delivered his death sentence to me. Numb and shocked, I looked around to see whether anyone was listening. Unable to respond to his brutal, life-crushing words, my father and I stood there motionless, without saying a word or asking any questions. The doctor said in a courteous but distant way that he would be sending his report to Dr. Gendelman and that it was a pleasure meeting me.

When we said goodbye and left the building, my father and I walked in silence across the parking lot to our car. Devastated by the doctor's death sentence and my father's inability to respond, I retreated uncomfortably into myself, completely at a loss about what to say or how to feel.

During the two-and-a-half hour drive home, which passed in uncomfortable silence, I sat in the passenger seat, looking out the window as tears rolled down my cheeks. I was glad when it got dark, so I could be alone with my tears, crying in my intense aloneness while separated by an unbridgeable abyss from my father, who focused on driving us home to New Jersey. I wanted my dad to reach out to me, to hold me, to share some feeling with me, to let me share my feelings, to comfort me, but that wasn't his style. As usual, I would have to bear this setback alone, accepting the unacceptable with all the courage my heart could muster. My father had just heard that his 21-year-old daughter would be in a wheelchair within four years and be dead by 40. How did he feel? How did I feel? I had heard such predictions before, but this time it felt real and couldn't be ignored. "No!" my soul cried inwardly. I was doing well in school, I had a profession that I loved, and I was graduating from college in six months. Surely, this can't be happening. A bizarre thought raced through my mind: How was I going to be an occupational therapist if I were in a wheelchair?

At one point we stopped to get some dinner, but still said nothing about the doctor's prognosis. During the meal I thought, "Now maybe he'll say something. Maybe he'll hold me and offer me some words of consolation." He said nothing. Like zombies, we sat eating our dinner and then got back into the car and continued our drive home.

Finally, I couldn't hold back any further. I decided to risk asking my father what he thought about the doctor's pronouncement. He replied, "The doctor shouldn't have spoken that way to you." He then discussed another issue, which had to do with a small party that the family was having the following weekend to celebrate my Nana's birthday. The party would be in her apartment in Manhattan, and our closest relatives would be there. He told me he didn't approve of Bob, my boyfriend, who was not welcome at the gathering.

Beneath my father's superficial conversation, I could feel the unspoken pain in his words and his attempt to deflect attention from the death sentence that had just been bestowed upon me. During the long drive home, I thought, "The doctor just told me I'm going to be in a wheelchair and die, and all my father cares about is harassing me about my boyfriend! What difference does it make who comes to the goddamn party? What difference does it make who my boyfriend is? What difference does anything make?"

I hated him so much at that moment that I could barely contain my anger with this distant, unemotional man. In my distress I wondered what my mother would say when I got home. The minute I saw her, I told her about the doctor's diagnosis and the hurtful way he delivered it, along with my father's ultimatum about Bob and the party. My mother immediately defended me about the party and was angry at my father for making such a big deal of it at this critical time in his daughter's life. "Who knows what's going to happen to Laura?" she said to him. "Who's going to want to marry her with her hands? Let her choose who she wants."

While I appreciated that my mother agreed with me about the party, I felt terribly alone and forced myself to hold in the pain.

Even though my future felt fragile and uncertain, life continued. I had many positive experiences at school, especially in my internships. I dedicated myself to relieving my patients' hardships and suffering, no matter what the illness. I channeled all my energy into becoming the best therapist I could. Despite my own physical challenges, I was excited about my future.

I received solace and support from many people during this period, including boyfriends, girlfriends, teachers, doctors, and my grandparents. Although I always had a network of caring people around me, the pain never went away. I wanted validation and support from my parents, the acknowledgment that what was happening to me was real, but that never came. Only years later did I acquire the wisdom to realize that they responded the best they could, based on their own sense of disempowerment, their own web of pain and suffering.

A Positive Experience

During my last semester before graduation, I returned to the A. Harry Moore School in Jersey City to fulfill my requirements in a pediatric internship. I was excited about working with Lois and other teachers who were familiar with me and my background. It was a great learning experience professionally and personally.

One day when I walked into the occupational therapy clinic, a little girl whom I had been working with asked me why I wasn't wearing my splint. Since the majority of students had some form of adaptive device, the school's safe environment allowed me to wear mine in public without being embarrassed. I would put the splint on when I arrived and take it off the minute I left. That day, however, I forgot to bring it with me, and I told her so. She then explained to me that she wore her braces every day because it helped her do better, and she suggested that I wear my splint because it would help me, too. This little three-year-old girl knew exactly what she was talking about, based on her life experience, and I was humbled by her brave words. From that day on, I never forgot my splint again. I then realized that because I had been normal before the onset of my disease, I often compared my current condition to the past and yearned to be normal again. But this child had nothing to compare her experience with. My internal fight involved comparing normal to disabled, always questioning my ability to do the smallest task, while this brave little girl knew only how to live with braces and splints, which were her only reality. She taught me a great deal about living in the present moment, without torturing thoughts about how life should be, but rather how it actually is.

I spent four months at the school, completed my internship, and graduated in the spring of 1977. Against all odds and despite all adversity, I had become an occupational therapist, and was ready to test the waters of my first job.

Stepping Into My Strength/Bridging the Gap Between Excitement and Fear

I applied to the top hospitals in the city, and was granted an interview at St. Luke's Hospital Medical Center for a position in community psychiatry. Many of my friends had decided they would take time off between graduation and work, but I knew I didn't have the freedom they did. I needed a job, and now. I had made the decision long ago to practice OT in the area of psychiatry because it would tax me less physically. With Tony's words as the touchstone of my career, I knew my assets and liabilities and how to accentuate my strengths professionally. I was elated when St. Luke's Hospital offered me the position. I was the first in my class to receive a job offer, and in honor of my achievement, I took one week off between my internship and my first day of work.

I really enjoyed the work and felt very accomplished. Fed by the internal strength that no one could take from me, I radiated the sense of being someone who could forge her own way through life. But the flip side of my sunny presence was shrouded in darkness, fearful of the unknown and of rejection. I was clearly motivated by fear, especially when it came to my intimate life. I always heard these words inside my head: "Who will ever want you with those hands?" No matter how well my life was unfolding, I always heard the frightful prediction, issued with medical authority, that I would be in a wheelchair by age 25. I decided I'd better provide for myself once I was physically bound to a wheelchair. Therefore, I applied to NYU for their advanced master's degree program in occupational therapy, which was designed for practicing therapists who wanted more theory and a stronger philosophical foundation. Since it wasn't a clinical program, it wouldn't require anything from me physically that would be confrontational or emotionally jarring. This program would prepare me with the necessary degree to teach and/or to apply my skills in a non-clinical arena if I were indeed wheelchair bound and physically compromised. I applied to the program and was accepted. The following fall I started my master's degree program by attending NYU two evenings a week. I would leave my job an hour early on those two evenings, take the A train to Washington Square Park, and walk to the OT building that I knew so well. I always felt a sense of joy being in the atmosphere of NYU, which symbolized something much greater than college memories. For me, it represented a leap into faith and trust, a call from the future that I could become something greater than I could conceive at the time. Better still, my best friend Judy from undergraduate school joined the program, as well.

Pervasive Thoughts

Many nights I would lie in bed praying to be married before I was in a wheelchair, so I could walk down the aisle on my own. I often cried myself to sleep, begging God to grant me this one wish. I often begged my boyfriend Bob to marry me before the inevitable deterioration set in. Fearful of the unknown, I felt so insulted by this grand injustice. Even though my career and personal life were fulfilling, I lived in perpetual anxiety because of the impending threat to my well-being.

Secretly, inwardly, I was always looking for "something" to help me get through my life. At the time I began having increased difficulty holding onto my eating utensils, so in self-preservation I learned it was easier to tell people I wasn't hungry. Time and time again, I refused to ask for help or to admit that my hand didn't have the muscle strength to hold the fork, the sandwich, the cup, or whatever object I wanted to grasp.

The denial of self was securely in place, and I hadn't even noticed how it happened. I developed what I refer to as an "eating disordered personality." While the embarrassment was huge and unmanageable, I ignored my body's needs and rationalized that I wanted to be thin anyway. I believed if my whole body was thin, no one would notice the muscular atrophy in my forearms and hands, and I would appear more normal that way.

While psychologically this denial of self controlled my life, I never became negligent of my health, and I watched everything that I ate. Usually, however, I ate when no one was looking for fear that I would feel embarrassed or ashamed. When I was in public, I would play a mind game to hide my shame from the world. I would order foods in restaurants that didn't require cutting or manual dexterity.

The summer after I graduated from college, I visited Dr. Steve Horowitz for the first time since I was in the hospital as a teenager. In my routine visit to Dr. Gendelman, I had continued to address the problem I was having with my right foot, and he suggested that I see Dr. Horowitz, who was now an attending neurologist and head of the EMG (electromyograph) Department at Long Island Jewish Hospital. I was excited to see him. I felt like a little girl. It had been eight years since I had last seen him, and I still had a crush on him. Would he remember me, the 15-year-old kid in the hospital? Would he think I had become an attractive woman? As soon as he saw me, Dr. Horowitz gave me a big hug and told me that because of my case he decided to specialize in the area of diagnostic testing. He then did an EMG on both my upper and lower extremities. What struck me the most from our encounter is what he said in response to a question I asked him: If I had children, would I pass my disease onto them? His answer disarmed me. "I'm not so concerned that your children would have the disease," he said, "but that you would watch them so closely in fear that they would." Dr. Horowitz's answer put to rest my anxieties about possible genetic or hereditary consequences of the disease.

CHAPTER 4

My First Marriage: Waking Up the Hard Way

IT'S AMAZING WHAT WE DO when we live in survival mode—the continuous cycle of protecting oneself from perceived pain and hurt, only to keep recapitulating the same theme over and over again.

I met my first husband just prior to my 25th birthday. As a staff OT on the inpatient unit at St. Luke's Hospital, I was waiting with my colleagues for morning rounds to begin when a gentleman walked in and sat down. Matthew, a postgraduate student from Columbia University, was volunteering one day a week on the unit. Matthew had just finished his undergraduate studies at Yale University and was taking postgraduate courses before applying to medical school. He wanted to become a psychiatrist, which is why he was volunteering on an adult psychiatric unit, and I was his supervisor.

Raised in a well educated, upper-class family, Matthew was extremely bright, good looking, and outgoing, exuding an air of confidence and sophistication. He was kind and thoughtful with the patients. Never having met anyone like him before, I was intrigued, and we developed a friendship. Although we were from very different backgrounds—I was Jewish and he was a W.A.S.P—we had a wonderful way of relating with each other. Six months after our first meeting, he asked me out on a date. I accepted, thus beginning our relationship outside the walls of the hospital. Right from the beginning, Matthew made me feel special. How was it possible that I, a woman with physical disabilities, had landed this amazing fellow? Through our relationship I was once again proving that I was someone with unforeseen potential. Within several months Matthew asked me to move with him to Boston, his hometown, where he wanted to live after completing his studies.

Besides basking in his love, moving to Boston was a great opportunity to start a new phase in my life, Excitedly, I sent out resumes with the hope of landing a great job. A month later Matthew and I rented a car and drove up to Boston to stay at his family's home in Lincoln, Massachusetts, while his parents were vacationing in Europe.

I had been to the house once before so I knew what to expect. Matthew took me to his favorite restaurants and showed me the places that were important to him as a child and as a young man. The next day I had an interview at the day hospital affiliated with Tufts-New England Medical Center in Dorchester, Mass., a facility that was looking for an occupational therapist to work in community-based psychiatry. When I arrived, Phil, the program supervisor who interviewed me, along with the rest of the staff, greeted me warmly. Everyone commented on my style of clothing, saying that I would fit in perfectly.

I was off to a good start, and the interview flowed with ease. I liked both Phil and the program's philosophy, and I left an hour later filled with excitement and anticipation. The following day I was called back for a second interview, with the director of psychiatry at the main campus in downtown Boston. Again, the interview went well, and I knew that this was the job I wanted. I also knew the staff was impressed by my clinical background, my enthusiasm, as well as the unique brand of occupational therapy that I would bring to the program.

After the interview, Matthew and I spent time looking for an apartment while enjoying Boston and the surrounding area. We found a brownstone on Beacon Street, right in the heart of Boston's beautiful Back Bay, where I wanted to live. Everything fell into place as we built the foundation for our new life together. I had never thought I could be so happy.

After completing the interviews and securing an apartment, we went to Nantucket (where his family owned a vacation home) to spend some time before returning to New York. On the drive to Nantucket, I received a call from Phil, who offered me the position as the group program supervisor. I was overjoyed. Everything I ever wanted was coming true. I breathed a sigh of relief, loving my life with a sense of trust and gratitude that I hadn't felt in a long time. Nantucket was a whole new world for me, and I was a little bowled over by the grandeur of it all. When we arrived there, Matthew's younger brother greeted us at the dock. At the house Matthew introduced me to his younger sister and then acquainted me with life in Nantucket. We had a romantic, magical time, which I took as a prelude to our new life together. Proud of my accomplishments and eager to embrace the future, I returned to New York and submitted my resignation to my supervisor at St. Luke's Hospital, where everyone shared in my excitement.

It Isn't Always As It Appears

In September, 1980, Matthew and I rented a moving van and drove to our apartment in Boston. I later made arrangements with NYU to finish my graduate studies at Harvard's extension program, and to complete my master's thesis while in Boston (which took me two years). When I said yes to relocating to Boston with Matthew, I was excited about a new start, a new city, and a new opportunity to be somewhere other than New York. The only other time I had entertained the thought of moving from New York was after I visited California for an occupational therapy convention just after I graduated from college. I thought that being accepted into the master's program for OT at the University of Southern California would be a great excuse to leave New York, but I never followed through. I didn't have the courage to leave my friends, my family, and even my connection to the medical world that I completely depended on. Now the opportunity to uproot my life and begin anew had arisen, and I jumped at the chance. It is certainly less scary to strike out into the unknown with a beloved partner. Matthew, who was everything I had ever hoped for, was someone I could love and trust as I did Michael. How wonderful to have an intimate relationship with someone who had a similar interest in practicing psychiatry and helping others. Matthew was a brilliant, sensitive man, and I felt honored that he wanted to spend his life with me.

After we first met, he said something I'll never forget. He said, "I'll heal your physical handicap with my love, and you'll heal my emotional handicap with your love." What powerful words! No one ever promised me that before, and I believed him with every beat of my heart. What caused Matthew great suffering were the emotional wounds he was carrying from his family upbringing. Although we came from very different backgrounds, we shared similar wounds that drew us together to be healed.

Because he was sophisticated and knowledgeable, I believed him; at least that's what I told myself. In reality, I believed him because I needed to believe him. Who else was I going to believe? My doctors offered me absolutely no solutions except "to keep my chin up." My belief stemmed from something much greater than gullibility: it stemmed from the need for survival. I was begging for a soul-level connection, and I thought I had found it. I also hungered for a new family like Matthew's, in which people engaged with one another, spent time together, and vacationed together. I wanted it all, so I said goodbye to my life in New York. Because Boston was only a four-hour drive up Interstate 84, I could easily remain in close contact with my friends and family in New York.

After we settled into our new home, it took only a few months for reality to hit. During these challenging and rewarding times, I soon discovered that my life with Matthew was complicated. We had a difficult relationship, and for the most part it didn't meet my hopes and expectations. I started working immediately at my new job, but Matthew struggled with the uncertainty of where to work and whether to apply to medical school or pursue additional premedical studies. This uncertainty about his future caused Matthew to become detached and emotionally unavailable. Usually he was preoccupied and withdrawn, except when he wanted me around, at which time he was kind and gentle. After having enough intimacy and socialization, he would withdraw into himself. I found this pattern hard to adapt to, especially since I needed consistency and predictability in our relationship. I never knew what to expect—whether he would be available or distant. So I learned by necessity to take care of myself.

Finally, Matthew decided to postpone medical school, and he took a job at a nearby private hospital as a psychiatric assistant. He continued with his pre-med studies, even though he had more than adequate course work for med school. He simply wasn't emotionally ready, and his hesitancy caused me distress. We spent quite a lot of time apart, both of us doing our own thing, independent of the other, and I was lonely and discouraged that the life I had anticipated wasn't materializing. Matthew kept promising me that things would change, that he loved me, and that everything would be fine. He even bought me a pre-engagement ring to prove that we would eventually be married. While that was a sweet gesture, I just wanted Matthew to pay attention to me, to open up his heart and let me into his world. In response to his withdrawal, I began to shut down and act extremely cautious around him. I never knew how to behave or how to react. But the more he distanced himself from me, the angrier I became, feeding his withdrawal even more.

One day he said to me, "I'm not in this world to make you happy." How could he make me happy when he was struggling to find his own voice and his place in the world? Again the feelings of rejection cut through me like a knife. I spent many days alone crying out to God for help and direction. In order to cope, I sought solace from my work, my friends, and my creative outlets, trusting that everything would eventually fall into place. Besides, life wasn't all that bad; we had good times, too, when we connected in a loving and meaningful way. I deeply loved this man, and I felt the intensity of his struggle. Somehow I could see beyond my own pain and empathize with him. I had done this before with Michael. The pattern was already carved into stone. I had faith that when he resolved his conflict, our life together would improve.

When reality becomes too uncomfortable, you live life blinded by illusions.

Foolish Pride

As I nurtured this belief for quite some time, I became ashamed at my foolishness for trusting him. I needed to trust him because I hadn't yet learned to trust myself. I withdrew and learned how to live alone in our relationship without depending on him for anything. This familiar way of living made it crystal clear that my romantic fairy tale had ended. I saw with painful clarity that Matthew wasn't the man I thought he was. Still, I wouldn't give up on our relationship, because I wasn't a quitter, and because I didn't have the courage to leave.

Matthew's detached and unavailable behavior felt very familiar to me. As the old pain of being unseen and uncared for resurfaced, countless times I wanted to gather up my strength and walk out the door. I didn't trust that I would be fine and that I deserved more than these meager crumbs of affection. What intensified my extreme loneliness was the daily encounter with my physical deterioration. My disease was progressing, and my heart again lived in fear. In panic, I clutched on to anyone or anything that might help me through this worsening crises. Outside work, I spent my free time reading, doing needlework, and searching for ways to bring peace and harmony into my life. I was struggling inwardly to find happiness in an uncomfortable environment.

Needlework, which was a form of meditation, brought me unparalleled joy. I never felt lonely or disabled when I engaged in this task. If I lacked physical strength, I always found a way to compensate; doing whatever it took to make it perfect. Thus I would use my teeth if my fingers were too tired or weak to pull the needle through the canvas. Needlework always made me feel normal, and everyone expressed awe and admiration at my ability to do this activity. Incredibly, I created some beautiful pieces while having almost no muscle strength in my fingers. What gave me the strength and the will to create works of beauty? I listened to my heart, which wanted me to know the joy of creative expression. Miraculously these works came through me.

I was happiest at my job, where I enjoyed my work and had nice friendships and professional connections. In fact, I thrived at work where I always did well. As the group program supervisor at a day hospital, I had clients who were adult psychiatric patients recently released from inpatient hospitalization. The day hospital provided a structured environment to facilitate the learning of skills they needed to cope in society. My job was to develop a task-oriented life skills program that would increase the patients' current level of functioning while fostering self-esteem and well-being. I always gave my patients the opportunity to feel purposeful and functional, through daily community cooking groups, pre-vocational work groups, and a total program that encouraged patients to feel worthwhile and important. What I wanted for my patients was, in fact, what all of us are seeking in this world. The patients responded to all the help and encouragement that we provided in our healing environment, and their positive responses brought me joy and made me feel valuable for contributing to their lives. At the same time, I was recognized for my professional skills. My friend Phil, the man who interviewed me, provided nonjudgmental personal and professional support for me, listening and assisting me with unconditional love. In addition, I had other caring, supportive friends who helped me get through the rough times with Matthew.

I felt safe at work. I could ask the staff for assistance when there was something I couldn't do physically. I would even ask the patients for help. I can't underestimate how critical it was to express my vulnerability in a safe environment and how therapeutic it was for my patients to see their caregiver receiving help, too. Because I never hid from them (and never had to), my patients related to my vulnerability. In so many ways, my job was my comfort zone.

During this time, my left hand, more than my right, continued to lose muscle strength, and my ability to function and manipulate fine motor tasks became more compromised. I received little support from Matthew, and I felt crushed. My need for his support pushed him into greater withdrawal. He didn't want to take care of anyone but himself, yet my low self-esteem and my survival fear kept me frozen in this relationship. Thankfully, I had friends who offered me support and compassion, and when I needed an extra dose of comfort and familiarity, I would travel to New York to visit my friends there. By now, I had realized that my unfulfilling, isolating life with Matthew was recapitulating the lonely experience that I had when I was growing up in my family. I was recreating with Matthew the same kind of emotional detachment and unavailability that I received from my parents. As a 26-year-old professional woman, I could seek the solace from friends and professionals, although the support I received never made up for the deep grief I felt with my significant other.

With my hand function was deteriorating, I knew I had to do something about it; I couldn't keep hiding out. I recalled that Dr. Steve Horowitz was involved with the Muscular Dystrophy Association. He told me that if I needed any resources, I should check into the association. I found out that my diagnosis fell within its guidelines, and MDA would cover me financially with any necessary medical intervention. I decided to research what was available in Boston, and found an affiliate at the Brigham's and Woman's Hospital. I quickly called to make an appointment for an evaluation. Even though this new lead was encouraging, the whole process broke my heart. Here I was again in search of help, another outside resource, to assist me with my disease process.

Even though I was an occupational therapist and a member of a department that could provide assistance, I chose to keep my appointment hidden from my work environment. I'm not sure why, but I did. I took a bus to the evaluation, feeling anxious and scared. Once again, I found myself looking out the window with tears sliding down my cheeks in anticipation of what I would learn. I couldn't imagine how MDA could help me. I resisted using any adaptive equipment, yet I was fighting a losing battle and would have to give in and try something new. I had no idea what, but I was desperate. Since my neurologist had nothing new to offer, I had to learn the difficult art of acceptance and compensation.

I recall meeting with a physician who sent me over to the occupational therapy department to be evaluated for a splint. In the waiting room at Brigham's and Women's Hospital, I looked around at the patients who where waiting alongside me. I had to fight back my desire to run away. It was surreal. "I'm a therapist," I thought, "not a patient." Feeling defeated, I asked myself, "What am I doing here?"

After an examination in the OT clinic, the physician and occupational therapist recommended that I have a splint made to manipulate my fingers with pulleys, giving me increased functional movement in each of my fingers. Called an outrigger splint, it would literally make my fingers move by external support. I sat there and said to myself, "There's no way I'm going to wear this splint. I'd rather be dead." This new contraption was not a simple lumbrical bar splint that I was given only a few years before. While I could hide that if I wanted to, I couldn't hide this one. Eying the device suspiciously, I thought, "My profession endorses this tool, yet I refuse to wear it. What's wrong with me? Why am I so resistant? And why am I not practicing what I preach?"

When the physician left, I told the occupational therapist that it was difficult for me as a professional to be on the receiving end as a patient, and would have to think about it. I cried the whole way home. I had spent years struggling, compensating for my physical differences and making everything work. How could I now succumb to a splint, an external support? Everyone would notice that there was something wrong with me. Did I want to experience this humiliation? After consideration, I went back and had OT make me a splint, but I never wore it. I put it under my bed, and that's where it stayed.

CHAPTER 5

My Hand Surgeon: Truly an Angel

I HAVE LEARNED THAT THERE is no such thing as coincidence. Somehow the universe always knows to send you exactly what you need. In my case, it was the gift of an angel in the form of a physician who would turn my life around, at least for a while.

In the summer of my 26th year, I developed a *granuloma*, a mass of inflamed tissue, under the nail bed of my right thumb, a problem that was unrelated to my disease. Phil, my colleague at work, suggested I go to the hand surgery department at the medical center. In the examining room, Dr. Mark Belsky, the attending physician, looked at my nail and recommended a quick outpatient surgical procedure to remove the infection. Dr. Belsky was gentle, kind, and considerate in the way he treated me, and I was grateful that he was the attending physician that day. What struck me most about our first encounter was that he didn't ask me about my hands. Instead, he focused on the immediate problem, unlike the majority of physicians who wanted a complete history of my disease. I had grown weary of physicians with their curiosity and constant questioning. As a human being with feelings and sensitivity, I was tired of explaining something that was inexplicable. I always wanted to give a quick retort and say it was arthritis, something clear and simple, but because I had struggled for so many years, I couldn't deny the truth of my experience.

I scheduled this simple surgical procedure, which would take an hour or two, after which I would return home and rest. My mother was in town for a visit and decided to stay an extra day in case I needed anything. On the morning of the surgery, my mother and I walked the few blocks to the hospital, and she stayed in the waiting room during the procedure. Because the surgery required only local anesthesia, I was fully awake and could speak to Dr. Belsky while he operated. During our conversation I learned that we had a lot in common. As a staff member of the hospital, I knew many of the same people he did. He had trained under the doctors in New York whom I knew from my clinical internships. We shared similar stories about our upbringing: We both grew up in New Jersey, and our fathers were both dentists. Because of his open, friendly, and warm demeanor, I didn't feel like just another patient. I felt strangely comfortable as he cut surgically into my nail bed.

Halfway through the procedure, Dr. Belsky inquired about my hands. I explained my history, my diagnosis, and my prognosis. After I shared my story, he said, "Even though you're not a hand patient, I'd like to help you function." Now here was an offer I couldn't refuse! I was grateful that this kind physician was willing to look "outside the box" and do everything possible to keep me from becoming completely disabled. Dr. Belsky suggested we meet to explore this further after I healed from the thumb surgery. He came into my life at a time when I desperately needed an angel to believe in me.

To Hide and Seek

Two weeks later, after my thumb had healed, I made the appointment. Feeling both curiosity and anxiety, I left work early and took a train to the hospital. I didn't know what Dr. Belsky would propose, but I knew that I was losing my hand function, a prospect that threatened my life, and I had to do something. His office was across the street from the medical center in what used to be the old medical school dormitory. As I walked into the office, I noticed pictures of his wife and baby boy, an endearing touch that made me feel comfortable with him and inspired me with trust at the same time.

Dr. Belsky proposed doing tendon transfers on my left hand. We knew that both hands would eventually require surgical intervention, but he suggested that we start with the left. In performing this reconstructive procedure, he would transfer healthy tendons just below my elbow and thread them into the diseased part of my lower arm, hand, and fingers. This would afford me the luxury of flexing my fingers in a fisted position so that I could hold objects in my hand. He suggested we spend a few months planning, researching, and reviewing all the possibilities. Above all, he wanted to proceed with caution and consideration for my needs.

Dr. Belsky suggested that prior to the surgery we make a video to document my current level of neuromotor functioning. We agreed that Dory, my best friend and an occupational therapist, would guide the session and provide emotional support. Dory asked me to perform daily living tasks: tying shoes, opening and closing jars, buttoning and zipping clothes, holding various implements (pen, fork, and knife), and doing other motor tasks that are usually involved in performing functional assessments on clients. We filmed this video in the occupational therapy department at the hospital where we worked, which was set up for this type of evaluation. I said yes only because Dory would be with me.

Even though I trusted Dr. Belsky and Dory because of their years of clinical experience together, it felt embarrassing to show them how incapacitated I was. On the morning of the filming, I walked into the room and immediately noticed the electric sewing machine. At that moment I wished I had the hand strength to sew curtains, as my future mother-in-law could. Dory sensed my nervousness, and her presence calmed me. She reassured me that Dr. Belsky was a wonderful man and that I should let him see me with complete candor and openness. Only in this way could he truly help me. I was grateful for Dory's support as a friend and colleague. Soon Dr. Belsky appeared with video camera in hand. I began performing the tasks one at a time. I struggled through each task shamefully as I showed my doctor and my friend how disabled I really was. A part of me remained emotionally detached from the experience as I struggled to do the best I could, while another part of me found this emotionally and physically draining. I was much more accustomed to the role of the evaluator, and it wasn't easy for me to be the patient under scrutiny.

Not until 12 years later did I watch the video, in the privacy of my home. I watched myself with my jaw hanging open. It was inconceivable to me that I was the woman in the video. I cried as I witnessed myself struggle with the simplest tasks, such as tying my shoes or grasping an object. When I spoke about the video to friends, I spoke with the objectivity and detachment of an occupational therapist speaking about a patient she had known 12 years ago. It shook me to the core to see how I had hidden from others and how I had compensated for my physical weakness to avoid humiliation and embarrassment. This video gave me a perspective about myself that I had never allowed myself to acknowledge.

Real Life

Because of my progressing disease, I had to think about everything I did—about the clothing I wore and the food I ate. I scrutinized every article of clothing that I purchased. On what side are the buttons? Is the zipper in the front, in the back, or on the side? Could I pull my boots up? Tie my shoe? Close my coat? Living life with dignity was all in the details. Would I be able to zip my jacket, snap my pants, button my shirt? I wanted life to be easy and thoughtless, but it never was, because it always presented me with choices I resented. When I was in the company of others, I had to carefully choose the food I ate. Predictably, I would go through the same mind game over and over again: Did I need a knife? Would I have to cut this or hold that? Oh, the embarrassment I felt when I couldn't manipulate something or hold my glass of water. I wanted to spread the butter on the deliciously warm French bread, but it was way too painful, so I didn't even reach for it.

Driving a car presented problems that most people never consider. For example, my first car was a Honda, the basic model without electric windows or electric door locks. I had trouble manipulating the door locks, and I always worried about whether I could get out of my car in a hurry in case of an accident. I hesitated to put my seat belt on because it was hard to unlatch the buckle.

The amount of time I spent worrying about my safety and other people's response was enormous. I used to envision myself being stuck in my car in a body of water, unable get the seatbelt off and the door unlocked. I felt embarrassed when I struggled to lift the change out of the change box to hand to the attendee at a parking lot or a tollbooth, and I hoped the people behind me wouldn't become upset because it took me so long. I felt like damaged merchandise and did everything possible to avoid exposing my frailties to others. Walking on eggshells, I lived in a constant state of anxiety. I was exhausted from having to think about every detail of my life, and I took absolutely nothing for granted. In my home I used adaptive devices to help me pull a zipper or button a shirt, and I kept a piece of sticky material called *dycem* by my front door to assist me in turning the knob to avoid the anxiety surrounding that seemingly simple action. My colleagues in the occupational therapy department gave me these adaptive devices as gifts that I would use in the privacy of my home.

When I was away from home, I would make a conscious decision as to how much I would allow other people to really see me. The choice always felt like a double-edged sword. On one hand, I was handicapped; but on the other, I didn't look handicapped. On the surface I looked normal to most people. If I decided to reveal my true condition, I had to trust that people would not injure me with their thoughtless comments, stares, or hurtful behavior. But when people were curious and asked me about my hands, I always shared the truth, and usually my honesty was rewarded with compassionate responses.

With all these challenges, I still led a full life. I attended the Harvard extension program two nights a week for my master's degree, worked full time, and continued to live a tumultuous existence with Matthew. I met with Dr. Belsky weekly, and we moved forward with a plan of reconstructive tendon transfers that would help me regain some functional ability. Dr. Belsky asked me if I would fly to New York and have a consultation with his teacher and mentor, Dr. Littler, the grandfather of hand surgery, who had developed the procedure Dr. Belsky would be performing. I knew Dr. Littler's name from my professional studies and was excited and honored for the opportunity to consult with him.

By now, I had become an expert in dissociating from my medical treatments. There was "Laura, the struggling patient," and there was "Laura, the curious woman seeking knowledge and clinical understanding." With that realization, I flew to New York City to meet the world-renowned Dr. Littler. On a beautiful, sunny day, feeling confident and hopeful, I strolled into his office on East 90th Street and Fifth Avenue. Dr. Littler was an elderly gentleman with a kind smile who spoke warmly of Dr. Belsky, whom he greatly admired. As he discussed the impending surgical procedure, he said, "Dr. Belsky is an excellent surgeon, and you're in great hands." I thanked him and told him of my confidence in Dr. Belsky, too. He recommended that I proceed with the surgery, and he was completely convinced that it would be tremendously beneficial. I left his office feeling joy, anticipating that finally I would have some relief.

After spending time with friends during the weekend, I flew back to Boston and made an appointment with Dr. Belsky. We reviewed my visit with Dr. Littler, and in great humility he offered me the option of having the surgery with Dr. Littler who, as Dr. Belsky stated, was "the best." He said he would not be insulted in the least if I chose the great surgeon to perform the procedure.

"It doesn't matter that Dr. Littler developed the surgical procedure and that he's the best," I said. "You're not only a tremendous surgeon, but, more importantly, you're a remarkable human being. I'll have the surgery only with you."

Dr. Belsky smiled gratefully at my compliment. Being number one in the world meant very little to me. I already had plenty of experiences with physicians who were number one, and what mattered to me most was how the doctor related to me, first as a person and then as a patient. Dr. Littler was a gifted, pleasant man, but I had established a deep relationship with Dr. Belsky based on honor and support, and that was all I needed. I wished more medical practitioners had his humility, grace and concern—the same qualities I had witnessed years before with Dr. Gendelman and Dr. Horowitz.

Between August 1981 and February 1982, I met with pre-op physicians and had a series of familiar diagnostic tests. Dr. Belsky referred me to Dr. Walter Bradley, an attending neurologist who specialized in Anterior Horn Cell Disease. To my great relief, he informed me that the disease was carried by a recessive genetic trait and would not be passed on to my children. "Perhaps in 10 years," he said, "medical science will invent a pill to arrest the neural diffusion in your spinal column." I found this possibility promising, but in the back of my mind, there lurked memories of past procedures and fears of future treatments.

The New England Medical Center, located hundreds of miles from the Mount Sinai Medical Center in Manhattan, now became my medical support system. This time around I was an active participant in my own process, rather than the passive observer I had been as a teenager.

In January 1982 I lost complete function of my thumbs, making the upcoming surgery even more critical. I eagerly hoped that something would turn this process around. With each phase of physical deterioration, I clung to Matthew, believing he would rescue me from this bitter reality. In the deep recesses of my heart, I waited for my parents to show up and ease this burden. At this point, my emotional anguish and the incessant physical insults caused by the disease were merging into one inseparable condition.

The surgery was scheduled for February 9, 1982. I arranged to be out of work for two weeks—one week in the hospital and one week to recuperate at my future in-laws' home. What troubled me a great deal was my patients' reaction to my disease and the surgery. Would their respect for me change? Would they still see me as the professional in charge? Much to my surprise, these misgivings proved to be groundless. As they openly shared their fear regarding my upcoming surgery, their outpouring of concern provided me with an opportunity to genuinely share my feelings with them. As I eased their fears, I eased my own.

My father was concerned that if something went wrong, I would be left with less functioning then I currently had. In response I said, "Dad, I have nothing to lose. I'm almost completely paralyzed anyway." I feared that if the surgery didn't work, I would have no other viable solutions. (The idea of wearing external splints was too devastating for me even to comprehend.) Having exhausted all my possibilities, I prayed this surgery would be the success Dr. Belsky envisioned.

Back to the Operating Room

On the day of the surgery, Matthew drove me to the hospital. The New England Medical Center had only double rooms, and I was thrilled this time to have not only one roommate, but one close to my age. I was also relieved that my father came to Boston to be with me during the surgery, since Matthew wasn't reliable enough to be present emotionally or physically. As an adult, I felt much different than when I was a teenager. For one thing, I no longer appreciated the residents' probing inquiries about my past medical history. I wanted to tell them to leave me alone; I was tired of sharing my story, of being exposed, literally and figuratively. The reality was that as a patient I was treated as a specimen, and the experience was degrading. On an affirmative note, I found life in the hospital to be less traumatic and frightening because of my age and maturity. I also found the hospital environment itself to be gentler. Since there were telephones and televisions in the room, I didn't have to leave my bed unless I chose to. The whole experience was more humane, and I felt a sense of pride in knowing this hospital as my place of employment.

In the morning I was wheeled to the operating room. As this was my first tendon transfer, I didn't know what to expect or what my hand would look like post-op. I simply closed my eyes, prayed, and hoped for the best.

The six-hour surgery had gone well, and I woke up in the recovery room feeling nauseous, with Dr. Belsky who was at my side, holding the infamous kidney-shaped bowl for me in case I threw up. I felt slightly embarrassed in almost the same way I felt after my first operation when my mother got to witness my post-op nausea. This time, however, Dr. Belsky made me feel comfortable and safe. Most of all, I trusted him with my life and well-being.

I was glad my father was standing at the entrance to my room. It was reassuring to have him at my bedside to help me cope with the physical pain and discomfort. My boyfriend, in contrast, was not often present. When he did visit, he remained detached and emotionally disconnected. Even my emotionally detached father commented on Matthew's inability to be available and supportive during my hospital stay. I did, however, have many other visitors, including colleagues from work, friends, and even my boyfriend's parents. Most comforting was having my father hold my hand through this traumatic time.

My arm was in a cast, placed inside a sling, and attached to an IV pole. The nurses encouraged me to sleep, which was a difficult feat with my arm suspended in mid-air. I persevered in my usual, uncomplaining way, and I managed to forget my arm and get some sleep. My father left after a few days, and I was discharged at the end of the week. Matthew's mother picked me up and brought me back to their home just outside Boston, where I spent the following week recuperating under the care of Matthew's loving family, who took care of me with love and attention. Matthew would visit after work and usually spend the night. All in all, I was grateful to be in a quiet, gentle environment where I could rest and heal.

A week after surgery, I went back to our apartment, and soon returned to work in a full arm cast, which stayed on for eight weeks. During this time, I became efficient doing tasks with one hand. I realized that life was easier when I was in a cast. I even had an excuse for my inability to perform certain tasks: I could simply explain that I broke my arm. While having my arm in a cast made me feel normal, I never went the way of fabricating stories about it. I discovered I didn't need to hide, and I could graciously accept assistance from others.

Ten days later I returned to Dr. Belsky's office to have the stitches removed. Lying on the table, I was filled with anticipation when he reached for his saw and split the cast in two. I hated the vibrations of the saw and the proximity of the blade to my skin. I trusted Dr. Belsky implicitly, yet I felt my anxiety rise as he pulled the cast apart. What would my hand look like? Where exactly were the scars? How ugly would I be?

When I saw my hand, my scars, and my swollen fingers, I was visibly upset. Dr. Belsky reassured me that the scars would fade, the swelling would go down, and I would relearn how to use my fingers again. He removed the stitches and re-casted me. I was glad to be in a cast because I wasn't ready to deal with the next step. Every two weeks I returned for a cast change. After eight weeks he removed the cast, and we both watched me wiggle my fingers. Success!

My friend Dory, who had accompanied me to the appointment, drove me home afterward. She bought a bottle of wine to celebrate the successful surgery, and she made a toast to "the restored strength and functioning of my left hand." Even with Dr. Belsky's reassurances, I constantly asked for hers, too; clearly, I had some doubts about regaining the use of my hand.

Matthew was not at the apartment when we arrived. He called to tell me that he was at a party with some friends. His absence upset me terribly, but I restrained myself, and when Dory left, I cried tears of inconsolable loneliness. Bruised emotionally and physically, I sat on the couch for two hours, staring at my hand and trying to wiggle my fingers. Red and swollen, my left hand had been altered. It was no longer the hand I was born with, and that boggled my mind. In the following weeks, Dory worked on me therapeutically, gently stretching and manipulating my fingers and wrist to increase mobility and decrease swelling. Through these simple range-of–motion exercises, I had to open my hand, close it, and grasp objects.

I felt that the surgery had to work because there was no other alternative. At night I slept in a resting splint to protect my hand. I was careful at home and work not to bump into anything. As the weeks passed, all my discipline with the exercises and careful behavior resulted in noticeable improvement. I was encouraged as I continued to increase my movement, and within a few months I had full flexion in my fingers, which gave me the ability to make a fist. I was so relieved. Dr. Belsky deemed the surgery a success, and I agreed because I could miraculously hold things that I had found beyond my capacity prior to surgery.

In my excitement I treated myself to a high-end, expensive sewing machine. I wanted to express myself creatively with my newly-repaired hand. Months earlier, when I walked into the occupational therapy department, I said to Dory, "Maybe someday, when I can use both hands, I'll sew on a machine." That day had now arrived. From then on I sat for hours, joyously creating beautiful curtains, duvet covers and quilts. People who viewed my work expressed amazed admiration at how my hands could produce such beautiful pieces.

I felt similar joy when I held chopsticks for the first time in my life. Granted, I didn't have a tight grip, but the pure excitement of doing something that was previously beyond my ability took my breath away. In those moments the disability, pain, and feelings of inadequacy disappeared. What might be deemed insignificant to others was monumental to me. One evening at dinner, when I was holding a sparerib, I said to Matthew, "Look what I can do!" These liberating moments brought great tears of joy. I knew that even though there was no cure, these small miracles helped me trust that my life would get easier.

Unfortunately, these successes were short-lived, and I soon required a second surgery. As I gained strength in my ability to flex my fingers (to hold in a grasp position), I lost the opposing motion of extension (being able to straighten my fingers). Dr. Belsky explained the delicate balance between the extensors (the tendons that allow the fingers to open) and the flexors (the tendons that allow the fingers to make a fist). Six months after the first surgery, my fingers went into a claw position (abnormal hyperextension of my third metacarpal joint). All I could do was pray that the next surgery would work. In October 1982 I scheduled another round of reconstructive tendon transfers.

Excuses, Excuses, Excuses

It amazes me how often I turned my cheek to not see what was happening in front of my face. How controlled I was by negative emotion, never believing I had a choice. When life becomes a game of holding on, you do just about anything to ignore the realities. If I only had the courage to step out of the trench I had dug for myself.

My personal life remained the same. I felt stuck and imprisoned by my own insecurities and fears. I would walk around the apartment, wondering where Matthew was and why we weren't spending more time together. For the most part, we lived separate lives. I pretended that the way we were living didn't matter to me, although it did, and I invented excuses about why I stayed with him. Sometimes I accused him of not caring about me and of having relations with others, both of which he denied. I was lonely and immobilized. Gazing out the window, I asked myself, "What am I doing? Why did I leave New York? Why did he ask me to come to Boston only to ignore me much of the time? Why am I staying? What's wrong with me? Why don't I respect myself more and find someone who will love and honor me?"

Although I had other outlets (friends, work, creative projects, and my studies), I again found myself in a situation without emotional and spiritual support from a significant loved one. Because I feared being alone and lacked the courage to leave, I stayed with Matthew and unconsciously relived the struggles with my family of origin. In fact, all I wanted was to get married and be safe. I desperately needed to know that someone would take care of me if and when I couldn't take care of myself. Thus, despite the discomfort, I stayed on, making excuses and rationalizations about our behavior without believing that I deserved something better.

The approach/avoidance scenario that Matthew and I enacted came from our damaged pasts and our struggle to survive. How can we love another when we're inwardly struggling to survive for ourselves and get our own needs met? In spite of my shortcomings, and his, I really did love Matthew. I loved him deeply. I loved the man I had met and the dreams and promises that we shared. I believed that with hard work and perseverance we could make our relationship work. The key word was *perseverance*. To me quitting wasn't an option. I steadfastly remained focused on the happy future I imagined rather than the disappointing present I was enduring. In retrospect I was continuing a pattern of codependency that would haunt me for many years to come. The damage was so deep, so imbedded in my cellular makeup, that I knew no other way to be.

Thankfully, the disease remained in the cervical and first thoracic vertebrae and didn't progress as the chief of neurology and the specialist from Philadelphia had predicted long ago. I was relieved and comforted that Dr. Belsky would do everything possible to help me regain functioning.

I had two more tendon transfers on my left hand while I lived in the Boston area—one in October, 1982 and the other in February, 1983. What I remember most about my second surgery was the comment my mother made shortly after my cast was removed. I called my parents, excited to let them know how quickly I regained movement in my fingers and how Dr. Belsky deemed the surgery a success. My mother responded with a remark about a new technique they were using in Utah. She said that the doctor's were implanting chips into the muscle belly itself to regain muscle movement in peoples arms and legs, and that, maybe, this would be available to me in the future when I needed it. As I listened to her speak, with my heart sinking to the pit of my stomach, I was enraged by her response, which completely ignored the accomplishment I shared with her. I hung up the phone screaming and crying, sharing with Matthew what had happened, determined never to speak with her again. Three days later I received the newspaper clipping of the procedure in the mail, with my mothers handwriting that said "keep this for future reference." I threw the paper in the garbage.

My parents disempowered me throughout my life. The pain was crushing every time. I never got use to the insults. I just wanted them to love me, and their lack of support hurt me to my core. It's almost as if they were fulfilling their own needs by keeping me in a disappointed, hurtful space

After the third surgery my overall hand functioning had improved and I felt great. Although the results weren't perfect (my left hand was far from normal), my hand looked and felt healthier than it had before.

Returning Home

In the late summer of 1983, Matthew and I returned to New York. Matthew started medical school in Westchester County, New York. I was excited about moving back and having the opportunity to be closer to my family and friends again. I felt strong and healthy and knew that Dr. Belsky was a quick three hours away. I wrote Dr. Belsky a thank-you card expressing my deepest gratitude. In part, I said, "How do you thank someone who has given you the greatest gift of all—the gift of functioning?" When friends and family called me on the phone, the first question was always "How are your hands doing?" I often felt shocked in responding to that question, because within a short time I had completely forgotten that I had a hand problem. For a few years I actually stopped identifying as the woman with "the disease."

A year after Matthew and I returned to New York, we got married. "Why not?" I said to myself. Neither of us had the courage to move ahead. We had struggled hard over the years on our relationship, and we were willing to keep working on it. Although the relationship continued to have weaknesses, I wanted to be married. So I married a man who was detached, disconnected and unavailable. He married a woman who was angry and tired, and who believed she was damaged merchandise. To make the marriage secure, I built a barrier around myself of supportive friends and the work that I loved.

I was thrilled when I was offered a position as the director of the occupational therapy department at a prestigious private psychiatric hospital. Professionally, I now had everything I wanted, and for the next three years I remained surgery free. I had few physical difficulties at work in the dual role of administrator and clinician. However, I once experienced deep embarrassment when one of the psychiatric residents said, "You should learn how to hold a fork correctly before you have children." His words struck me as unnecessary and humiliating. I explained to him about the series of surgeries on my hand and how this was the best I could do. I never understood why people said such cruel things, and his comment often replayed in my mind and brought me pain. But in spite of such rare occurrences, I continued to excel at work and felt included and honored for the person I truly was.

Although my marriage was filled with strife, I desperately wanted to have a child. I wanted to hold someone, love someone, and felt a child would fill the hole in my heart. At first, I desired a son. I believed a son would bring me the unconditional love I was seeking. I had always heard that sons love their mothers. Then, years later, after reading so many books on mothers and daughters I felt I was ready for the challenge of a daughter. Little did I know what that challenge would look like.

A year later I gave birth to my daughter Jessica, and had five months of maternity leave to be home and enjoy the gift of my new baby. I had loved being pregnant. I felt a sense of aliveness and health I hadn't felt in a very long time. I cherished my time with her, especially since time off for me had usually meant recovery from surgeries. I remember being filled with anticipation about how I would be as mother. I knew I never wanted to repeat the relationship I had with my own mother and did everything I could to not recapitulate that.

Jessica would indeed be a mirror for me to heal the relationship with my own mother. We certainly are given every opportunity to work through our baggage—we're just required to be awake enough to notice. It would take me quite some time before I fully understood.

Jessica was the joy of my life, and I felt blessed to have such quality time with her away from work. With her birth came other challenges. I was showered with beautiful gifts for her after her birth, delicate little dresses and outfits fit for a princess. Unfortunately for me, these became another trauma, another confrontation, and another reality check. As much as my hands had become more functional, I found it virtually impossible for me to manipulate the small tasks associated with motherhood. I broke out in tears when I tried without success to button one of her delicate dresses. Sometimes I had to use my teeth, and once in awhile I broke the button that way. I hated myself when I had to struggle so hard, and all the frustrations around my sense of inadequacy surfaced. The cruel realities of my life intensified with her as once again I removed diaper tabs with my teeth (Thank God there were no longer diaper pins). I shopped for my daughter's clothes in the same way I shopped for mine, scrutinizing every part of the outfit to make sure that on a good day I could handle whatever physical challenges it posed. It saddened me that I couldn't put Jessica's hair up in pretty little ponytails and ribbons like the other toddlers. I couldn't wait until she was older, when she wouldn't need me for these burdensome tasks. So I asked the babysitter to do things that I, her mother, should do. As tears ran down my cheeks, I often apologized to Jessica for my inadequacies and for the intense frustration I felt.

I experienced a chronic underlying sense of inadequacy and unworthiness over the smallest issues at home. Work didn't challenge me in the same way. I don't know why there was such a discrepancy between my personal and professional life. Clearly, the burden of feeling damaged played itself out to a much greater extent in my personal, intimate world than it did in my professional world.

To succeed in both worlds took inconceivable strength and determination. At home I could accomplish incredible feats if I wasn't burdened by people's reactions to my inventive ways of doing things. In the comfort of my own home, I could do most everything, in part because I had an unconquerable spirit. I also consciously had to conserve the energy I expended to avoid tiring myself and being in pain. After all, my husband was in medical school, I was working full time, and I carried the brunt of our family's responsibilities.

Unfortunately, my hand started to show signs of weakness again, and the joint in my left pinky had become immobilized. My fingers were beginning to contract, and another surgery was inevitable. Dr. Belsky, now the chief of hand surgery at The Newton-Wellesley Hospital Center in Newton, Mass., explained to me that the tendons had stretched out in time. Thus when Jessica was 15 months old, I had a fourth hand surgery. "Here we go again," I thought.

This became more of an undertaking because of the physical distance involved. We were grateful for Matthew's parents, who lived outside of Boston, where Jessica and I stayed while I was recuperating. Matthew accompanied me to the hospital, stayed for the surgery, then returned to his studies in New York. The morning of surgery, as I stepped into the hospital elevator, I said to Matthew, "I don't know if I can go through this again. What if I don't wake up? I have a child to take care of now." Thankfully, I did wake up, and continued the joyous task of being Jessica's mom. I often wondered as Jessica grew older how she would react to her mother's disfigured hands. Years later I received Jessica's response. I will never forget her words. She said, "My biggest fear is that at 13 I will have hands like yours and be depressed like dad." That was quite a burden for any 12-year-old child to bear. As I held her in my arms I reassured her that this would not happen.

I repeated this process twice over the next year, each time driving to Boston for my scheduled pre-and post-op visits. Altogether, in a period of six years, I had seven surgeries on my left hand. By now my hand had regained enough strength that I was feeling strong and healthy. I had six pounds of muscle strength, which was significantly better than none. Jessica was 16 months old, and Matthew, who had graduated from medical school, was doing his residency. Professionally, I decided to shift my area of concentration to pediatric occupational therapy. I wanted flexibility in my work hours, so I explored being an independent contractor or a consultant.

I had a strong desire to work with children, so I left the position as the director of occupational therapy and accepted a position as an independent contractor working with children at the Citywide Autistic Unit in the Bronx. In the past, working with children in therapy and physically manipulating them would have been impossible, but now I wanted to give it a try. It represented a new beginning for me. After working in the field of adult psychiatry, I held the belief that if I worked with children, they could avoid becoming psychiatric patients as adults. Feeling healthy and motivated, I acquainted myself with the therapeutic modalities currently used in school-based practice. I enjoyed the physicality of working with young children. It was all "hands on" work, which reinforced my ability rather than my disability.

Working with the autistic population was demanding and required some muscle strength. The children had a tendency to bolt down the hall, and my biggest concern was whether I was physically strong enough to hold their hands tightly enough to avoid this from happening. As much as it was exhausting and physically wearing, I was up for the challenge.

Matthew and I both wanted to have another child. When Jessica was 3 years old, I gave birth to Benjamin. During the early part of my pregnancy I was diagnosed with Placenta Previa (a condition where the placenta rides low in the uterus) and my physician warned me that I could hemorrhage if I chose to carry this pregnancy to term. My only option was to remain on bed rest. Nothing was going to interfere with me having this baby, so for the next six weeks I stayed in bed, reading, resting and communicating with the child inside me, grateful that the pregnancy provided me an opportunity to get off the roller-coaster ride and rest. After six weeks the placenta corrected itself and I was able to return to work. At 30 weeks I found out I was having a son and I was thrilled. I knew this child came to me for many reasons yet unknown. I felt the tremendous gift of having my two children, remembering how fearful I had been to even consider having children, believing I might genetically pass my disease to them.

My commute to the Bronx from Brewster, N.Y. took an hour each way. When Benjamin was a year old, I decided to bring my practice closer to home. I wanted the opportunity to be closer to my children, so I became a full-time therapist in a local school district, working with children from ages 5 to 15. The work was physical, and I had to use my body as a therapeutic modality. This meant "waking up" the child's body through sensory motor integration, a practice that improves his or her ability to function. As an occupational therapist, I was helping others to like themselves, to feel worthy, and to become more functional. I gave them exactly the same message I gave to myself. I knew of no other way to keep going.

Life with Matthew hadn't changed, and neither had our marriage, which continued with all its trials and tribulations. Matthew agreed to try couple's therapy to help resolve our conflicts, but the progress was minimal. When Matthew completed his residency program and accepted a position as an attending psychiatrist at a nearby community hospital, our life became a little easier. Or maybe I just viewed it differently. I told myself that at least now he was supporting me financially and that he was contributing to my life. Matthew was as distant with the children as he was with me, and the burden of feeling like a single parent exasperated my already stressed body. To lessen the load, I hired Joyce, who came to the house to care for the children while I was working. Joyce, and her husband Gus, became a surrogate family for my children. I knew I could always depend on them, which helped me tremendously. I was the mother of two small children, holding a full-time professional job, and dealing with ongoing medical intervention to keep me functioning. I felt betrayed by the world, and the anger crept deeper and deeper into my soul. I wasn't happy, and my body responded with panic attacks as my anxiety levels skyrocketed. For example, I recall anxiously walking down the streets of New York City and becoming terrified that a stranger making snickering sexual comments would harm me. I was living a life dominated by fear and anxiety.

While things were tense in my marriage, I made a significant breakthrough in another area of my life. The despair and the disconnection I felt with my parents, mostly my mother, were ongoing. I realized at this time that in order for me to survive, I had to "divorce" her on an emotional-spiritual level. I made a conscious decision to relinquish any remaining desire to be loved and honored by her. I was tired of her hostility and detachment, as well as the sadness and grief I harbored within me. This decision to divorce her gave me the courage to muster the strength two years later to divorce my husband. Once I could divorce my mother, I could divorce anyone. I was finally done being mistreated and devalued, and I was beginning to stand on my own strength.

I enjoyed my children, my friends, and my work, but consciously I knew my marriage wasn't working. I was also tired of pretending that things would improve. Lying awake in bed at night, I yearned to be with someone who would be more available as a husband and father. Matthew had promised me that he would be more available when he had finished his medical studies, and although I wanted to believe him, in my heart I knew it would never happen. As I faced the prospect of living without him, I was haunted by my mother's words uttered so long ago: "Who will want you with those hands?"

Matthew was now a practicing psychiatrist, and I was a successful occupational therapist. By all appearances, we were an attractive couple, with two beautiful children, a nice home, and promising futures. However, I had stayed trapped in a marriage that wasn't nourishing because I was wounded and couldn't rise above the self-image of being handicapped. I stayed despite receiving little emotional and spiritual nourishment. I stayed until I thought my soul would die.

In the fall of 1992, I met Sam, who caught my eye at services on the High Holidays. A mutual friend introduced us because we were both occupational therapists. We became friends, and I enjoyed spending time with this likable, fun-loving man. I soon learned that there were many other people in the world with whom I could relate, and this realization provided enough incentive for me to finally make the difficult decision to end my marriage.

After a stressful weekend away with Matthew, I decided I couldn't continue anymore. I decided that life alone, with all its stresses and uncertainties, was far better than this secure but difficult marriage in which my soul was suffocating. I had a full-time job and a full-time babysitter, and I was staying for one reason only: fear. I was 37 years old, and I deserved more than this.

We were both relieved when our 13-year relationship finally ended. Even though I wanted this divorce, going through it was extremely painful. My heart had yearned for the love and happiness of family life, and with my persevering spirit, I did everything humanly possible to continue my marriage with Matthew. We had been through so much together, and it broke my heart when we finally admitted our failure to make the marriage work. In the spring of 1993, a few months after Matthew and I separated, when Jessica was 7 and Benjamin was 4, I began to date Sam.

CHAPTER 6

My Knight in Shining Armor

I WAS HUNGRY TO BELIEVE I was worth loving. I begged the universe to send me someone who was willing to love me the way I believed I deserved to be loved. What I didn't realize was that I had to love myself first before someone else could. That was the pearl of wisdom I was missing.

From the moment I saw Sam, I knew I wanted to be with him. Was it the twinkle in his eye, the lightness in his step, or the way he held his infant daughter? My soul drew me to him, and I opened to the experience. As we started spending time together, I could feel the joy and excitement of being with someone who knew how to be available. This longing for heartfelt intimacy had been growing in me all my life, and unlike the frustration I felt with Matthew, I now experienced sweetness and an upbeat way of relating with Sam that led to endless hours of closeness based on the freedom to speak from the heart. And unlike Matthew, with Sam I knew that he was listening and that my thoughts and feelings mattered to him.

There were a few red flags, but I chose to ignore them because the positive outweighed the negative. When Sam came into my life, he brought with him many complicated and unresolved family issues as a result of his first wife's death and his quick remarriage to a woman he knew from work. He had two children from his first marriage:

a 19-year-old daughter and a 17-year-old son. He also had a one-year-old daughter from his second marriage. Clearly, he had a lot of emotional and physical responsibilities, and I, of course, had my own two children.

Sam was an affectionate, physical man, and it felt wonderful to be held by a man who adored me. When I married Matthew, I often said that I wanted a family man who would participate in family activities, such as going to the Bronx Zoo with the children. Unconsciously, I attracted a partner who was recapitulating a similar sense of loneliness and isolation that I experienced as a child in my family. I was exhausted from these feelings of alienation. With Sam they never came up, because he was open and more emotionally present.

After a year of dating, Sam and I knew that we wanted to live together. After careful consideration, we decided that I would move into his home, and sell the one that Matthew and I had owned. Sam and I spent hours sketching, redesigning, and reconfiguring how to fit five children into our home. His older children, who were in college, spent the majority of time away from home, while his youngest child visited every other weekend. My children were excited about the move, although we knew it would be a major adjustment for all of us.

When Sam married his second wife, he was still grieving the loss of his first wife, and was attached to many of her belongings. His second wife lived among these constant reminders of that former marriage. In preparation for our relationship, I was determined to make that house my home, and was unwilling to share it with any other woman, past or present.

My children and I moved into the house in August, 1994 after the remodeling was finished. I brought my creative energy, while Sam brought his sensitivity and understanding. Together, we established a beautiful new home for the seven of us. My children quickly found friends in the neighborhood, which eased their transition, and they loved Sam, who was like a father to them. My children visited Matthew every other weekend, but Sam had become their dad. His presence was a gift to them as well as me.

Although he was the perfect family man with my children, Sam had problems with his own, which caused great anguish and resentment with his two older children, who still mourned the loss of their mother. Sam believed that I had the ability to blend our two families together and step in as the new mother figure. Although Sam's family was dealing with complex emotional pain, unresolved anger, and grief, I never doubted that I could cope with whatever situation arose. However, I underestimated the enormity of the task, and the next few years witnessed unforeseen stresses and strains in our relationship.

I brought my own insecurities to the relationship. Would I be good enough? Would his children accept me? Would I feel that this was my home? His children were angry and resented my intrusion into their lives. They resented that their father's need to be loved and cared for took precedence over their need to be nurtured. I wondered whether Sam's friends would accept me as they continued to mourn the loss of his first wife, their beloved friend.

I found myself once again in an environment where I was shut out. Sam's older children wouldn't accept the changes, and being excluded and ostracized opened deep wounds that caused me great pain. At that time, I wasn't conscious or wise enough to cope with my own feelings, and I often became angry and detached. Sam understood how hard it was for me to be excluded, but he was conflicted between his children's unresolved emotional needs and his own. I wanted Sam to love me, make me feel safe, take care of me, and support me emotionally. I wanted to love him, make him feel safe, and take care of him. Together we were dealing with our contentious divorces, struggling with our children, and forging ahead to make the life of our dreams. We both ached to matter to someone, anyone who could see us, hear us, and love us. We gave those gifts to each other, even when we were being emotionally challenged in every direction.

Sam and I were both practicing occupational therapists, so we could share our professional life. Our interconnected personal and professional lives felt glorious for a while. We gave each other what we needed most, and I loved him deeply. I encouraged him to respect and honor himself, and he encouraged me to try things I never felt physically capable of doing. Sam urged me to join him in the activities that he loved so much, and because I trusted him, I took the risk, let go of my old fears, and jumped right in. I felt safe knowing that he would be there if anything happened to me. With his encouragement and support, I challenged myself and engaged in activities I never could have imagined doing. For example, I bought myself a 21-speed bike and took 50-mile bike rides, skied in the beautiful mountains of Canada, and engaged in many other outdoor activities that I had dropped since the early onset of the disease.

I loved riding a bike and joining my new friends for extensive bike rides. I had a custom bicycle made with gears placed on the left side. I still had enough remaining strength in my left hand to manipulate the gears, whereas my right hand had grown too weak to manipulate the gear handle. Even by restructuring the gear to favor my left hand, my grasp was tenuous at best. Every time I went over the tiniest pebble in the road, I held on for dear life, feeling that I would be thrown off the bike. However, the joy and excitement of feeling able, rather than disabled, was comfort enough. My heart knew that I was safe and that my beloved partner was at my side whenever I needed him.

The only experience greater than biking was skiing. When I was younger, my doctors would not permit me to engage in these activities for fear that I would fall and cause more damage. Now, at age 38, I was ready to listen more to myself and to bring joy in my life by being part of a group that engaged in exciting, adventurous outdoor activities.

The first time I went skiing I was terrified that I wouldn't be able to ski at all. Not only was I afraid of the physical demands involved, but I was also afraid of my inability to look like everyone else on the slopes. I figured out that if I wrapped the ski pole strap around my wrist, no one would notice that I didn't have the actual muscle strength to hold the pole with a natural grip. It was a hassle to do this, and not at all safe. Since I had the straps wrapped around my wrist, I couldn't drop them when I fell, and risked landing on them. Other skiers, who simply held the poles with the straps as support, could more easily let go during a fall and avoid these mishaps.

In retrospect, the amount of energy I expended trying to figure out the best way to ski and look normal brings a smile to my face today. My son Benjamin at age 6 reminded me that new skiers learn without poles and suggested that I drop mine. He said, "Mom, I'm not using poles, and you don't have to, either." I was touched by his innocent wisdom.

The first run without poles was so glorious that it transformed skiing for me forever. I stopped worrying about what other people thought and gave up the need to look like everyone else. Grateful for my son's sensitivity, I learned to ski—and to do it well. I felt empowered and elated, alive with freedom and health, when I glided down the mountain, unencumbered by false props.

For the next 10 years I skied without poles with speed and ease as I traversed most trails as well as other skiers. Standing on top of a mountain was exhilarating; without disease or weakness, I was just another skier flying through the air, feeling the wind, and witnessing the beauty of the snow-covered terrain all around me.

Sam had opened the door for me to this joyous activity; he showed me the way, and my heart grabbed the opportunity. I never gave up, nor did I allow my fear to stand in the way. In all the years I skied, I never hurt my precious hands, not once. Thanks to Sam's encouragement, I'm glad I refused to be limited by the doctors' fears.

Because of my weaker hands, donning the ski boots, ski gloves, jackets, helmets, and goggles was arduous. I often cried in frustration over the difficulty in putting on the equipment, something others could do without a second thought. This humiliation gave me a reminder of how the disease was present and progressing. Thankfully, Sam was always at my side to assist me and take away my embarrassment. He witnessed all my fears and frustrations. I never hid these feelings from him.

In early March of 1995, I noticed that I was losing strength and dexterity in my right hand. It had been 13 years since the first hand surgery on my left hand, and once again I found myself disengaging from certain activities and covering up, so people wouldn't notice my handicap. I hated being so weak, a shameful feeling that burned at the core of my being.

I knew that Dr. Belsky would help me, just as he had done for the past 13 years. I simply wanted a life without embarrassment, pain, and constant intrusion. I silently cried out to Dr. Belsky, "Please save me again."

The Angels Meet

Sam and I drove to Boston to visit Dr. Belsky. When I had begun to lose my grip while holding a pen or fork for more than a few minutes, I knew it was time to seek medical attention for my right hand. Although somewhere in the back of my mind I knew the progression of the disease in my right hand was inevitable, the reality of its happening didn't make it any easier.

As a right-handed person, I found it troublesome to have paralysis in my left hand, but paralysis in my right hand was terrifying. For many years I had worried about how I would manage when my right hand started to show similar signs of deterioration.

I felt blessed that Sam was in my life, so I wouldn't have to go through this process alone, as I did when I was married to Matthew. At the same time, I was excited to have Sam and Dr. Belsky meet each other, since they were both important men in my life. I knew that whatever happened next, Sam would be at my side, holding me, supporting me, and loving me. At such moments I forgot the drama concerning his children, the sadness that our life didn't flow with more ease, or, for that matter, anything else in my life that continued to be negative or disruptive.

Emotionally, this was a difficult time as I struggled with feelings of inadequacy and doubt. I received little support, if any, from my parents; the underlying fear that I was not acceptable was always present. Sometimes I could avoid the pain that it caused me, while other times I could not.

Sam and I became engaged just prior to our visit with Dr. Belsky. The commitment soothed my desperate need to believe that someone was there for me, that this time I would not have to go it alone. Somehow I felt that marriage would ease the pain of the challenges to come. I was comforted by the prospect of looking at the ring on my finger of my left hand post-op, seeing a sparkling diamond that would give me the courage to face the future.

While the meeting between Sam and Dr. Belsky was warm and friendly, the visit confirmed that I needed surgery. My left hand had stabilized, and it was time for the same reconstructive tendon transfers in my right hand. Dr. Belsky said he would fuse the thumb joints in order to give me a functional grasp, which is the positioning of the thumb and first finger in opposition to hold an object securely. I didn't need the surgery with my left hand, but as a right-handed person, this was a critical component in the reconstruction process.

After leaving Dr. Belsky's office, Sam and I spent the night in Boston before traveling to our home in upper Westchester County. We found a restaurant in Quincy Market, had a few glasses of wine, and I broke out in tears. Once again, I had to endure the endless pain and the fear of walking into the unknown.

I was overwhelmed by the thought of repeating the marathon of surgeries I had endured before in healing my left hand. The prospect of going through it on my right hand terrified and exhausted me. Sam sat and listened patiently as I spewed out my anger and pain on him. Projecting my anger on him was an easy way to deflect the painful reality that confronted me. The wine afforded me an opportunity to touch and release some of my deepest wounds.

My Right Hand

The surgery was scheduled for May, just days before my 40th birthday. Overwhelmed with fear, I couldn't imagine how I would function in daily life without the use of my right hand. On an emotional level, this surgery differed from the earlier ones. In the past I relied on the function of my right hand when my left one was impaired. The disease had now robbed me of both hands, a condition that brought a new level of despair. I grieved over the fact that both hands would never feel natural again. The tendon transfers and fusions would make me feel "rigged up" for the rest of my life.

The only blessing was that Sam would be there. My children would have to witness their mother's suffering again, a painful fact that made Jessica quite anxious. One day prior to surgery she said, "I don't know what to do around you when you're sad and your hand hurts so much." My children were older and had a better understanding about the process of surgery and recuperation, but still the process took an emotional toll on everyone.

Knowing I would have a series of surgeries, I requested a five-month leave of absence from my job. I was employed as a full-time occupational therapist in a local school district, and as a right-handed person, I couldn't perform certain tasks with my arm in a full cast. For example, I couldn't hold a pen, use the keyboard, or use my arms freely to engage in occupational therapy interventions with the children. Knowing ahead of time that I would have multiply surgeries, one after another, made it impossible to return to work as I had done in the past. In fact, I never returned to full-time status again.

Sam and I drove to The Newton-Wellesley Hospital just outside Boston, where Dr. Belsky once again performed hand surgery. We planned the most support for everyone: Our close friends volunteered to stay with Jessica and Benjamin, and Sam chose to spend the night at a nearby hotel, so he could be as close as possible. I was tired of the whole ordeal: the pre-op procedure, the surgery, the recovery room, the nausea, and the hospital visits. I was such a familiar face that the hospital staff recognized me when I arrived.

The best part of surgery was having Sam at my side. When I returned to the room after surgery, Sam crawled into my bed, so I could rest in his comforting arms. Later that evening, when I was ready to ingest some nutrients, he brought me a delicious milkshake. The hospital staff even let Sam stay in my room the second night because the bed next to mine was unoccupied. No one had ever loved me so completely. Because of Sam's love, the memories of the physical pain and anguish didn't feel so overwhelming as with my previous surgeries.

We returned home three days later. I remained in a cast for the next six weeks. Every two weeks, I returned to Boston for cast changes, stitch removal and follow-up visits to ensure that I was healing appropriately. The visits were always a reality check, painful both emotionally and physically. Sam, my friends, and my father made the trip with me, so I never had to do it alone as I did in the years with Matthew. This time the trips to Boston entailed shopping and dining excursions, which made the pain of the medical visit more bearable.

I suppressed the pain by buying lots of clothes. I would see Mark (I was now on a first name basis with Dr. Belsky), receive whatever medical intervention was required, and head to the stores at Harvard Square or on Commonwealth Avenue. I put enough painkillers into my system to keep the physical pain at bay and I avoided the emotional pain by shopping at my favorite stores and eating at my favorite restaurants. If I had to drive three hours to Boston, I damn well was going to experience some pleasure! Shopping was truly a survival mechanism, and the clothing I purchased filled a void that ran deep in my soul.

Although Sam was wonderful in many ways, resentment continued to build between us because of the ongoing drama around his older children. Their anger and jealously were deeply embedded. It never occurred to me that perhaps they imagined he might not have enough love to give us all.

Sam lived two separate lives, one with his older children and one with his new family, a schism that eventually cracked the foundation of our relationship. His children drove a wedge between us, and Sam allowed it to happen. The one thing Sam was clear about was that he would do anything not to risk the loss of his daughter, even at our expense. I had a hard time understanding this, because I needed to trust that my future husband put me first, thus building a strong foundation for dealing effectively with the children.

Sam, who was riddled with his own abandonment issues, found himself in situations where he had to choose between his children and me. For example, on Mother's Day, which took place a few days after surgery, while we were lying together in bed with my head resting on his chest, Sam telephoned his daughter to say hello. This was a difficult day for her since the loss of her mother, and I was privy to their conversation. When I realized that she never asked about me, I felt pain and separation. Even though I already knew the answer, I asked him, "Did she say anything about me?" When he replied she had not, I said, "Do you know how unseen and unacknowledged that makes me feel?" He said that he understood why I was upset, agreed it would have been nice if she had asked about me, and then defended her behavior, attributing it to her sorrow. He said, "I don't want to lose my daughter, and I'll do anything to keep from letting that happen."

He never rocked the boat or even questioned his children's actions. He accepted at face value that whatever they did was justified. Being the tenacious person I was, I never understood why he wouldn't speak up. Because he would voice his internal conflict with me, I wanted him to honor himself enough to be forthright in expressing his true self to his children.

There was another force driving Sam's actions and reactions that had little to do with me. He was dealing with his own feelings of guilt, shame, and remorse based on actions that took place after his first wife's death. His children were enraged at his past behavior, and each of them acted out in protest. Frightened of losing them, he based his actions on fear rather than on respect, honor, and self-awareness. At that time I, too, did not have enough self-respect and awareness to avoid taking his behavior personally. We suffered from a combination of low self-esteem and co-dependency.

Despite his unresolved issues, Sam had a much deeper side to him. When that side surfaced, I loved being with the man I had always desired. For instance, he lit up with passion and depth when he did psychodrama with people. After witnessing this for the first time, I said to him, "Now that's the man I love." But most of the time he didn't reside in those soulful depths, and as we continued our dance, our core differences kept resurfacing,

As my sense of injustice drove me to inquire more deeply into the root of Sam's behavior, I assumed the role of coach. I was driven by my need to heal my wounds and Sam's and by my desire for Sam to find his voice, to resist passivity, to act more assertively in our family. He willingly accepted that I could step up to the plate and push him into self-awareness, even when everything in him was in resistance. That's what I do best: fight for the highest and best within a person because playing the survival game isn't enough. My deep love for Sam allowed me to put my armor on and fight for him, and in the process fight for us both. Sam invited me in to help fill the void in his family life, and I did so with great passion. Unfortunately, my own unhealed grief and pain didn't add well to the mixture. I, too, was still in survival mode and couldn't act with unconditional love.

In retrospect, both of us were struggling to be seen and heard. The family was surviving, we were surviving, and there was no way Sam could please everyone. Some days I questioned what I was doing and why I was trying so hard. God only knew I had enough to deal with, but I loved Sam to the core, and I knew that no matter what, he loved me, too.

Along with everything else, my selfish need to be in a big, happy family got in the way, and I didn't want to live with more disharmonies. I recognize today that my strength and conviction came from my own yearnings, my own survival needs, and in all fairness to Sam, my expectations were unrealistic. It wasn't my place to make anything happen. It was exhausting at times, but we had our own method of recovery as we found our way back into each other's heart.

Between 1995 and 1997 I had a series of seven surgeries on my right hand. Dr. Belsky decided to do the surgical procedure in stages rather than all at once as he had done with my left hand. The first stage involved surgically fusing my thumb in a functional position with pins and wires, and the second stage included transferring tendons. I returned approximately every two months for each procedure, with almost no time in between surgeries. The procedures were extremely painful, and the entire routine was exhausting. It included driving three hours to Boston, being labeled a patient, wearing a hospital gown, feeling probed, sliced, and stitched in surgery, not to mention enduring the numerous follow-up visits that each surgery required. I no longer could sublimate my feelings through shopping and dining extravaganzas. Dr. Belsky had to redo the thumb fusion multiple times before he found a position in which the thumb and the first finger rested in their optimal place. Both my thumb and first joint of each finger were then fused for stability. It felt as if my children never saw me without a cast on. I can't even imagine their fears, wondering what would happen to their mother. I remember how frightened Jessica was and how Benjamin would sit beside me and range my little pinky finger because it became so contracted. Each child handled the situation differently.

Five months later I returned to work on a part-time basis. I had a difficult time maintaining the strength required to successfully complete my work with integrity. My thumb was fused, my tendons were repositioned, and my muscle strength was zero. Writing became an arduous task, and the physicality required to handle the children was extremely taxing. I used all the compensatory skills I had, but I couldn't compensate for what was non-existent. In order to use my hands, I had to use the muscles in my entire upper extremity (arm and shoulder), and that was painfully exhausting.

Because I could return only to part-time status, I applied for compensation from my private disability company. This limitation to part-time status and the ensuing financial concern felt like a lightening bolt through my heart. I never wanted to rely on assistance, but because I was the queen of rationalizing, I convinced myself that the money would ease the guilt over my inability to contribute financially to our marriage, something I had always done in the past. On the inside my heart was broken, filled with resentment and anguish over the choices I was forced to make. The ongoing support of my colleagues and supervisor at work sustained me while I continued to figure out how to adjust to my situation. Deep down I knew that something was shifting and that my priorities were about to change.

My life as a professional was slipping away, and I felt enormous pain, a depth of anger and rage at life's cruelty. I was tired of struggling just to survive, tired of holding everything together while inwardly I felt myself shrinking away. I had just completed a series of surgeries, yet my prospects for the future were dismal. I was tired of the anger, despair, depression, and the ceaseless series of losses I continued to experience both physically and emotionally. In addition, while my parents remained detached and unavailable, I still grieved for their love and support as my own world was turning upside down.

In the fall of 1997, Dr. Belsky suggested that I stop even my part-time work. "If you don't," he said, "you won't have hands by the time you're 50." This bold statement came from a man who always had an answer and a procedure to rectify every situation. Now there was no more magic: there were no more tendons to transfer and no more quick fixes. The only solution was to stop every thing I was doing, and work was the most obvious place to start. Although I was flooded with emotion and despair, I knew I had to heed his counsel. This new development felt like defeat, life's cruel reminder that I had finally lost the battle.

In an attempt to turn things around and to perceive my situation as an opportunity to stop struggling so hard, I questioned myself. "What's wrong with being a housewife and mother?" I asked. "Haven't I always wanted to spend more time with the children?" I asked my friends for their advice, even though I knew quite well there was no choice. My body, not my mind, was making all the decisions now.

I was grateful that my right hand didn't deteriorate until I was with Sam, who would support me emotionally and physically. I was also thankful that my children, Jessica and Benjamin, were not babies and were old enough, at ages 9 and 6, to be somewhat independent in their daily activities.

Life Changes Times Two

When it rains it pours. Everything was shifting and somehow I would have to learn how to ride the shift. There wasn't much of a choice so I just kept going.

Sam and I had been living together for more than four years when my divorce with Matthew became finalized. Three months later, on Election Day, November 4, 1997, we were married. We made a conscious decision to have our wedding in two stages (with so much going on, I needed some time to adjust). The first stage involved a very intimate wedding ceremony, with only our closest friends in attendance. The second stage followed a few weeks later when we celebrated our marriage with all our friends and family. Having previously experienced the glitz of big weddings, this time we chose a small, intimate gathering without fanfare. Sam and I asked each of our best friends and their respective spouses, along with my children Jessica and Benjamin, to join us under the canopy. Sam's older children declined the invitation.

During the beautiful wedding ceremony, Sam and I stood under the *chuppah* (wedding canopy) as our beloved rabbi officiated the service. As we recited our vows, my children, my friend Pattie, and Sam's friend Rudy each held a pole that supported the chuppah. The ceremony was tender and loving, filled with the promise of joy and new beginnings. After the ceremony we had an intimate reception at a small, elegant restaurant nearby.

Two weeks after our wedding, I terminated my position at the school district that had been so patient with me. The surgeries had finally taken their toll. While I was at work, I couldn't take the residual bone pain and the constant aches due to the tightness of reconfigured tendons. I could no longer rely on the compensatory skills I had used to stay functional for the better part of my life. It hurt to hold a pen and write for more than a few minutes at a time. It was exhausting to hold a fork, prepare food, and take care of myself (let alone everyone else around me). Clearly, I had been overdoing it, and life had finally caught up with me.

I was 43 years old, and had two children who needed their mother to function. I continued to treat the handful of children I was currently working with in my private practice, and I found consulting work (only six hours a week) to fill the void.

I didn't completely disengage from my profession until 1999, when I stopped renewing my license to practice. By relinquishing this attachment to my profession, I could no longer hang on to any hidden belief that I was still an occupational therapist.

Certainty Within Uncertainty

Even before our wedding day, Sam and I felt the uncertainty of our lives prior to our decision to marry. Always present were Sam's ongoing parenting struggles with his older children, coping with his younger daughter's problems, my physical deterioration, the stress of my children's attempt to adapt to all the change in their lives, along with the tensions that we as a couple were dealing with from our former spouses. Deep within my core I knew my soul would never survive another relationship loss, so Sam and I kept recommitting to our shared journey.

Four weeks after our wedding day, in early December 1997, Sam and I invited friends and family to a celebratory dinner at a nearby restaurant. Everyone attended except Sam's two older children. I had entered a time of mixed blessings. I was happy to be married yet terrified of the prospects confronting me. For this occasion I put on an elegant dress and a happy face to celebrate the joy of life.

Throughout the day I felt cold, not because of the weather, but because of a piercing chill that permeated my being. I felt sad and depressed because I had lost my physical strength and the independence that I cherished so highly. I felt oddly thin, as if my life force was diminishing, and I was wasting away in the process. I also felt fragile: I realized that I was now surviving without really thriving and I had lost most of my will to be alive. But I kept these thoughts to myself, enjoyed the festive company, and looked every bit the happy new bride. I danced, ate, and drank away my fears and unease as I wondered silently to myself, "What will become of me after this wonderful day is over?" My apprehension didn't concern Sam, but the deep despair over the new life I had committed to embrace.

Embracing the Mountain

Without faith in my ability to make a positive change, life became a heavy burden for me to carry, fraught with fear, suffering and negative feelings. I was exhausted and afraid of spiraling downward.

During winter recess from school, we decided to drive to Canada for our annual ski trip. I knew the children would love it, and I thought the thrill of skiing would rejuvenate my spirits. Unfortunately, that emotional lift never happened. Standing on top of the mountain, I wondered if it was best to end my life. Gazing at the valley below, which at that moment represented the depth of my despair, I thought, "How easy it would be to ski off the mountain and plunge to my death." I had no idea how to free myself from the darkness in which I was engulfed. How could I survive the trauma of losing everything I had worked so hard for—my independence, my functioning and my career?

Again that ominous thought assailed me: I could ski right off the mountain and put an abrupt end to my struggle. But no matter how dark the cloud, I couldn't take my own life. As tears streamed down my eyes and love filled my heart, I knew that my children needed me, and I could never abandon them to fend for themselves.

As I stood on the mountaintop that day, I chose not to die but to live. Moments later, I was captivated by the panoramic view of snow-covered mountains and treetops and an abundance of sunlight streaming through the clouds and glistening in the snow. An overwhelming feeling of beauty surrounded me, and I felt a sense of contentment, freedom, bliss, ease, and grace within my soul as I realized that I had the power to do anything I chose. Not others, but I and I alone had the answers to all my dilemmas and perplexities.

Shaken, I skied down the mountain and shared with my husband, that evening, what had happened to me on the slope earlier that day.

Even though I felt a transcendent moment of aliveness, I still lived in the valley of dark, depressing feelings. I needed time and space for healing.

During the months that followed, I would lie in bed, staring out the window while avoiding any physical contact with Sam, totally consumed in tears. I was terrified of connection, because of the emptiness I felt, often wishing I could just end my life. I had absolutely no clue how I was going to survive such tremendous pain and loss. I told Sam, "I could see myself driving off a cliff." The following day I made an appointment with a psychiatrist my friend recommended.

The Gift Brought Forward

My children grew up witnessing much of my pain, fears and soul confusion as well as my tenacity to survive and thrive on both the personal and professional level. It was a blessing for them to see just how capable people with a disability can be. I told my children, "It's not what you have, it's what you do with it that counts." This insight took on great importance, since both my children were diagnosed with Attention Deficit Hyperactivity Disorder. Because of my ability to overcome labels, I wouldn't allow them to use their diagnosis as an excuse for their actions. My children witnessed firsthand (no pun intended) how to be successful despite any disease or disability, and this attitude, this gift, has served them all their lives.

Unfortunately, my feelings of despair remained. I isolated myself by not wanting to share the depth of my sadness with others. To bring much-needed joy into my life, we adopted a sickly two-month old puppy named Zoe. Nursing this little puppy back to health brought me joy and melted away some of my despair. In a way, healing her helped heal me at the same time. By channeling my energy into little Zoe, I also avoided burdening my children with the responsibility of bearing my pain and despair.

By 1999 my relationship with Sam was on the rocks. His son had withdrawn completely from our lives, and Sam was hanging on by a thread, trying to secure a relationship with his older daughter. We had hit a wall, and we were floating in a sea of hard feelings. Feeling shut out by him, I responded by withdrawing and becoming less intimate. While he remained physically present, he was emotionally guarded, staying in the fortress of his surface self while pushing away all feelings of openness and vulnerability. For me, too, the potential for loss and rejection was such a high price to pay that I withdrew into the safety of my own cocoon.

The residual pain of my early years had once again reared its ugly head. The anger, hurt, and rejection had surfaced as Sam and I went through our family drama. No matter how destructive the family dynamics, we played our parts eloquently. Neither of us had a clue about how to cope with unresolved feelings of inadequacy or with the emptiness we both felt so deeply. The only difference between us was that I was willing to work with it and he wasn't. I never took a passive or complacent attitude, and I certainly wouldn't deny the depth of emotional work we needed to do. Unfortunately for me, Sam was more comfortable in the passive role.

On a more positive note, Sam and I provided a safe place for my children and his youngest daughter to grow up with wonderful family memories. We had a circle of supportive, loving friends whom we enjoyed sharing our lives with and who constantly showered them with love and attention. Our best friends, Gail and Rudy, loved the children and treated them as if they were part of their own family. We shared many years of joint family holidays and gatherings. All in all, my children grew up knowing they were loved.

Sam was a wonderful father to my children, always available to pick up the slack when I didn't have the emotional or physical strength to be present. In many ways I was an unavailable parent because of my chronic state of despair. I would get frustrated with my inadequacies and exhaustion and would spend hours in bed not wanting to do anything. I struggled to take care of myself, with repeated infections, and a new diagnosis of fibromyalgia. At that time in my life, I had very little energy or desire to transport the children to their sports and after school activities. Instead, I stayed in my bed in a fetal position and was relieved that no one was home to hear me cry myself to sleep.

So despite our differences about how to parent our children, Sam and I were able to form a partnership that became a huge blessing for me. We shared a beautiful home, had wonderful supportive friends and held each other's hands through family crises and losses. Through all the ups and downs, we carried the heavy load of our family's responsibilities. But in the end these turned out to be too much.

Since I was working only a few hours a week, I spent my days reading and getting together with friends, a lifestyle unfamiliar to me. Riddled with sadness, I continued moving in and out of depression as I searched for meaning and purpose in my life. While there were many joyful times, often I felt that I couldn't handle one more day. Just to survive, I had to sublimate my energy by expressing my creativity, enjoying my friends, and planning my daughter's *bat mitzvah*. How I could create anything with my hands in that weakened condition still amazes me. Today I realize that my soul was channeling healing energy from my heart to my hands.

CHAPTER 7

The Great Fall

*Like the Phoenix, I had to go down
in order to rise again.*

TRANSITIONING FROM A STRONG, SUCCESSFUL professional to "doing nothing" was quite painful. I had difficulty coping with my new status as an unemployed person living on disability. I plunged into a state of emptiness and darkness, what the mystics call the Dark Night of the Soul. Each morning I asked myself, "Who am I if I'm not the occupational therapist who fought so hard to survive? What am I going to do with my life? How can I live without purpose or meaning?"

My husband, who was generally supportive, didn't appear to mind that I was disabled and unemployed. He wanted to take care of me, and perhaps hoped that without work I would lavish more time and affection on him, something he desperately wanted. I was haunted by the message I heard long ago when my disease started to progress: *I couldn't survive on my own without having someone else to take care of me.* Despite all my effort to avoid being in such a situation, severely limited by a loss of independence, my greatest fear had come true.

Hole in My Soul

In hindsight it feels as if Spirit had perfectly orchestrated everything from the very beginning. Looking within, I became quiet and introspective, seeking solace and peace to fill up the hole in my soul. In my meditations, I visualized myself descending a mountain and resting in the quiet valley below, knowing that someday, somehow, I would rise up and climb to the peak of another mountain. This vision gave me strength and comfort. One day I stood in the driveway and shared with Sam my emerging inner life, and although he listened attentively, he didn't fully understand my need for quiet and solitude. Actually, neither did I. I said to him, "I've changed. I didn't ask to change, but I did. I don't mean to hurt you; this is all about me and the changes within."

Interesting opportunities began to emerge. Once I was having lunch at an upscale pizzeria with my friend Pattie and her children when I received a telephone call from Nan, the rabbi's assistant. The rabbi wanted to know whether I would teach fourth grade religion the following fall. Shortly before our wedding, Sam and I had joined the temple so that Jessica could pursue *bat mitzvah* training and religious studies, as well as enjoy a community of new friends. Excited and intimidated by the offer, I told her that I had absolutely no understanding of Jewish history, laws, and traditions. True, I was Jewish, but in name only.

The rabbi felt I would be a wonderful teacher, and Nan encouraged me to take the position. "I'll think about it," I told her, knowing quite well that no one says no to the rabbi. Several days later I accepted the offer. I was honored that he thought me competent enough for the job, but secretly I suspected that he had a hidden reason in offering me the position. In those days I was not feeling so competent, even though I had spent years working with children. Theoretically, there was no reason why I couldn't learn my religion and successfully teach others about it.

A Leap of Faith

As I entered this new, uncharted territory, I quickly fell in love with teaching. I began reading about Jewish history and culture, and I sat at the computer for hours designing lesson plans. Because I was contributing to others, I regained some purpose in my otherwise small, insignificant life. Teaching provided a venue for my own growth and creativity to emerge as I spent hours each week planning lessons and developing activities to share with my students.

Jessica and Benjamin were involved in religious studies, so we drove to the temple together each Sunday morning. Benjamin was a student in the first class I taught, an experience we both enjoyed. The formal study of Jewish culture was a new experience for both Benjamin and myself, and the classroom provided the opportunity for us to share in the teaching-learning process together.

My involvement in the temple opened the door for spiritual renewal in my life. Besides becoming involved in various temple activities, I also attended two classes with the rabbi. One explored ancient teachings of the Kabbalah, the mystical tradition of Judaism. The second was a Hebrew language class for beginners.

A new world of intellectual and spiritual depth was opening to me as I spent time devouring one book after another. I read about Hasidic masters, Jewish Renewal, and the holy scriptures of the Torah and the Tanakh. I read contemporary and traditional texts by Martin Buber, Z'ev ben Shimon Halevi, Rabbis Abraham Heschel, Aryeh Kaplan, Lawrence Kushner, David Cooper, Arthur Green, Zalman Schachter-Shalomi, and many others. The readings introduced me to a side of the Jewish faith with which I was unfamiliar, filled with deep compassion, truth, and joy. The more I read, the more grounded I felt. I soon realized that I had found a new home for my soul, and that a process of spiritual transformation was under way.

During this glorious time, I spent hours on the soft, cozy couch in the sunroom, completely immersed in my books. My wonderful companions, Zoe and Jake (we had adopted a second mini-poodle to keep Zoe company) would jump on the couch and cuddle alongside me. The room, which was predominantly windows with a cathedral ceiling, was filled with the light and warmth of the sun. The house itself was sequestered in the middle of the woods. When I looked out the windows, I felt surrounded by the lushness of the trees. What a perfect place to relax! I cherished the peace and tranquility in the house after Sam and the children left to start their days.

While my mind felt invigorated by what I was learning, the gentleness of this quiet wisdom tradition soothed my soul. The books focused on acceptance, love, wisdom, truth, and humility. I recognized that in those readings I was finding my true self, the self I wanted to be.

Time To Let Go

My surgeries were over. Dr. Belsky could do no more because he had used all the tendons I had. I had to accept my hands as they were. I continued to visit Mark's office annually, where we documented the changes and filled out the necessary forms for my disability insurance to continue. My hands felt mechanical, and I joked that I felt like the bionic woman.

Mark's surgeries had helped me in many ways. I could hold a pen again (my own adapted version), but I had to hold a fork with my left hand. Determined to stay as functional as possible, I carefully monitored my expenditure of energy to avoid overtiring my muscles to a state of exhaustion. Because of the repositioning of my right thumb after surgery, I had to stop bicycle riding, since I could no longer hold the handlebar. However, I could continue skiing because it didn't require the use of my hands. Sam was upset and angry when I had to give up biking, and his anger cut through me like a knife.

I no longer had the dexterity to do needlepoint, but I could still use my sewing machine and enjoy quilting. I spent hours designing my creations as gifts for my friends and family. These creative activities continued to feed my soul. I firmly believe they helped keep my body alive.

Psychiatry Meets Spirituality

Shortly after I married Sam, I started seeing a psychiatrist, Dr. C., who was originally recommended by my children' pediatrician, for my daughter. After the first visit, I decided I would see him myself. An elderly gentleman with a wonderful European accent and gentle presence, he had such a spiritual nature that our sessions helped me begin to love myself by letting go and just being.

Dr. C. challenged my story by asking me why I hated my hands. He said, "When you speak, your hands dance." I explained to him that my hands caused me much pain and feelings of inadequacy. I told him about being in a store recently and struggling with embarrassment to get change out of my wallet. The experience intensified my sense of inadequacy. He replied, "Those are the hands with which you caress and love your children." He helped me to see things differently. Later that night I changed my AOL screen name to *Dancinghands,* having made a conscious decision to view my hands positively.

The next time I was in a store struggling for change in my wallet, my attitude shifted, and I said to the clerk, "I'm sorry, but this is difficult for me, so please be patient." The clerk immediately offered me assistance. What a different scene it was when I didn't have to hide in self-loathing! With Dr. C cheering me on, I realized that I was doing my best. In time I became more relaxed, patient, and self-accepting. By introducing me to the concept of *being* rather than *doing*, Dr. C gave me permission to be without having to justify being alive through constant activity. In other words, he placed importance on being as the foundation of doing. I had given up doing when I left my profession behind, and now, having disentangled my sense of self-worth from external activity, I was exploring who I was in my essential self, and who I wished to become. Dr. C. helped me by introducing me to my spiritual side. I never before had a therapist who brought spirituality into the practice of psychiatry.

Over the next two years as my therapist, he bridged the medical and spiritual worlds as he guided me on my healing journey.

Six months after I started seeing Dr. C., Sam began his own sessions. We occasionally saw him as a couple, and even our children had sessions with him from time to time. Dr. C. became such a household name that we honored him by naming our newest puppy, Teddy, after him.

By early 1999 my relationship with Sam was in perilous condition. In November, with the help of Dr. C., we declared a "time out," an emotional separation, to see whether we could reconcile our differences. We moved to separate bedrooms and committed to more time in our personal space.

I felt smothered in trying to find a new place for me in the world. I needed emotional and physical space, and Sam had a difficult time accepting this. Although he demanded a great deal of my time and energy, I needed to step back and let him resolve his own conflicts, make his own choices, fight his own battles. I had enough to do in my own life.

I began to bounce back from the survival mode through the connection to my temple and my teaching. This entry in my journal, dated 11/99, expresses my growing awareness:

"What is this total connection to my culture and my religion? It may appear that I'm going overboard, but really I'm not. I feel safe, secure, challenged intellectually, with a wonderful opportunity to be myself. Why wouldn't I want to be affiliated with the temple if I am receiving all these blessings? I love the community and the feeling of family. I have met some wonderful people, and I love learning the songs and hearing the cheerfulness of the music. I found the home I was looking for, and I'm content. I can give and receive: My soul is filled to overflowing, and I pour forth my love to others. I love my new spiritual life! Who could have imagined that I would love spending my time reading, learning, loving, and just being? I have the time to grow, reflect and make things right. It's too bad that everyone can't stop working long enough to settle inwardly and connect with the soul. Of course, there is a sacrifice involved in arriving at this understanding, and that's not working. I don't appreciate the pain that goes along

with the reason I'm not working. It's a high price to pay, so I better make the best of it. Was this all in God's plan?"

It didn't take long to realize why the rabbi wanted me to teach. I was beginning to settle and center myself while finding some peacefulness within my broken-down body. I was learning that I could rest in the valley for awhile.

PART II

DROPPING THE STORY

Trust that you deserve to live a happy and healthy life and you will heal your soul.

CHAPTER 8

Spiritual Awakening

"God was in this place and I, i didn't know."
—Genesis 28:16

FOR THE NEXT TEN YEARS I focused on healing myself emotionally
and spiritually as I became acquainted with God in a whole new way. My
friends and I started a group called the Kabbalah Sisters, our version of
a book club dedicated to the study of Kabbalah. The word "Kabbalah,"
which means received wisdom, refers to the esoteric, mystical teachings
in Judaism. Although the group didn't last long, our joyful time of
sharing food and Judaism's wisdom tweaked my interest to delve deeper.
It was during this time that I read *God is a Verb*, a beautiful book by
Rabbi David Cooper.

Retreating and Renewing

Once, while reading a Kabbalistic text, I came across a reference to Elat
Chayyim, a Jewish Retreat and Healing Center in Accord, New York,
90 minutes from my home. The center, which focuses on healing by
drawing on the ancient wisdom of the Jewish tradition, is a place of

celebration and renewal that uses dance, song, prayer, and ritual to help participants find holiness within themselves. My friend Joanne and I decided to attend a weekend retreat there in late April 2001. We hadn't an inkling of what to expect or what was expected of us; neither of us had attended a spiritual retreat before. The minute we drove onto the access road, I felt a sense of peace, as well as excitement and anticipation about what lay ahead. As we drove down the long road to the entrance, we breathed in the beauty of the land, the vast expansiveness of green rolling hills, and breathtaking mountains in the distance. The grounds contained a swimming pool, yurts for chanting and prayer, instructional buildings, and a dormitory for sleeping.

As I walked through the entrance of the main building, I felt a sense of having returned home, a deep serenity and loving presence that filled my entire being. The main building housed the dining room and the sanctuary where most activities took place, including Shabbat and Torah services. In the main room there was a sunken area called the "pit," where people sat on steps circling the others who were sitting on the floor. I loved the pit, which was welcoming, cozy, and safe, and it quickly became my resting spot.

What captured my heart outside was the gate, which was made of uneven broad wood slats that seem to fit together perfectly. Something about the unevenness of the slats joined together always fascinated me, as if it was a metaphor for how I felt. I spent many hours taking in its beauty, reflecting that I, too, felt unevenness inside as I allowed myself to discover my own beauty in new ways.

Jason Shulman, an internationally known spiritual teacher and modern day kabbalist, led the retreat, which was based on his work at the school he founded, A Society of Souls. His curriculum promoted the belief that healing can occur as we deepen our understanding of our true selves and awaken to God's presence. The retreat was powerful in many ways. Jason's emphasis on self-healing through awakening the human spirit, opening to the God-self, and returning to wholeness, spoke loudly to me. Although the concept of healing was new to me, I was receptive and eager to hear what he had to say.

Surrounded by like-minded people, Joanne and I spent three days absorbing wisdom, joy, and grace. I was learning that God lies within, and we ourselves can heal our wounds. When Joanne retired to our room to get some sleep, I sat with new friends into the late hours of the night, sharing experiences of our personal journeys of healing. Shabbat service was festive and joyful, with dancing, chanting, and drumming.

Elat Chayyim is a warm, inviting home to spiritual seekers learning to surrender to the present moment. A place of joy and community, learning and exploring, it encourages people to expand their consciousness and to become acquainted with God transcendent, as well as God immanent. When I left this house of many blessings, I knew that I would return many times.

A few months after the retreat, I made contact with A Society of Souls and asked for help in locating a kabbalistic healer in my area. Through the awakening of Spirit, the realization that God is within us, I was ready to explore inner healing, which was vastly different from finding a cure through the medical route. A Society of Souls referred me to Katherine (Kat for short), who as a licensed clinical social worker served as a bridge for me between the spiritual and the medical world.

I met with Kat every other week for sessions that lasted an hour and a half. During the first 45 minutes, I sat across from her, discussing my current concerns, history, challenges, desires, and dreams. In the second 45 minutes, I would lie down on the healing table, and Kat would place her hands on me. She called this practice the Healing of Immanence, or the channeling of source energy to the client.

This was my first experience with energy healing, and I found it fascinating and restorative. It offered me the opportunity to allow my body to receive the grace of healing energy, a practice that represented a major shift in my approach to getting healthier. Rather than relying on surgery to correct physical problems, I was receiving non-physical energy and letting it stream though my body to do its healing work. Rather than using my head to figure out how therapy should take place,

I opened myself to the healing sensations without any thoughts at all. As my understanding deepened, I thought, "There must be a reason why I've gone through the medical route and have had the grace to study Kabbalah and contact God within me."

I became more openhearted, compassionate and receptive as Kat guided me in embracing both my past and my present circumstances. She saw my potential for wisdom and encouraged me to continue on the path as a seeker and healer. "You're done being a warrior who meets challenges with courage and strength," she said. "Now you must become a *tzaddik* (a wise teacher)." With Kat's encouragement I was ready to shift gears by dropping my weapons and picking up my angel wings. Tired of fighting, I was learning to accept myself unconditionally, hands and all.

I continued to see Kat for the next year and a half as I delved deeper in my spiritual explorations. As a seeker of truth, I remained open to anything that brought peace and understanding. I was beginning to see the emotional baggage I was carrying as a mirror of my physical disease.

I met Rabbi David Cooper in November at a meditation conference in New York City. I had read his book, *God is a Verb* and was deeply moved by the energy of his words in between the lines. Because of this, I decided to attend the conference and meet him personally. The session was an introduction to meditation through the practice of chanting or *davenning*. Devotional chanting awakens a longing in the heart for the experience of inner silence, boundless love, and union with the divine. The Hebrew words of the chants opened my heart and penetrated me with what felt like ancient soul memories. Afterward, I spoke with David and shared how meaningful the session was and how his book had touched me. I left the conference with his chanting CD, *Songs of Prayer*.

From that day onward, I listened to the CD and chanted the songs of prayer every morning. I felt the stirrings deep within; as the Hebrew words penetrated my soul, tears streamed down my cheeks, and I lost myself in ecstatic devotion.

Silence is Golden

Four weeks later, drawn by an urgency in my soul, I attended my first week-long silent meditation retreat with Rabbi Cooper at Elat Chayyim. Other retreat leaders included his wife, Shoshana Cooper, Eliezar Sobel, and Rabbi Jeff Roth. Throughout the week, the only opportunities to speak came during group instruction or group and individual interviews. Dialogue took place solely between teachers and retreatants. To facilitate introspection, we observed silence at all times and practiced mindfulness of eye contact and body language.

At 5 a.m. a volunteer sounding the bell would walk down the hall. Our day began with morning meditation, followed by yoga, brunch, davenning, walking meditation, instructional time, and more meditations, both walking and sitting. At 5:00 p.m. dinner was served, followed by seated meditation and an evening of Torah Talk (biblical or Hasidic teachings).

These long days were sometimes joyful, sometimes overwhelming, and always insightful. To amuse myself, I often sat in the pit looking at people's socks and figuring out personalities based on what socks they wore. I distracted myself because I couldn't get comfortable with all the silence. Why had I chosen to be here? I came to daven, experience Rabbi Cooper, and have some quiet time away from Sam and the kids. Now that I was immersed in round-the-clock silence, I felt overwhelmed. Without a daily meditation practice, I had never been this quiet before. When I realized there was nowhere else to go but within, I began to appreciate the power of silence. I realized how peaceful it was avoiding small talk and responding to everyone's chatter. Silence offered me a respite from my life back home, and I found myself contacting and releasing a plethora of emotions that normally got buried under the busy-ness of daily life. What an amazing healing experiences this was.

On the second day I went to the 6 a.m. yoga class. Yoga was a mixed blessing for me because I found it difficult to assume postures that required weight bearing on my arms. Concerned about looking good and keeping up with everyone else, I pushed myself to the point of pain as I held back the tears.

After the session I spoke to Dov, the instructor. I made a conscious decision to be honest with him about my limitations and asked for his guidance to help me find alternative options for my yoga practice. It was a risky conversation for me, since I generally didn't allow myself to be so vulnerable. I told myself, "Stop hiding, risk being real, and let people help you." I stood there crying as I explained to Dov the quandary I was in—wanting to engage in yoga but not being willing to suffer the pain created by some of the postures.

He gently suggested I allow myself to feel the struggle, and offered to work with me in finding alternative solutions. I also shared with him how painful it was to maintain a cross-legged position for a 45-minute sit, due to Lyme disease stiffness. He offered his meditation bench as a possible solution to the discomfort. I gave him a big hug as he complimented me on my willingness and determination to make yoga a joyful, successful experience.

When I had the courage to ask for help, I received exactly what I needed from this gentle, generous man, who gave me not only yoga lessons, but lessons in loving myself.

Breaking Through/The Edge

I had a significant breakthrough on the third day, when during walking meditation, intense feelings came to awareness. Flooded with painful memories from earlier in life, I cried a thousand tears and thought I was going to have a breakdown. I asked myself, "Would anyone know that I was having a psychotic break on this rural back road?" Despite my fear, I kept walking until I found myself at the entrance of a small play area. I walked over to the swing and began to pump high off the ground. I looked up into the sky and desperately asked God, "Are you there? Do you know that I'm here?"

I held on by wrapping my arms together to secure my grasp so I wouldn't fall, swinging as high as I could while looking up into the beautiful winter sky. Suddenly my feelings of sadness broke, and I started singing one of Jason Shulman's chants entitled *Hold Me Closer, God.* A sense of joy, peace, and harmony flooded my being. When I came down from the swing and walked back into the main room, I had a smile as wide as my face. I had asked God whether I was alone, and I received a definite answer: "No, you're never alone." The next day I asked Rabbi Cooper what had happened, and he said, "You went to the edge. Good for you!"

I spent the rest of the week noticing my feelings and witnessing how I reacted to them.

My favorite part of the program was davening in the pit. Every morning I sat wrapped in my *tallit* (a prayer shawl), feeling the warmth and comfort it provided me. Devotional chanting took me deep into my intuitive self, allowing my emotions to surface and to be expressed through song and tears. One morning I knew with overwhelming clarity that my disease wasn't some haphazard suffering inflicted on me. I had to have this disease, which was integral to my very core.

During the morning chant, as David spoke about God always being present, I felt a magnificent chill rush through me. I sat with my eyes welling up in tears, again recognizing that I was never alone; God had always been guiding me, even when I didn't know it. While David spoke about the biblical patriarch Jacob's journey to God, I found myself identifying with it. Jacob wrestled with an angel and got hurt in the process. The familiar tale, when seen through the eyes of my own suffering, resonated within me because of its theme of woundedness, the search for God, and liberation into truth. Jacob's experience represents transformation from injury to wholeness.

This disease was my personal Jacob's ladder. I began to see the disease in a different way, realizing that like Jacob, I, too, had the ability to go from injury to wholeness. I was awestruck that God had given me this grand opportunity to love myself completely, from the inside of my body to every person and circumstance in my life. I began to view my body as a teacher, and to see my disease as an opportunity, not a curse. My disease was located in the gray matter of the vertebrae in the spine. Gray matter is responsible for movement and motion. I wondered whether there was a connection between gray matter and the feeling that I never "mattered." What an interesting play on words, I thought. That day I wrote in my journal: *"To transform my life, I must get a handle on my feelings and learn to hold them with loving kindness. I kept hearing these words: Follow your heart and listen to yourself; your soul is trying to tell you something. And in response I cry out to God, 'Hear me, please hear my cry to you. I can't do this alone.'"*

At the time, these revelatory experiences were new to me, and I didn't know quite what to do with them. I simply took them in, and later discussed my insights with David when he was available.

Constriction

I now recognized how I had lived with constriction my whole life. When I met Sam, I felt freed, but when I started to feel pain, I constricted again. I began to coach myself to notice the pain before I constricted, to talk to it and set it free. When I did this, my hands became more flexible and opened ever so slightly. With an *aha!* of understanding, I realized that my physical condition was directly related to my feelings of self-love and acceptance.

The retreat opened my heart. I began learning that I was perfect just the way I was. I felt a total sense of belonging, a sense of community, without judgment, criticism, or separateness. I returned home seven days later with a better understanding of the dynamics between Sam and me and the relationship I had to my disease.

The meditation week introduced me to the invaluable gift that silence can bring to the body and the soul. The shift was clear: I had returned home a quieter, more inner-directed person. The need for shopping, running around and filling up my time by watching television and going to movies now took a back seat to silence. I wanted an environment that was calm, quiet, and still. I began to feel the difference between the expansive feelings I had felt during the retreat and the constrictive feelings I had felt for most of my life. However, this deeply reflective process inevitably widened the gap between Sam and myself. He was extremely outgoing, and here I was transformed, wanting to go deep inside. We seldom did much together, and it soon became apparent that our lifestyles were discordant.

As part of my new outlook, I asked myself whether I needed to be alone for awhile. Other questions arose: Am I seeking solitude to continue this path of self-discovery, and is this the only way? Can Sam and I maintain a relationship and stay together with all the changes that are occurring? Is Sam on the same journey I am, and if not, should I accept our differences and stop trying so hard to change things? And if the inward journey leads me to another way of being in the world, what keeps me from moving on?

I asked God these questions before I fell asleep at night. I needed guidance in making difficult decisions that I intuitively knew lay ahead of me. Sam and I struggled during this period, confronting the issue of whether or not to end our relationship. No matter how deep our differences, we held on to the remote possibility that we could work it out. On a soul level our love was deep. On a personality level, we unconsciously hurt each other time and time again.

After the retreat I became deeply involved in Jewish Renewal and the individual task of healing my spirit. Because my meditation teachers were involved in Buddhist, Sufi, and Eastern philosophy, I, too, broadened my understanding beyond Judaism, and spent the following months reading, absorbing, and learning about other spiritual traditions, belief systems and practices. These exciting studies were creating a very different me. The Buddhist teachings in particular helped me learn how to be gentler with myself as well as others. They helped me learn self-acceptance, one of the fundamental principles on the journey to true wisdom.

As a result of my inner work, I started to believe I was not damaged merchandise. I understood that the disease in my spine was necessary for my growth in this lifetime. I also knew that without this disease, I wouldn't be the person I am today. I felt empowered and determined to love myself—all of me.

My Rebbe

I connected deeply with Rabbi David Cooper. During the first retreat David and I had a wonderful talk and he encouraged me to join the Jewish Meditation Advanced Training (JMAT), a program that consisted of four weeklong retreats during a two-year period. I had already learned how wonderful silence could be, and I knew the insights and wisdom that I was drawing from the instructors and the community of Elat Chayyim were invaluable on my path. I wanted to continue my teaching-learning relationship with David. What lay ahead of me was the opportunity for immense personal growth and transformation. David, another angel, became my spiritual guide, my *rebbe*, for the next five years. I would not be the person I am today without his guidance, wisdom, and openhearted love. David saw me, heard me, and appreciated me as his gentle strength nurtured my heart and repaired my soul.

The following June I attended the first JMAT session. I continued to experience illuminating moments as I surrendered to my True Self and continued my search for understanding and spiritual awakening. I found myself in deep exploration, opening my heart more and more as I sat among intimate gatherings of like-minded people. Privately, David spoke about the pain I had endured because of betraying my Inner Self, and about the necessity now to choose fearless trust in its healing presence and guidance. I no longer wanted to identify myself as a victim who needed to be rescued. I was attempting to step outside my family history, with its limiting perceptions and painful experiences, in order to view life from a new, expansive, self-empowering perspective.

CHAPTER 9

Necessary Action

It's about listening to the deepest part of your soul. Your soul always knows the truth of who you are. It's the personality self that gives us trouble and makes life complicated.

In late August, 2002 Sam and I decided to get divorced. We had struggled with our marriage for many years, had tried everything to salvage it, and we were both exhausted from trying to reconcile our differences. I still loved Sam, who had received all of me: my anger and disappointments; my frustrations with life; my joy, hopes, and desires; my passion and the weariness that comes from broken dreams. But even though we still felt affection for one another, we could no longer live together.

I wanted a partner who loved himself enough to step up to the plate, as I was doing. I wanted Sam to have enough self-respect to believe in himself and to strive for a higher life. The problem was that I wanted him to reach for these things himself. Sam had difficulty maintaining his strength, and I became weary of coaching him. We had been sleeping in separate bedrooms for a year and a half, struggling to keep our marriage alive, and now, having exhausted all possibilities, I could do nothing else but mourn the loss of us.

When I told my 13-year-old son that the marriage was finally over, he asked me whether there was anything about Sam that I still loved.

I replied, "There's nothing left, and I don't think we're good for each other." Benjamin said, "Mom, you need someone like me, who's deep, sensitive and emotional." Such wisdom from the mouth of babes! Ben was wise and had depth far in advance of his age. Like a mirror, he reflected back to me what I couldn't see for myself: I needed a lifestyle of depth and quiet, but I had clung to my present life because of my fears and insecurities.

Sam offered me something no one had offered me before: emotional availability, family, and loving support. Sam would do anything for me—except explore the depths and share them with me. Sam loved me more than anyone had ever loved me before. I didn't ask for that to change, but when I went on my journey of transformation, everything changed, including us. Dr. C. once said to me, "Sam didn't ask for this, but when one person changes, the dynamic of the relationship is bound to change."

I had promised to be his wife until "death do us part." For the first time in my life, I had experienced a real family. But my heart yearned for something else. Sam put great demands on my time and space, and I felt suffocated. At the same time, something was calling me to go deeper, to become more spiritual, and to explore unknown, uncharted territory. My days of "living in the box" were coming to an end. A whole new world was opening to me where I would find solace. In the past I set high standards for myself, and I pushed others to reach for those same high standards. I always wanted more, and it disturbed me that other people didn't have the same thirst, the same passion and strength to go for the gold. If I didn't have my drive and tenacity, I never could have survived all that I had, emotionally, physically and spiritually.

Sam didn't hold that high spiritual space with me, but my spiritual community did. I wanted to be surrounded by the energy of soulful depth. That's why I gravitated to books that instilled a sense of wholeness and a belief in something other than sense-based perception. Clearly, Sam and I were on different paths, and we had to honor our own truth, even if that meant ending our relationship.

CHAPTER 10

Moving On

THERE IS A DEEP SENSE of knowing when it is time to make a life change. It is as if your cells are speaking to you. All we have to do is get quiet and listen to the song of your heart.

In the fall of 2002 we filed for divorce, put our house on the market and went our separate ways. I stayed in the same town to provide continuity for my children's education; I didn't want to add to the disruption caused by the breakup. While it was a difficult time for me, I felt a newfound freedom that I had been searching for. Within a few months I purchased a beautiful house, located a few miles from our current home. It was set back from the road in a wooded area and offered a retreat-like serenity. The small house was perfect for the three of us, and the property was exquisite, with beautiful gardens, a stone patio, and a view through the woods to a lake. Sam, who bought his own house approximately 10 miles away in the next town, promised to stay involved with the children.

On January 3, 2003, I sat in my new house with my children, praying that I had made the right decision. I hadn't lived alone since I was 24, when I lived and worked in New York City. This transition felt different, because I was solely responsible for my two children, as well as my new home.

That thought alone was frightening. I had never shouldered the burden of owning a home independently. I sat in the living room confronting the future with a mixture of excitement and terror. "What have I done?" I cried out to God. "How am I going to do this alone?" Part of me was proud that I could leave the safety of my life with Sam. The other part was scared to death.

When I separated from Matthew, I lived alone in my townhouse, but Sam provided backup to help me manage. This time I was completely alone with my 16-year-old daughter and my 13 year-old son. Although I had started to date a man who visited me every other weekend from Boston, I clearly was on my own.

I had a difficult time doing everything involved in maintaining the upkeep of the house, because of my diminished hand strength. I often broke down in tears when I couldn't do such simple things as opening the canister lid on my water filter. I had blisters on my hands after shoveling snow or mowing the lawn. I constantly asked myself, "Why have I put myself in this position?"

I didn't have the finances to pay someone to do the maintenance, so with the assistance of my teenage children, I took charge of the job. Once again I was confronted by my lack of strength and ability. I did experience a minor victory when I found a lightweight electric lawn mower, so I could do the task myself. I had never given in to dependence throughout my illness, and I wasn't going to start now. I would prove once again that I could take care of myself.

Heart Broken Open

My children responded to the move differently. Benjamin liked our new home and quickly made friends in the neighborhood. In many ways, this transition enabled him to put the past behind him and to experience new beginnings. For one thing, he ended his lifelong passion for basketball and began to immerse himself in skateboarding. He transitioned from engaging in team sports to an individual activity that brought him internal joy and inner peace. Because both children loved

Sam, they felt his loss acutely, as well as the loss of their father, Matthew. Matthew's personal life had become so chaotic and destructive that both children chose not to see him for the next five years.

Shortly before the move, Jessica's behavior became erratic and disconcerting. In addition to the losses associated with family changes, she felt the insecurity of a teenage girl struggling through adolescence and the heartbreak of breaking up with her boyfriend during the junior year of high school. She became depressed and apathetic, and her behavior took a huge toll on Benjamin. It took a toll on me, too, as I struggled to keep things together for both my children as they wrestled with their deepest challenges and wounds.

An added stress for Jessica and Ben was their biological father's change in support. Matthew stopped paying child support and alimony, which added a financial responsibility that brought me great anxiety. Sam saw the children occasionally, but there was no male figure regularly available to them. Basically, I had to hold the family together by myself.

By the end of Jessica's junior year in high school, I could no longer deal with her apathy and disruptive behavior. Something had to shift in our living arrangement. Because she rarely attended her classes, her guidance counselor informed me that she wouldn't graduate the following year if she didn't shape up. I became increasingly concerned, and under the guidance of her therapist, I knew I had to do something to alter the course she was on. With the financial support of her paternal grandparents, Jessica agreed to attend the Hyde School, a private boarding school in northeast Connecticut that promised to help her turn her life around. She would matriculate as a second year junior (the Hyde school didn't take students entering their senior year). Jessica was smart enough to recognize she was in trouble and needed help getting back on track. I was grateful for my ex-in-laws' involvement and hopeful that Jessica, with our support, would find some healing in her new environment.

I was so exhausted by mid-summer that I contracted shingles, a painful skin disorder brought on by an overabundance of stress. My body was responding to the stress, and by now I understood the process all too well. By the end of the summer, I found myself engulfed in emotional despair as I dealt with survival issues. I was devastated by Jessica's pain. Her risky behavior made me fear for her life. I lay awake at night waiting for the phone call from the police telling me my little girl was dead. I didn't know what else to do, and I naturally absorbed the pain, as any mother would. My beautiful little girl wasn't supposed to be hurting this deeply. I felt powerless because she needed significant outside help. Once again I was emotionally and physically exhausted. Once again life wasn't following the expected plan. I had hoped that Jessica would finish high school and go off to college. But that dream had been squashed, and now my girl was leaving home ahead of schedule to gain control of her life in a safe, disciplined environment.

Benjamin witnessed the despair and confusion both his sister and I felt, and this had to affect him on a deep level, even though he didn't let on. Basically, we were all he had, and he would say that to me when he shared his pain over the loss of his father and his stepfather. My heart ached for him.

Holding On

Situated in the Connecticut countryside about two hours from our home, the Hyde School was based on character development, emphasizing such virtues as integrity, truth, and honor. Parental involvement was required, although Jessica's biological father chose not to participate. I found it the perfect place for our new family of three. and became actively involved with the family program, which included monthly meetings and weekend retreats with and without the student present. The school soon became my focus. It fed me on a soul level. The program's emphasis on truth, honor, and integrity validated my own journey to wholeness. I learned the important lesson of stepping aside and allowing my daughter to be what she needed to be, not what I wanted her to be. I drew strength from my involvement, which was a magnificent experience that not only helped me with Jessica, but helped me see my own history differently.

During this tumultuous time I was overwhelmed with all I had to deal with. In his deep anguish over his sister and father's destructive behavior, Benjamin started to display signs of inner turmoil. He masked his sadness and grief with humor and became the class clown, a fact, that was disturbing to his teachers and me. I received numerous phone calls from his teachers, who expressed concern over his sliding grades, his behavior, his inability to accept the boundaries set by authority figures. I was holding on by a thread. I was relieved that Jessica was away at school so I could stay as present as possible with Benjamin. I know I disappointed him many times with my lack of energy and willingness to drive him places, and to be there the way he needed me to be there. I became angry, short tempered, and quick to react because I was beaten down by my life circumstances. Yet we always found a way to maintain a healthy connection, a way to share our hurt and clear our hearts. Benjamin often said, "I'm not okay if you're not okay." I always felt the burden of those words and tried even harder to do the best I could.

All in all, I had two children who were acting out, an exhausted body, and a depth of sadness that permeated my soul. The separation from Sam had profoundly unsettled them; their father's abandonment weighed heavily on my children's hearts. Burdened by my choice, I had to continually remind myself that the divorce was necessary for my personal growth. I would ask God, "Why is my life filled with such unrest and turmoil?" Although I blamed myself for everything that had gone wrong, I forged ahead and endured the harsh realities that my children and I were facing. As I continued seeking the truth, I went deeper and deeper within to find the answers. Through all my experience—my involvement in the school program, my meditation retreats, and my individual work with Kat—I was learning to stay present and to be available to my children and myself.

As I continued going within and acknowledging all the aspects of my newly developing self, I began to let go of the self-loathing. I started to see others differently, and with less judgment. I could accept them for who they were. I even began to see Sam differently—not as the man I wanted him to be, but the man he truly was.

Through my involvement in the JMAT program, I became friends with Roberta, the woman who ran the bookstore at Elat Chayyim. I offered to volunteer my time whenever I could get away from my responsibilities at home. I craved being in the peaceful energy of Elat Chayyim, and volunteering offered me opportunities for deep spiritual conversation with Roberta and others who resided on the premises. I was in total joy when I was there, and I spent hours immersed in the energy that emanated from these books of wisdom. I assisted Roberta in restructuring and reorganizing the bookstores operations and inventory system. Often I stayed overnight at Elat Chayyim and either engaged in the program or simply enjoyed the respite from my normal life.

My second meditation retreat in June 2003 brought continued awakening on many levels. My journal records what was unfolding in my life at that time:

"There's only one way to go when you're silent and that's inside. As I meditate and chant, I'm beginning to explore the causes and the necessity of my disease, as well as my higher purpose. I feel a sense of wholeness as I peel away layers of old conditions and beliefs. As I stop being angry, what emerges is a blessed feeling of thankfulness that I'm alive, not in a wheelchair or dead.

"I'm beginning to understand that everything happens for a reason. The disease had to manifest itself; all I had to do was understand the process. Yet with my seeking mind, I continue to wrestle and deal with the pain and discomfort of being fully present. I am all too aware of an internal struggle going on, based on a lifetime of fear and anxiety, deep confusion and uncertainty. I have known a lifetime of begging, too. To whom am I begging? I haven't a clue. All I know is that I'm bargaining with someone, begging for an opportunity to see life through normal eyes, to live one day without thinking of every movement I make. I hope to wake up one day and to do what normal people do. Somehow I knew that I was fighting something bigger than myself and that I had the right to be alive and to know the reason this disease was happening to me. I also wanted to outsmart all those untouchable doctors whom I believed were right because they were the experts.

"I'm struggling for answers, and bit by bit they come to me. All those years I had to stay alive, so I hardened my heart and I faked it. I pretended I was fine. I drank and danced and smiled my fears away. I dressed myself perfectly to hide the imperfections. I tried to stay as thin as possible, so my body would not give away the fact that the muscles in my upper extremities were wasting away. I played games with myself, survival of the fittest, as they say.

"I decided that if I couldn't beat them, I would join them, so I became an occupational therapist. I took numerous classes at the university medical center where learned professors told me everything about my disease. I was a disease. I became my disease. I listened to the death sentence issued by the doctors, and for the next 22 years, I worked with various disabilities and diseases, encouraging people to fight for their lives. In reality, I took on both sides—therapist and patient—to deepen my understanding as I searched for my own truth. I held both sides of the duality, choosing a profession based on my limitations. I struggled to gain clarity about my illness and to offer strength to my clients and patients, so they, too, could see their assets, not just their limitations. I encouraged parents and professionals to cultivate their children's self esteem, which is critically important to their fragile existence.

"My professional strength stemmed from my intimate knowledge on a soul level of the internal struggles disabled people go through. I learned after many tears and bouts of anger that being disabled didn't mean that people aren't capable of being the best they can be. As my personal journey shows, spiritual awakening involves accepting oneself, not being perfect. That I have a disease in the structural center of my body is not coincidental. No superficial disease for me! No broken bones or easy fixes! I'm beginning to realize that I'm never alone in the process and that the still, small voice within has always encouraged me to stay on my path."

It took a few years after this retreat to really understand what I was talking about. As the journey continued and I later wrote, *"Shame, fear, and inadequacy are like a big stop sign; they disallow my true nature from emerging and keep my dancing soul from taking its own authentic steps."* Years later I labeled my healing practice SoulDancing.

During this retreat I made progress in practicing yoga. As Dov coached me, I stopped struggling against my physical limitations, as well as judging myself against an external standard of performance. When I forgot my fears, I increased my participation. Even with some physical discomfort, it didn't hurt anymore. I saw clearly that fear kept my soul from its true expression by keeping me stuck in woundedness. By opening my heart to the fear and embracing it, I was learning to accept and befriend myself with love and mercy. At the same time, I deepened my commitment to help others through their struggles, trusting that there's light at the end of the darkest tunnel. I was beginning realize what it meant to heal the soul.

CHAPTER 11

The Return of Hope

I CONTINUED TO STRUGGLE WITH the belief that I had power to co-create my own destiny. I was locked in the web of old patterns of security.

Though living apart, Sam and I would see each other on occasion. Sometimes he came to my house to visit the children. One evening we went to dinner, and when he kissed me goodnight, I felt desire for him and drove away crying. That I had stirrings for him was disconcerting. He called me on his cell phone as he was driving home to share the same sentiment. I never quite knew how to handle my mixed emotions for him. These feelings lingered for quite some time.

In October, 2003, ten months after we separated, I was at High Holy Day services, and began to yearn for the life Sam and I had shared. I missed our joyful times together and the feeling of being cared for. Things felt different for me the few times I had seen him. I wanted to believe that we both had changed and that perhaps we could rejuvenate our relationship. I had become gentler and more tolerant of other people's lifestyles. I also had a clearer understanding of what had made our marriage dysfunctional, and what drove us apart. I convinced myself that I had been unfair and that I had not honored his truth, I had only honored my own.

Much about my relationship with Sam surfaced during the Hyde School family meetings. I began questioning myself as I listened to other struggling couples. If I done X or tried Y, I asked myself, would things have been different? As I watched other families' struggles, I thought about how I had behaved with Sam and how I had reacted to him. Everyone was playing the blame game. I wanted to tell people, "Stay in the relationship and do your inner work. Don't blame the relationship for your problems; take responsibility and work on yourself." I hadn't had the opportunity to follow my own words, and now I wanted it. How I wished things could have been different. The profoundly deep work at the family meetings opened a door for me, enabling me to see things from a different perspective than when I was entangled in the marriage. I was beginning to surrender and to let go.

A Wish and a Prayer

We learn to stay even in our despair because it is safer to stay with what we know than to risk the unknown. How little we trust ourselves and how much uneasiness we allow living with our past programming.

Now that I had changed, I hoped that we could try again to heal our relationship. I conveniently forgot about the difficult times, the dishonesty, the clinging, the inability of Sam to hold his center and to stand in his integrity, as well as the suffocation I felt by his neediness.

I was tired of being alone and carrying the weight of the family by myself. I wanted to live in a real family, and ours, for all its problems, was the best I had ever known. Thus one day I decided to e-mail him and tenderly share these feelings with him. He responded to my e-mail and invited me over for dinner to show me his new home. He wanted me to approve. When I walked in the door, I felt such sadness looking around at what we once had together. I surveyed the pictures, the furnishing, the wedding gifts—years of shared dreams and memories that we had created together. They now evoked feelings of painful separation in my heart. After dinner we took a walk, hand in hand, and shared our feelings, desperately hoping we had grown enough and that maybe we could build a healthy relationship.

We started to see each other. But it didn't take long for old, unhealthy behavior patterns to surface, the same ones that had led to our downfall years before. This time, however, I chose to ignore them. After each painful episode, we addressed the issues and hoped that with awareness and time the problems would heal organically. I wanted desperately to find my way back to him, no matter what the emotional cost. I told myself to take things slowly and let them evolve naturally. But the whole time, I was fighting my own inner wisdom, and I was well aware of it. In fact, I didn't listen to my inner voice at all. I listened instead to my fears and loneliness, which urged me not to go through life alone.

Despite the game-playing nonsense that resurfaced, Sam and I loved each other deeply. I continued to believe that if we could keep the channel of communication open, and took care not to hurt each other, we could have the relationship that we had always wanted. In March 2004 we dissolved our legal separation and were once again a married couple. Sam spent most of his time at my house, even though his was only 20 minutes away. After a few months we decided to sell his house. With the proceeds we built onto mine, making a beautiful new addition for our blended families.

In a way, we were doing exactly what we had done 10 years earlier. Once again we were a family. I had grown from my spiritual practice to see with greater clarity and compassion. We both had a great desire to love and be loved, so we recommitted to each other, believing that this time it would last forever.

It didn't. Four years later we would file for divorce. But those four years were filled with healing and grace. Sam and I each grew in individual awareness. He became involved in the Hyde School program, and we aligned as parents, assisting Jessica in her growth. He once again became Jessica and Ben's dad. Sam supported me through extremely trying times with Jessica and my never-ending legal issues with Matthew. I encouraged Sam's spiritual growth to help him heal his own deepest wounds and the dissension within his own family. In time, his oldest daughter and I reconciled our differences and became dear friends. During those four years we brought healing to the incomplete parts of ourselves, and closure to our life together.

Seeking, Seeking, Seeking

Although I was deeply engaged in my spiritual work at Elat Chayyim, I found myself gravitating to alternative healing modalities, such as shamanic healing, therapeutic massage, and Jin Shin Jyutsu, which facilitates the restoration and balance of body, mind and spirit through touch and acupressure on the meridians lines. As I explored each healer's personal version of healing and wisdom, new levels of personal growth unfolded.

For example, my friend Joanne, who was deeply involved in shamanic healing, suggested I meet with Val, a shamanic healer. Shamanic healing is therapy at the spiritual level, retrieving lost parts of our soul and removing blocks from our physical bodies and our non-physical energy fields. The shamanic healing sessions with Val were incredibly revealing, helping me piece together the reasons for my despair and sadness. Val told me I suffered my first soul loss when I was descending the birth canal and a second soul loss when I was three years old. Soul loss occurs in response to trauma. The experience may be too painful for us to be bear in full awareness, so a part of our soul leaves and takes refuge in non-ordinary reality. I soon realized that I carried sadness and grief from my paternal ancestors and victimization and abuse from my maternal ancestors. She told me I was holding disempowerment in my third *chakra*. (Chakras are energy centers through which energy flows in the body. The third chakra, or solar plexus, focuses on being self-confident, having self-worth, and feeling in control of our lives).

Val explained that as a sensitive soul I felt the sadness and pain of my ancestors. She explained I entered life with that sensitivity, and one of my tasks was to use it to heal personal and ancestral suffering. The notion of soul loss made so much sense to me, especially since I was born two months premature, and at age three I felt the pain of my biological father's death and my own transition to a new home in faraway Newfoundland. Val explained that to heal I must hold that three-year-old spirit in my arms and love her with the unconditional acceptance I needed as a child but never received.

During a shamanic healing session, I would lie on the floor on a blanket as she drew the "spirits" out of me. The healing energy often triggered physical sensations, such as severe back pain, difficulty breathing, and at times convulsions and violent shaking. As she worked, Val chanted and made strange sounds that I had never heard before, while I held onto healing stones to ground and tune my energy. This whole experience was new and bizarre, to say the least, but I left each session feeling more complete.

The day after receiving information about healing my three-year-old spirit, I found pictures of myself at that age and began speaking to my child, the little girl who was still holding the pain. I told her that I loved and missed her and that it was safe for her to return to me, so we could be whole.

The journey of exploring different healing modalities was fascinating and terrifying. Despite their differences, they all worked together to heal body, mind, and soul. But each in its own way often made me experience a roller coaster of emotion. Old feelings of inadequacy, hurt, fear, and terror still resided deep within me. No matter what I did on this psycho-spiritual path, I still remained stuck, and tripped myself up. I asked myself, "What's still hidden from me? How can I get unstuck? I am working hard, but is it enough?"

Sam's support was boundless. He, too, became involved in most of the healing techniques that I discovered. Once I encouraged him to attend Elat Chayyim for a weekend with Rabbi Zalman-Schachter Shalomi, the grandfather of Jewish Renewal, and even gave Sam a beautiful, new tallit for morning davenning. I encouraged him to follow his heart and live a more spiritual life, and he soon became involved with Elat Chayyim. Although we were now both participating in events at Elat Chayyim, only once did we participate as a couple. While it appeared we were on the same path, in reality we were not.

I noticed that he was plugged into my energy for his spiritual growth, and the energy imbalance left me feeling drained. I wanted someone to spiritually feed me as much as I fed him. I longed to be fed with wisdom and knowledge from a true partner in life, and because it wasn't forthcoming, I continued to feel the emptiness of not having this match. I wanted to be with my beloved husband as a partner, not as his coach. I wanted to be on equal footing. Old feelings were beginning to emerge. We knew that this time there was no denying them.

Painful Realities

Besides dealing with marriage issues, I had to face Jessica's verbal attacks. Because I was vulnerable to her painful outbursts, I reverted to my usual behavior when my world was shaken: I retreated into survival mode. I spent so much energy just surviving Jessica's verbal assaults that I became weakened emotionally and physically. How could I separate from Jessica and let her go? As her mother, I was supposed to keep her safe from harm and pain, but I couldn't. The pain was so deep that it tore at my soul. I wanted a relationship with my daughter based on love and support, yet ironically I felt my relationship with my daughter was mimicking the relationship I had with my own mother. Jessica's withdrawal and detachment caused a deep wound. I didn't know how I could survive another detached person in my life. I had been there twice before, with my mother and my first husband, and had learned all too well how to go within and protect myself. As much as I desired Sam to comfort me, my own survival instincts took over. Terrified of my own vulnerability, filled with tremendous stress and heartache, I wondered, "How can I feel safe to be vulnerable when I'm in the survival mode?" I was surviving Jessica and Matthew while struggling to stay present for Sam and Ben.

I experienced enormous tension, anxiety, and fear at this time. Matthew, with his financial withdrawal, the constant courtroom battles regarding his support violations, and his abandonment of his children, caused us great anguish. Sam, too, continued to have difficulties with his own children, as well as his ongoing internal struggle with trust and intimacy in our relationship.

Once again, the overwhelming stress brought up all my unresolved fears. In October, 2004, I wrote: *"I awoke at 7:20 this morning with an incredible insight: I'm back to surviving. My body and soul are out of sync again, and I'm no longer journeying toward healing. Sam wants me to share my sadness and pain with him, but he doesn't bring his to me. We're both so stuck in our own guardedness and fear of intimacy that we can't seem to trust each other enough to let go and allow the other in. We want to, we long to, but we don't do it."*

Going Down Head First

Jessica's painful behavior catapulted me to my eventual breakdown. She was the last straw. I could feel my life force draining out of me.

I now gave less attention to my inner work. I stopped meditating, chanting, reading, and taking care of my soul. Instead, I became preoccupied with building the addition to our house, which was extremely stressful in itself, and with Jessica, who had returned home after one year at the Hyde School and placed on probation for her non-compliance at school. With her return, Jessica's behavior escalated to the point that it required tough love. For example, when we returned from vacation, Jessica had broken into our home, determined to do as she pleased. Without any remorse on her part, we were clueless how to continue supporting her when her behavior was clearly out of control. She continued to set herself up to fail in everything she did. Sam, Ben, and I constantly had to defend ourselves from Jessica's angry behavior. With support from her therapists, we told Jessica that she could no longer live with us. "I honor myself too much to allow you to stay," I told her. The next morning I sat with her and watched her pack. She left without an argument.

This was the hardest thing I ever did, but the teachings of the Hyde School taught me how to let go. I knew there was no other option. When we allowed Jessica to return home four months later, after being thrown out of the home she had been living in, we vowed we would do everything we could to help her through this difficult period. But it was apparent to all involved that there was little that Sam and I could do that would be meaningful and constructive.

In this environment, I could hardly catch my breath. I continued to seek out healers, but once home I couldn't maintain the positive energy I experienced during each session. I struggled to hold on, but I no longer felt strong. My body, mind, and spirit were broken.

By February 2005 I was in constant pain. Besides having severe pain in my left hip and knee, I was often dizzy and exhausted, constantly sick with one sinus infection after another. I had a difficult time engaging in any physical activity, including walking, practicing yoga, or even chanting for any length of time. My left hip was so painful that I stumbled out of bed each morning because my hip would literally give out.

I had no clue what was happening to my body, why I was losing the sense of health and well being I had felt just two years before. I called Jed, a Jin Shin Jyutsu practitioner whom a friend at Elat Chayyim had recommended to me a few months before, praying he could help me.

I was tired, my body ached, and I needed someone to take a good look at me. When I looked in the mirror, I was shocked at the lifelessness in my eyes, which were vacant, with no light, sparkle or life. I was disconcerted that my life force had vanished. I was thin and drawn, as if I was dying physically and spiritually. I was simply disappearing, devoid of energy to give to anyone. In a word, I was done.

In April, 2005, as I stood at my back door looking out the glass pane, I said to myself, "If I were to fall down, I would never get up again. I have nothing left in me. This must be what bone cancer feels like." I stood there with tears in my eyes, motionless, not knowing how to feel, and how not to feel, this deep truth. Looking back, I think that the thought of bone cancer came to me because I felt the pain and despair deeply within my bones, within the very core of my being. In reality, I was in intense physical pain: My neck, shoulders, and back hurt from overcompensating for the weakness in my arms, along with the relatively new pain in my hip and knee. The emotional and spiritual pain was just as deep, pervasive, and ever-present, but thankfully Sam was at my side to help me bear the burden.

We had just completed construction on our home, having spent top dollar to buy the best for our simple yet elegant living space. I used all my energy making sure everything was perfect. Little did I know that my desperation for perfection and control was my attempt to keep me from unraveling. I was consumed with perfection and, in fact, everything was perfect on the outside. But on the inside my spirit was gone. The continuous drama around Jessica was the final blow to my soul, and as I hung on by a thread, my body collapsed. In a state of complete desperation, I vowed I would do anything to get to the source of my pain.

CHAPTER 12

The Appearance of Angels In the Form of Healers

TO BE TRULY GUIDED MEANS to lay down your weapons and pick up your angel wings. I began to recognize just how guided I have been, long before I even knew what the word meant.

Jed was aware that something major was happening in my body. One day, when I was on the healing table, he said, "Something is about to shift, and you'll be going through a major transformation in your life. You need to be physically strong to handle what's coming in." He recommended I have a session with Maria, a medical intuitive he knew from Colorado, who could access important information held in my body and spirit and get to the source of my difficulties. Medical intuitives can tune in to the subtle energy of the body and use intuition to find the source of people's physical and emotional conditions. They look at the effects of emotional energy, past and present, on our physical health, as well as past traumatic experiences that might alter the frequencies of cells and the integrity of our energy system.

A Colorado Shaman

Maria, a shaman as well as a clinical psychologist, lived in Colorado, while I was in New York. Even though I had experienced shamanic healing and other energy healings, I was relieved that she had a degree in clinical psychology. Energy healing from a distance was new to me, and I liked the fact that she had a foot in both worlds, the familiar world of Western psychology and the unfamiliar world of shamanic healing. Despite my apprehensions, I sensed that Maria would be my next healer and that I had been guided to call her.

When I phoned to make an appointment, she asked a few questions, and then said, "I have to ask the Spirits if you're ready to do the work. I'll get back to you in four days." My experiences had acquainted me with the unusual techniques of shamanic and kabbalistic work, but I had never come across anything like that before. But I trusted her (after all, Jed had referred me) and I was willing to try anything.

Four days later she returned my call, relaying the message from Spirit that I was ready to do the work. She set our appointment for three weeks later. In preparation for our session, which she called a ceremony, she asked for my birth name and birth date. Since the session would be over the phone, she requested that I mail her a photo of me taken within the week of our ceremony. As a shaman, Maria called the Spirits to guide her as she worked with my body, uncovering old beliefs, traumas, and wounds that I held deeply inside my cellular makeup.

My three-hour ceremony took place in May, 2005, 17 days shy of my 50th birthday. I was in my bedroom behind locked doors, since the pounding of the builders downstairs doing construction work made me anxious. I was so nervous about my first session that when Maria answered the phone, she immediately said, "We (meaning she and Spirit) need to make you feel less anxious." Those comforting words set the tone for a comfortable session. She then asked me to remove any jewelry I was wearing because she was sensitive to metal. I immediately panicked; I always had such a difficult time putting on and taking off jewelry because of my hands. I felt anxious that I couldn't meet Maria's expectations, but she allayed my fears by again telling me to calm down, to take my time, and to be at ease. I laughed inwardly and thought, "This wise woman knows me already!" When I was ready, I lay on the floor, feeling the subtle energy moving through my body. It amazed me that I could actually feel energy moving through me, as if I was lying on a healing table right next to her in the same room.

What she and Spirit presented was astonishing. Throughout the entire session, she referred to "we," meaning that she and the spirits were in partnership. Maria first commented that my body was in immense, pervasive exhaustion. She referred to the anxiety, fear, and terror that had plagued me throughout my lifetime. She listed every vertebra in my spinal column that was affected by my neurological disease and identified my current disabling hip and knee pain. She identified systemic Candida, adrenal gland depletion, spastic colon, and much more as she and the spirits walked through each organ and told me about the secrets my body held. She read my body as if she had an autobiographical sketch and an MRI. She knew me from the inside out, and I felt completely safe with her.

Deep-rooted emotional and spiritual issues emerged during the session validating what I had already suspected. Maria described the fight-or-flight patterns in my life and how they affected my adrenal glands. She pointed out many of my life issues, such as control, trust, self-judgment, perfectionism and self-criticism. She spoke of my self-contempt, decreased self-esteem, low self-image, self-doubt and lack of confidence. She also identified cycles of depression throughout my life that I rarely allowed myself to have.

Maria described the volatile nature of my mother's marriages and the terror Buddy had of dying. She explained that because of my parents' unavailability, I retreated into myself as a child, becoming invisible in an effort to escape. She said that my survival skills had helped me cope with pain and annihilation, but in the process I experienced severe abandonment, feeling cut off from Source and from creation.

She spoke about my parents, in particular my deceased biological father, and she identified where I held the energy of my life's experiences inside my body. She also explained that all throughout my life I had made decisions based on the fear of abandonment and my need for being perfect.

What I found particularly insightful was her exploration of the difference between the birthright of creation vs. the family of origin birthright. The former, which was permeated by unconditional love, had boundless freedom and potential, while the latter, conditioned, and fearful, led to restriction and painful loving. As a demonstration, she asked me to open my arms fully to the side as she said, "This is your birthright of creation." She then said, "Now bring your hands six, no four inches apart. This is your birthright from your family of origin." This demonstration brought tears to my eyes. Never having heard this distinction before, I was reminded how much I had never felt accepted as a child.

Maria described each one of my organs and explained how my body held the energy of past emotions on a cellular level. For example, she said that my lungs continued to hold my mother, father, and biological father with sadness and grief, while my liver was filled with anger at my mother because I had to live in reaction. She explained that when a child is always living in reaction, she doesn't really know who she is; she only knows what she doesn't want to become. I also felt angry at my biological father, Buddy, for leaving me when I was so young.

Maria addressed my whole being—body, mind, heart and soul. She knew what made me tick: where the tears were and where the pain resided in my body on cellular level. Since the physical body had translated feelings of anger, sadness, grief and fear into disease, to get unstuck I would have to release these toxic memories and feelings on that same cellular level. This new concept struck a cord deep within.

I was in awe of how Maria and Spirit could see right to the very marrow of my being. The spiritual intimacy that we shared, her recognition of my essential self, and the permission she extended to me to just *be*: All this validated me and was healing in itself. She gave me the assurance and the confidence that I would heal and that I had a lot more to do in this world. She also instilled in me the awareness that

I had the power to change my existence, and I was excited and ready to take on the challenge. This three-hour phone appointment with a shamanic healer, who lived halfway across the country from me, was the catalyst for me to change my life forever.

After I finished the session with Maria, my whole body tingled from the energy exchange I had just experienced. As I was gathering my thoughts, Jessica knocked on the door; it was time to drive her to evening classes. We spoke for a few minutes, and I asked if I could hug her. She responded with a hug and said, "I don't want you to hate me." I responded, "I love you, Jessica, but you don't want my love right now. I have to allow you to find your own way, while remaining open to you, and not feeling rejected or hurt by your actions." Clearly, I needed to learn not to take Jessica's actions personally. She had her own work to do independent of our relationship, and I didn't want to interfere. I felt a new surge of strength as I spoke to her, a sense of solidity and clarity about my boundaries. The session with Maria had helped me gain a different perspective. If I am who I am as a result of my cellular damage, then I was ready to release it all.

One week later, a few days before my 50th birthday, I stood before my husband and said with a calm, clear voice, "I'm done being sick. I'm going to heal. If I can't heal in this house, I will leave." I said it and I meant it. I knew in my gut I meant it. The words came from my depths with a conviction of spirit and utter confidence.

My true healing began when I said yes after my session with Maria. Her words echoed in my mind, "You will heal and have a lot of teaching to do." Her words empowered me to believe that I was greater than my physical body. I was much more than what I had been conditioned to believe. At this turning point, my way forward was clear: I had to get out of my way and trust that with Spirit's presence I could live my life differently.

People had often said that I was a spiritual being, a bright light, but that's hard to believe when you're in immense physical and spiritual pain, burdened by emotional baggage and old belief systems. I now had an opportunity to dismantle my old conditioning on a cellular level.

Maria was the angel to guide me through the process. Her intuitive healing session empowered me to change my destiny. I was now more than ready to let go of it all, and with that decision my life began to change.

I continued my work with Maria for the next eight months. Because of my extreme adrenal fatigue, Maria suggested bed rest for approximately four weeks. She recommended that I change my diet by eliminating wheat and dairy, gave me a list of herbal remedies, and suggested that a naturopathic doctor do a stress test on my adrenal glands. When I did, the naturopathic doctor confirmed what Maria had seen energetically. Maria and I continued with weekly phone sessions, and when she travelled to New York, I experienced her healing energy in person on two occasions. On the healing table, Maria probed deeply into the blocks that remained embedded in my cells. The depth of Maria's spiritual gifts and her energetic healing continually fascinated me.

To deal with my continued physical exhaustion, Maria recommended that I see Alice, an herbalist/iridologist in Buffalo, New York, whom she and Jed both knew well. My body clearly needed additional help, since the herbal supplements and adrenal support that Maria recommended weren't strong enough to keep my body from remaining in crisis.

An Herbalist from Buffalo

On July 12, 2005, I boarded a plane for Buffalo. I was a little apprehensive about the trip because I had hoped to find someone closer to home. However, Maria's recommendation washed away my concerns; I knew Alice was the best herbalist for me.

When I arrived in Buffalo, I found a taxi and gave the driver Alice's address. Twenty minutes later we arrived at a strange-looking building in a Buffalo suburb. The friendly taxi driver asked how long my appointment would take, and I told him to pick me up in two hours.

As I got out of the taxi, I began questioning myself. "What am I doing here?" I thought. "I must be insane." I walked around to the back of the building, where her office was located. The receptionist was friendly, and within 15 minutes Alice greeted me in her office with a warm, loving smile. Alice, who was in her 70's, had a radiant glow that made her look years younger. I knew within five minutes that she was a blessing and that her positive energy would help me heal. She took one look at me and said, "You're in crisis, but you *will* heal." Relief flooded my system, soothing my anxiety.

Alice held a small glass instrument to my eye and proceeded to tell me what I had inherited genetically from my parents. First, she looked into my right eye (paternal side) and then my left (maternal side). She then evaluated the color of each eye behind the iris, a procedure that defines the amount of toxicity in the body. She explained that when the eye is brown, it is filled with toxins and disease. As healing occurs and the toxins are removed, the eye color changes to clear blue. My eyes, she pointed out, were muddy brown.

"Are you planning to make a major change in your life?" Alice asked. Looking into my eyes, she said, "You're constantly thinking about changing your life." After another penetrating glance, she asked, "What happened between the age of 5 and 6, and again around 13 and 14?"

Her first question alone convinced me that she knew what she was doing. She saw trauma to my head at these key points in my life. "I hit my head in the back of a convertible car when I was fooling around with my sister at age five," I replied. "When I was 13, my neurological disease presented itself." "Instead of taking you to the eye doctor after you hit your head," she said, "your parents should have taken you to the emergency room, but they didn't know." She felt that my head trauma was the precipitating event leading to my neurological disease. As she continued to look into my eye, she kept repeating "What a constitution you have." She repeated this phrase frequently throughout the two-hour session.

Through her study of my eyes, Alice revealed that I had received my great strength from my mother, and that we were similar, except that my mother got stuck and I didn't. Alice spoke in detail about the emotional connection between my biological father and my mother. I was amazed at her insights. Through the practice of iridology, she knew detailed information regarding the emotional baggage between my parents. Alice said that my mother never understood why Buddy treated her the way he did, and that from then on she never trusted again. "Your mother is held together by Scotch tape," she said. "It's very old adhesion, and there's no changing her now. Just love her for who she is, and this acceptance will be healing."

Alice continued to gather information while making marks on my eye chart, delineating the areas in my body that were stressed and unhealthy. She told me that the ADHD in the family came from my maternal grandfather, and that Buddy had difficulty with mood swings because of blood sugar issues. She told me I had suffered from bouts of depression throughout my life, but I never allowed myself to be depressed (I had heard the same thing from Maria.) She then listed the genetic disposition affecting my body from my father's side. This included the adrenal glands, spine, thyroid, ribs, spleen, liver, upper intestine and colon. She said that every vertebra and organ was inflamed, and that I had systemic Candida and parasites. The area from my jaw to my coccyx was totally out of alignment, and the small lymph nodes throughout my body were swollen. I explained how my eyesight had worsened over the past two years, and she said, "How can your eyesight not be affected when your body has all this going on?"

On the maternal side, she linked pain in my left breast and a cyst on my left ovary to lack of maternal nurturing. She told me that I had three pregnancies, having lost the third one in a miscarriage. She said that my mother identifies me with Buddy, and that both of us were still holding onto him. "You need to let him go," Alice said. "Letting go of Jessica would also help you let go of the deep hurt you carry around your mother. It's time to take care of yourself."

She explained how my mother completely shut down after her marriage to my biological father and would never allow anyone in again. "She gave you her story, with the abuse she felt from Buddy and her inability to trust again," Alice said. "She passed all of this down to her children." These were quite a profound statements, and I took it all in.

She described me as a private person, even though I was gregarious and outgoing. She said I was totally different from anyone else in my family. She spoke about my body being riddled with toxins from extensive surgeries, inflammation, and medications.

As I listened, I was amazed. Everything she said made sense. The anecdotes she revealed about my mother were liberating, and for the first time I felt my mother's pain and frustration. Alice affirmed the significance of Buddy's biological and energetic connection, which helped me understand the deep yearning I always felt for him.

I was comfortable with Alice. Even as she continued to list just about everything that could possibly be wrong with someone, I didn't feel overwhelmed or scared. Because of her kindhearted, loving nature, I felt hopeful, trusting that she could help me heal myself.

After an hour and a half, she asked me to stand up, because she needed to do a hands-on adjustment to my body. She said, "I never do this on the first visit, but I feel it's necessary because you're in such crisis." Then she adjusted my jaw, shoulder, cervical and pelvic area, after which I felt much better.

Then we discussed how to alleviate the problem areas. Alice sat at her desk and listed on one side of the paper all the foods I had to give up, as well as the foods I had to begin eating on a regular basis. The list was exhaustive. I had to drop all foods that contained caffeine, sugar of any kind, (including all fruits), and foods with chemical preservatives. The prohibited list included all fermented foods, vinegar, wheat, dairy, red meat and alcohol. I had to eat four to six servings of raw vegetables twice a day. Thank goodness I was a salad eater! Of course, I would now have to eat salad with lemon and oil instead of my usual Caesar or Italian dressing. "Oh well, I told myself, I can handle that." I saw clearly that my new eating habits would be costly, more in keeping with health food stores than with the typical food store chains I was accustomed to. I felt overwhelmed, but determined to make this radical change in order to survive.

Alice flipped the paper over and began writing down an extensive list of supplements, vitamins and herbs that I had to start taking immediately. As the list grew longer and longer, I thought, "You've got to be kidding! How am I going to afford all this?" She listed supplements that I had never heard of, and she was adamant about my taking them. She said, "This is where your determination, perseverance, and dedication will come in handy."

I shared with Alice my concern about the expense, but it didn't seem to affect her at all. She wouldn't budge when it came to the essentials of my healing process, and I saw her point. "If I had cancer," I thought to myself, "I would spare no cost in order to heal." Thankfully, I had enough money to proceed . . . at least for a while.

I trusted Alice, just as I did Maria, because these women healers who read me so accurately, who were trustworthy and believable, knew me so well, Maybe I was naïve, or maybe I was willing to go out on a limb, believing that I was safe and people weren't going to hurt me. Whatever the reason, I decided to believe in them, in myself and in the power to heal. I had to believe. What other choice did I have? Expensive supplements or not, I was going to heal!

Alice said that we must alleviate my systemic inflammation, and this step was a major commitment to my healing process. She told me that I would move beyond my biology and genetics and that I would heal.

I left her office two hours later filled with hope. The taxi driver who promised to be back was indeed there and took me to the airport. As I sat waiting for my flight to arrive, lost in contemplation, I pulled out a little notebook and wrote down everything Alice had said. I sat there with calmness as I watched people running from here to there on their journeys. My inner journey would be demanding and even grueling at times, but healing was the only thing that mattered at this point in my life. When I arrived home a few hours later, Sam picked me up at the airport, and I shared with him my experience and new beginning. He was right there with me.

To clean myself out on a cellular level, I took herbs and drank liquids I had never heard of before. I swallowed more than 40 pills three times a day, along with herbal teas, liquid herbal supplements, and a protein shake filled with gross-tasting liquid drops, every morning. I also found myself cooking in ways I had never imagined, preparing dishes with only fresh and natural ingredients. No more frozen or ready-made meals.

For the first time in my life, I was taking good care of myself. In fact, I was nurturing myself on a physical and emotional level by paying attention to everything I put in my mouth. I chose every morsel of food with careful deliberation. Talk about mindfulness! All of my meditation and awareness practices came to life through this process. I was feeding my body and nurturing my soul with complete love and acceptance as I cleaned out the toxins that had overrun my system.

At the beginning of my food revolution, I looked in my pantry and read the labels on every jar, can, and box of food I had. I was aghast at how many items I had to discard. I took a trip to Trader Joe's with two bags of canned and jarred goods to return. The supervisor, who understood my food restrictions, allowed me to return the products, because they all had some ingredients that I couldn't have on my restricted diet, including sugar, wheat, vinegar and salt. My list of prohibited foods had nothing bad in it for the normal person, but they were no longer acceptable for my new food regime.

At first, changing my diet was exhausting. Once, I called Jed in a state of complete frustration and said to him, "What am I going to eat?" However, with patience and resourcefulness, I slowly found my way through. I learned to read every label and discern what I could and couldn't have. I became Laura, the fully conscious eater, and I followed this program without wavering. Even when we went out to dinner, I didn't waver. I put forth a 100 percent effort, because healing had become greater than anything else in my life.

In this regard, I wrote a poem on July 17, 2005:

Healing is Greater Than Anything Else

I have begun to move from a place of sadness and suffering
To let go and trust in the universe:
To take the risk and do the journey;
To travel from a place of fear and loneliness
To a place of compassion and awareness;
To recognize that life will give me the necessary tools,
Providing me with mirrors to witness who I AM.
My body needs to heal from the inside out;
My body knows the truth.
It is the body that holds the suffering and injustices
Deep within my cells.
My body is tired of the charade of perfection
And is asking for my soul's compassion to heal.
My body has had enough,
My being needs to heal.
As I continue to take the steps to empty and open,
I invite myself to reach out to others,
Those who may not be able to ask for my openheartedness.
With a depth of knowingness, I need to do this to heal,
And healing is greater than anything else.

As this poem shows, I had recognized that healing comes from the heart, on the inside, while cure comes from something outside ourselves.

It didn't take long to realize how life-altering Alice's program was. I quickly recognized that my healing was so much bigger than just the food I ate. It involved being receptive, forgiving, and totally accepting of myself and everyone else in my world. It also called for letting go and moving beyond my rigid definitions that divided the world into black and white, good and bad, for and against. As these new, healthy attitudes went deeply into my soul, I began detaching myself from others, without having to take everything so personally. I could nurture and celebrate myself, no matter what others did to me! Best of all, I could lighten the burden of my life by being fully present to healing and health.

As my cellular cleansing program brought heightened awareness and amplified my transformation, I began to see my relationships differently. I accepted my mother, father, Sam, and Jessica for who they were, and I stopped trying to change or fix them.

One night I wanted a glass of wine when things were difficult at home. I realized, of course, that wine wasn't part of my program, and I asked myself why I even entertained such a desire. That evening, as I questioned my yearning and looked deeper at what was driving my desire, I learned a lot about myself. In the past I simply would have grabbed a wine glass and opened a bottle. Now, with honest reflection, I realized I didn't drink for the taste, but for the effect that wine had on me. Wine always took me a little out of my body, a pleasant distraction that made coping so much easier. Now I had to learn a different coping strategy. I would never jeopardize my healing process by drinking wine that was loaded with sugar, my number one enemy at the time. During moments like these, I acknowledged just how deep the healing really went.

Six weeks later I returned to Buffalo for my first checkup, excited to visit Alice again. I felt confident that I was making good progress by following the program, taking all my supplements, and beginning to honor myself. I also knew that I was changing because from time to time I would experience waves of emotion that accompany a state of heightened awareness. When I arrived, Alice said immediately that I looked much better and that the toxicity was moving quickly out of my brain. She was pleased that I had embraced the program so completely.

"Many emotions are surfacing," I told her, "and I'm riding these waves without understanding why."

"It's all part of the detoxification process," she explained. "Many deep-seated issues are coming to the surface as part of the releasing process. You're getting in touch with the maternal, feminine side of yourself, as well as recognizing the strengths and gifts that your mother gave you. Just accept yourself as you are, and allow the process to unfold. As the toxicity is released, the past will come zooming in your face. If you witness it as it leaves you, you'll be aware, not depressed. Look at it and kiss it goodbye. By releasing it, you're saying goodbye to it on a cellular level."

Alice noticed a clearing in my lungs, an indication that I had given up clinging to old patterns regarding my father Buddy. "As you clear out," she warned, "fear will rise to the surface. Don't get hysterical about it; just be aware. Take consolation in the knowledge that the worst is over."

I left Alice's office feeling wonderful about my progress. I was inspired to keep up with my new healing program with 100 percent commitment. I continued to visit Alice every six months to keep abreast of my progress and to see whether any changes needed to take place.

CHAPTER 13

Trusting in the Universe and Its Messages

Trust is the name of the game.

I CONTINUED MY INDIVIDUAL WORK with Maria, and soon Sam and I agreed to do sessions with her together. Confident that with Maria's guidance we had a chance of working through our problems, we committed to a period of six months in which to heal our marriage.

In my individual phone sessions with Maria, we explored my relationship with Sam and the traumatic events from earlier in my life that were causing conflict in our relationship. With great clarity, I saw how my wounded inner child, who suffered from loneliness, abandonment, and unworthiness, contaminated the present with unmet needs from the past.

With Maria's help, I got in touch with deep inner pain stemming from when I was three and four years old, times of profound humiliation and separation, when my chronic fears, lack of trust, and ongoing wounds were all seeded. She explained that a great inner conflict was also playing itself out—my fear of dependence and yet my great desire to have someone upon whom I could depend. These sessions helped me accept my feelings and express myself, despite my uncertainty.

"Your mother holds you responsible for your actions as a four-year-old," Maria said one day. "She continues to humiliate you in front of others by telling you that you're stupid."

I recalled how my mother would often tell people the story of how my sister pushed me down the stairs when I was four years old. In my stupidity, my mother claimed, I would allow my sister to do anything she wanted to me. As Maria explained, "When your mother labeled you stupid, she didn't have to be accountable for *her* lack of mothering, which took her conveniently and guiltlessly out of the picture."

As a young child I received the message that I shouldn't desire anything for myself because of my inherent unworthiness. I bought into the belief that I was the bad guy, a theme I subconsciously recapitulated over and over again in my close relationships.

I have vivid memories of these sessions with Maria. I would create a sacred space in my bedroom by drawing the curtains closed, turning off the light, lying on the rug, and listening to Maria on the other end of the phone. She would ask me to recall an early childhood memory. As I retrieved an incident from my past, she would encourage me to enter the world of feelings of my three-year-old child. I would begin to merge with my little girl, and sometimes I merged so completely that I no longer felt linked to the present. As I allowed myself to open to the experience, I could feel energy flowing through me, releasing feelings that had been withheld for a very long time. In the safety of my room, Maria guided me through releasing the emotional impact of old traumas, including the incident of my pretending to be a dog. I lay sobbing in a fetal position, realizing the impact of such damaging events. Working through these memories with Maria, allowing myself to embrace the grief and the pain, I would sob as the cellular memory of each event was dredged up, experienced and released.

This experience had a profound impact on me. I saw clearly where my psychological issues originated and how deeply my past experiences continued to intrude on my later relationships. My fear of intimacy and abandonment became real to me—not just a story I made up for survival.

Maria encouraged me to hang pictures in my room of me as a three-year-old girl. I made a collage and hung it directly across from my bed, and when I awoke each morning I spoke to little Laura, saying, "I love you so much, and I am here for you, holding you and loving you. You don't have to be afraid of being a bad girl. I wish I were your mother because I would love you so much you wouldn't have to be afraid anymore." Speaking tearfully in this simple, heartfelt language to my inner child brought about enormous healing in my soul.

For many months I would lie in bed and gaze at little Laura while speaking gently to her. As I cried for all the humiliation, isolation and shame she had to endure, I felt a profound shift in myself. Over time I recognized that she had an inner beauty and radiated it as an adorable being of light. I often wrapped my arms around myself while sobbing, as I told little Laura that I loved her smile, her eyes and her depth of spirit. I re-parented myself by constantly reminding my inner child how her smile brightened my life and how I loved her very much. I even wrote poems inviting her out of her imprisonment.

The work with Maria helped me look within to understand where my pain and grief originated, after which I began to view my life and relationships differently. In challenging relationships I started to observe and not react to what people said and did. I appreciated other people's pain without taking it personally. I also began to receive and process information intuitively, knowing things with surprising clarity. These shifts gave me clear proof that I was changing dramatically.

With uncanny accuracy, my journals predicted these changes. I wrote with great foresight that I would experience major shifts between the ages of fifty and fifty-five. On October 20, 2005, I wrote: *Stay pure in your thoughts. Stay pure, and once and for all get rid of the baggage. What life brings you will just happen. You don't need to do anything. Just clean yourself out down to the cellular level. The rest will fall into place.*

As much as I considered myself to be aware, I still couldn't fathom the depth of my pain. I couldn't grasp how much pain I had pushed under the carpet of my being in an attempt to appear strong. Maria helped me connect to my emotional abandonment and lack of trust that stemmed from my birth trauma. As with Alice, I wanted to clean out on a cellular level because I was through being a victim. With our inner work, I reconnected with how my lost soul and troubled heart had given birth to the physical disease that manifested in my adolescence. On November 4, 2005, I wrote in my journal: *I am letting go of the hurt, the loneliness, and the abandonment. I am letting go of the child who felt shamed and unworthy.*

In a testimonial to Maria, I wrote that working with Maria means to "heal for real."

In retrospect, I learned that the wounds locked deep inside the inner child are very real. I spent years reading John Bradshaw's work on the inner child, which helped me understand the damage it can inflict when its presence goes unacknowledged and unhealed. Not until I experienced the depth of my wounds energetically, however, did I progress in freeing myself as an adult.

I discovered that my inner child had been so wounded that I had a hard time differentiating between feelings and perceptions that belonged to me and those belonging to others. This confusion between self and other, inner and outer, led to a lot of uneasiness in my relationships. The problem kept me stagnant, holding on to the emotional and spiritual disconnection I originally felt as a child.

The struggle to be fully seen and heard continued to influence my life. As I started to disentangle my adult self from my wounded inner child, I could finally distinguish between my perceptions and those of others. I then had the choice of staying stuck in my victim stance or changing my viewpoint. Too often I still held on to my disempowerment in intimate relationships—and, conversely, disempowered my partners just as my parents had disempowered me. I was so scared of being loved conditionally that I rejected whatever love I was given. This pattern attracted partners who were detached or had abandonment issues that mirrored mine. In needing to be strong, I became critical, judgmental and controlling. In reality, I was desperately trying to stay in charge, unaware of the underlying dynamic that was driving me. In my rigidity, I couldn't bend and adapt to other people's truths. Worse, I recapitulated all the patterns of my upbringing by attracting the same energy I had experienced. In effect, I kept attracting me.

Psychic Revelations

After many months of flirting with the prospect of having a psychic reading, I finally gave in. In the spring, Joanne had a reading with a woman named Judy, and she felt this psychic's intuition was keen. Having had a fascinating past-life regression in Sedona, Arizona, during the summer, I was curious to find out what Judy's predictions would be. Little did I know that our meeting would propel me into the world of metaphysics, intuition and psychic probabilities.

On November 9, 2005 I walked into Judy's office, and within a few minutes the depth of her intuition stunned me. Judy's reading, consistent with those of Maria and Alice, revealed that she saw me healing completely. "The disease originated in your brain," she said. "Everything affecting your body has its home in the brain." She told me I was in the middle of a major transformation and that I was destined to be a teacher and healer. "You have major work to do," she said, "so be prepared, for your life will change radically."

Judy predicted I would soon be moving. She said that she didn't see me staying married to Sam. The reading went on in more detail with names and future events. I walked out of her office in awe, feeling even stronger about my capacity to heal, change my life, and be a co-creator of my own destiny. I was determined to heal, transforming into a new, upgraded version of myself.

After this first reading, I became obsessed with readings, healings and predictions, and for good reason. They helped me believe that no matter what was happening at home with my children and my husband, I was going to have the life I truly desired. I believed that I could work through my history and step into a future that would be happier, healthier, and more graceful. The readings motivated me to envision a new life.

I began to feel a strong attraction toward doing healing work with others. Up until then, I had never entertained any thought of being in the workforce again. As I continued to learn and grow through my healing process, however, I realized I had a gift to share with others, and a renewed sense of passion to work with children and their parents. Now I was seeing through a softer lens, through healing eyes, not through the eyes of a clinician. With this growing sense of purpose, I wrote a paper entitled "Seeing through the Eyes of the Child," in which I described a new model of healing between parent and child. As I wrote it, I kept hearing Judy's words: "Whatever happens to you will be wonderful."

By the end of 2005, I began to trust that everything would fall into place. I believed in the unbelievable, that I would have the life I had always desired. Although my relationship with Sam became easier, we both knew we would not remain together. We tried everything we could to keep the marriage alive, but despite our transformational work we simply couldn't salvage it.

Although I knew what I wanted, I was afraid to completely let him go. I continued to slip into old fears and my need for security. I asked myself, "Is Sam right for me? That's all that really matters." I went back and forth for another two years as I focused on healing and became friends with the metaphysical world. I continued my morning davening, which helped to center and ground me. "When do I shift from being out of control to giving up control?" I frequently asked myself in prayer.

A Different Kind of Control

Healing helped me let go of my drama on a practical level. After much consideration, I informed Jessica that if she wasn't attending college as a full-time student she was old enough to live on her own. Her continued insults empowered me to stand up and honor myself, and the home I shared with Sam and Benjamin. "I carried you for nineteen years," I told her. "It's your turn to carry yourself." There was nothing more I could do. She had made her choices, and I no longer questioned her actions. My relationship with my daughter became less tumultuous. Nine months later, with my love and blessings, Jessica moved to Boston. On December 7, 2005, I wrote her a letter expressing my sentiments.

Dearest Jessica,

As you move forward in your new life, I'd like you to view this time as your second birthing. This time it's not your mother giving birth to you, but you, Jessica, giving birth to yourself. I love you deeply and wish you the most wonderful, fulfilling life in every conceivable way. Of course, you'll have challenges to contend with; you'll always have those. Live life to the fullest—all of it—the good, the bad, and the ugly. The trick is to learn from it all, not just the sweet stuff. Hard times make us strong and help us appreciate the good times. To live life to the fullest, embrace all of it. Staying only in the middle often brings you safety, but rarely meets the passionate yearnings of the soul.

Moving out on your own is a huge developmental step. At almost twenty, you have your whole life ahead of you. All you have learned up until now will guide you. My daughter, my heart, I love you, and I truly hope you know in the depth of your soul that my teaching, guidance, and mothering were meant to help you be the best you can be in this world. I am always here for you, body, heart, and soul. I am excited for you and look forward to the next phase of our journey together. Jessica, I had my own learning to do, and I have grown up in many ways. The teachings of the Hyde School have come alive for me in a gentle, loving, nonattached way. This past year has helped me see the world differently. May my calmness, new sense of balance, and wellness be a support to you in your continuing growth.

Happy Birth-day, my beautiful daughter.
With all my love, Mom

Obviously, I was learning the art of allowing and letting go while still being fully present. I was beginning to learn this invaluable lesson in other areas of my life, too.

On January 3, 2006, Sam and I drove Jessica to her new home in Boston, and I slipped her a month's rent. I was no longer battling Jessica for control of her life. I gave her back the ability to make her own choices. We had both grown up. Jessica's move away from home gave us both the distance required to heal our relationship and ourselves. She needed to find her authentic self, and because I loved and honored her, as I did myself, I was not afraid to let her go.

On January 16, 2006, I had my third visit with Alice. This time I met her at Jed's home in Woodstock, New York, an easy two-hour car ride. As before, the visit was encouraging. Her first words to me were: "You're done with nervous breakdowns." I replied, "I know."

As she placed her glass ring up to my eyes, she said, "Your heart and lungs are clear, and your right side has cleared out in such a short period of time!" (The right side holds the paternal biology. The left, the maternal or feminine side, had not cleared as much.) Then she said, "You don't have a disease!"

I replied instantly, "I know."

She told me my brain had cleared out the toxins and that I should continue my good work. She, like Judy, foresaw the promising future that lay ahead of me, and I now had sufficient proof to believe in them and in my transformation, because while monitoring the progress of my hands I noticed that when I went deep inside, either in meditation or davening, my fingers felt straighter and softer, clawing a little less. And as I davened, I opened my hands to God in an offering position, as if to say, "Here I am; open me up."

In my journal entry dated January 17, 2006, I wrote: *"I don't quite understand how my hands can heal with all my tendon transfers and bone fusions, but God works in strange ways. Who am I to question God? I will continue to open and graciously accept all that you present me."*

Maria further explained that the disease had resulted from a "toxic mixture of restriction and rage" and that was what had crippled me.

"You had toxic despair in every breath you took," she said. "You were fighting between staying alive and wanting to die, which was the split you carried in this lifetime. Your hands constricted and closed inward, due to the emptiness and loneliness you felt so deeply within you. All you could possibly do was to offer it back to the universe, because you couldn't hold on to that depth of despair and alienation."

I wept as I listened to her words: "Your work with Alice will free you. It will heal the fusions and tendon transfers. Remember, this level of healing transcends the body as we know it." I had heard this message repeatedly from the different healers who had crossed my path, and now I was embodying this truth on a cellular level.

At the end of January, I wrote in my journal: *"I'm not holding on for dear life anymore."*

In early February I added: *"I can't help but notice that my right hand is opening; it's softer, more agile. I'm stronger and have much more energy. I want to make others aware that alienation from one's environment can actually damage the body on a cellular level. The pain represents a plea, a cry for help from people who don't feel they belong in this world."*

Here's the formula for how some people get sick: *Alienation from others + alienation from self = disease.*

This Magic Moment

IN MID-FEBRUARY, 2006, I VISITED my sister in northern Virginia, with the intention of staying a week, but ended up staying for three. My sister introduced me to her friend Rose, a psychic. This was the first time I socialized with someone who had intuitive abilities, and the three of us opened immediately to intuitive play. Rose sensed the presence of guides and angels around me, as well as the energy that radiated from me. Like other intuitives and visionaries, she was certain my disease would heal and that I myself was a healer.

Early one morning, during meditation, I felt an external source of light move into and through my body, flexing my thumbs at the joints as if they were normal, which caused them to tingle. While getting up a few minutes later, I noticed for the first time in twenty-five years that I could move my left thumb, bending it at the joint closest to the base. Overcome with exhilaration, I shouted, "Thank you, God! Thank you, God!" I had just experienced a miracle.

That day Rose recommended that I have a reading with Marcus, a minister at a metaphysical church in Washington, D.C. I acted on her advice, and in my reading Marcus said, "You will fully heal and play a significant role in the spiritual movement."

One evening soon after, my sister and Rose and I decided to attend our first message circle, where we could receive brief channeled messages from multiple psychics as they share insights received directly from Spirit. These are the messages I received from the various intuitive readers that evening:

- I was on a new path that required me to make decisions and push fear aside.
- I had to move on because I had accepted "the comfort of discomfort," the solace of having an identity rooted in adapting to pain.
- I needed to speak publicly in the metaphysical world because others could benefit from my healing skills.
- I was to stop denying my own bright radiant light and not be afraid to use this gift.
- The intuitive side of my nature, long hidden from view, wanted to blast out of me and be used in the service of others.

The messages from the metaphysical world were clear and consistent—I would move forward, and my life would change. I would become the healer I was meant to be. I could no longer remain stuck because of my fear of the future.

When I returned home from Virginia, I knew it was time to come out of hibernation. I told Sam I was finished with our couples work with Maria, and he agreed.

As the year wore on, I noticed slight yet significant changes in my hands. I could make more of a fist with my right hand, bringing my thumb closer to my index finger, which enabled me to manipulate small objects. I also had some independent movement in my fingers, which I had lost as a result of the tendon transfer surgeries. The pinky finger on my left hand that had contracted at the middle joint was now beginning to fully extend, as was the middle finger of my right hand. The other fingers of my right hand were almost fully extended.

As I continued to unravel my emotional self, progress in my physical body continued to manifest, generally in little spurts that almost eluded me. I could hold my pen with ease a little longer than before, handle small objects better, and not feel pain in my arms and shoulders while lifting packages or doing housework. Day by day I was feeling stronger and struggling less in a world that was becoming far more tolerable.

CHAPTER 14

Immersion in the Metaphysical World

Shifting from Being Out of Control to Giving Up Control

I BELIEVED THAT THE UNIVERSE could do a better job with my life than I could, so I chose to step out of the way and I became more accepting and gentle with myself. My life started to revolve around my interest in the metaphysical world. I started reading about vibrational medicine, energy work and hands-on healing. I spent hours at Awakenings, a metaphysical bookstore in Katonah, New York, spiritually and intuitively connecting with healers and readers. With this new exposure, I was strengthening my readiness to become a healer and to take healing into my own hands.

Once, when I was at a healing fair, I met Drew, a hypnotist. When he saw me, he immediately said, "You know you're a psychic." I laughed and replied, "Why does everybody keep saying this to me? Is this for real?" As we continued the conversation, Drew told me that it was time for me to move on and that my relationship with Sam was complete. "You only need to decide that you're ready to heal, and you will," he said. "You don't love yourself enough, so you need to carry your pain. When you find the courage, you'll let go of your fear and move on." I had three more sessions with Drew, who focused on teaching me skills and practices to release old energy. Like many of the angels I attracted into my life, he encouraged me to be the best I could be and to become fully present.

In July, I returned to my sister's house to visit my new intuitive friends. I decided to have a reading with Melody, a woman I had met at the message circle in February. Her reading was significant because she introduced to me to the relevance of past-life experiences in current situations. Melody told me I had many past lives as a crippled child who died before the age of 10. She said, "This is this lifetime in which you heal." She explained how unconditional love promotes health while conditional love undermines it, as witnessed by my past lives as a crippled child. I thought her explanation was interesting in lieu of my current family pattern of conditional love and acceptance.

Melody also explained to me about brain shifts. "You've had four or five experiences of them," she said. "These near death-experiences alter your consciousness and remind you to stay on your path. You experienced one during birth and another years later." Immediately I remembered passing out in the hospital when I was 15. "Now it's time to get rid of this disease," Melody said, "and you can." At the end of the session, she suggested I contact David Slater, a healer who lived in Colorado and who worked with vibrational medicine.

Readings like Melody's reiterated the same theme. It felt ridiculous to keep spending money on readings, but the messages helped to reinforce my healing process.

One day when I was visiting Awakenings, I met Graham, an energy healer who offered me a free session, and I enthusiastically said yes. A week later when I met with him, he asked if I had been abused early in my life. He said, "You took that abusive energy in, and your hands closed up as a result. Stress caused your hands to contract as early as 2 to 3 years of age, but the physical manifestation didn't show up until you were 14. There's no doubt you're in the process of healing."

Earth Angel

My next reading was special and requires proper introduction. In August, 2006 I met Roland, a medium who channels spirit from the other side. I hadn't been to a medium before. Linda, the owner of Awakenings, knew him well and invited me to join her in a message circle he was leading. There were 40 people in the room. Roland approached each one of us individually and channeled a message from the other side. I was amazed at what I observed. From halfway across the room, Roland turned to me and said, "Your father is sorry that he had to leave you so young. He loves you, he loves you, he loves you. You want to know if you'll get through it, and if your hands have strength. Your father is sending healing energy into your hands." Never having experienced anyone channel my father before, I sat there in shock, tears streaming down my cheeks. Roland, who was standing far away from me, couldn't possibly have seen my hands.

He then spoke about my mother's cancer and my life as a teenager, reassuring me repeatedly how much my father loved me. When he asked whether anyone present had a picture of a person who had crossed over, I held up a picture of Buddy, my biological father. Actually, Roland doesn't even need to look at a photograph; he picks up the energy vibration that the picture holds and speaks from his intuitive knowing.

"Your father had to leave you when you were very young," Roland said. "He didn't want to. He's sorry he didn't have more time on Earth to love you. He's been around you as a presence for a very long time. He regrets having to leave you." Roland kept repeating how sorry Buddy was for leaving. After the session Linda and I, excited and awestruck, spoke of Roland's abilities. To be in contact with my father was something I had longed for my entire life, and I wanted more opportunities to hear Buddy's words. I left that evening thanking God for all the validation and support the universe kept bestowing upon me.

Two days later I returned for a private session. "You're in the midst of a transformation, moving from the unsettled into the settled," Roland said. "You're going to be all right." He said that energy was moving out of my hands and asked me whether my hands hurt because as an empath (an intuitive who absorbs the feelings that another person feels) he felt tightness in his own hands "Yes," I answered. "They feel tight because of my surgeries."

"Are they getting better," he asked. And he answered the question himself: "Yes, they're getting better; you're hands are healing. The guides want you to expose your hands—back and front—to the sun's healing rays for nine days. Let the sun nurture your hands, and you'll release all the tension that's coming out through them. Your hands are better, but when you're stressed, your hands are tighter. Stress has caused your hands to be unsettled."

At the end of the session, I asked Roland whether he saw my hands healing. "Absolutely," he replied. "Keep stretching the fingers. You are a miracle. You're meant to be alive and to share with others how you worked with the healing energy to restore you to health. Other people need to hear your story and to be inspired by it."

Like Alice and Judy, Roland didn't see any disease. I left my session with him quietly and calmly absorbing his encouraging words.

Every day brought new awareness and confirmed that I was ready to leap into my new life. I was awestruck how angels continued to show up to guide me forward on my journey. My soul yearned for much more than my present life offered. Every healer and every reading affirmed that I had a higher purpose. In order to step out of my present life into the new one that was calling me, I would have to learn to completely trust in the universe and its messages.

The Ultimate Trust

My life with Sam was a lie and unfair to both of us. We needed to look beyond our fear, let go and trust that we would be absolutely fine. The marriage was over, just as life as I had known it was over. As Roland said, "It's time for you to find peace, freedom and serenity by learning to love yourself enough." To begin a new life called for courage, a leap of faith and a belief that I was all right. I had to completely trust in the universe and my Higher Self that I was meant to have a new life, one in which I would receive all that I wished for. I had been working diligently to heal and to trust by dropping my story, both energetically and emotionally, of grief and limitation. Ever since my session with Roland, I had watched the puzzle pieces fall into place.

Sam and I separated our bedrooms but agreed to live together for one more year until Ben graduated from high school. We agreed to remain civil by stepping beyond the ego, with its pain, hurt and blame. In accepting that it was best to move on, I wanted to rise above the anger, disappointment and pain I felt and learn to live as friends with Sam. By living in a gracious, kind and open way, I knew that the opportunity for our personal growth was tremendous.

During the time we remained in the house, we had many moments of real friendship and tenderness, as well as many difficult and trying times. We saw both as opportunities to learn how to live from our heart center, rather than from our ego, with its rootedness in fear. I had the intuitive awareness that in order for my physical healing to progress, I had to live in a loving environment.

Benjamin, my 17-year-old son, who was transitioning into the next phase of his life, found this to be a trying time. He had a deep core of spiritual knowing that made him less reactive than his sister and more capable of adapting to the inevitable changes that he knew were coming. Jessica, living in Boston and consumed with her own life, was less directly affected by the changes playing out in our home. I knew our separation would affect her as well, and we kept in regular contact with one another to talk through the feelings and emotions that arose.

Roland once spoke about Benjamin in my reading. "Benjamin is a spiritual being, an old soul," he said. "Your son came into this lifetime to heal you. You have a unique spiritual connection."

Benjamin and I had always acknowledged that spiritual connection. I told him recently that he was the only person who loved me unconditionally and that his love empowered me to heal. Even with this understanding, I worried how the divorce would affect him. Yet my son put his personal issues aside by insisting that I needed to separate from Sam. "You need to trust God," Benjamin said. "God knows who you are, and He will always take care of you. He knows that everyone you touch heals."

To my knowledge, Benjamin didn't even believe in God. What was surfacing in my 17-year-old son was trust in the Higher Self, the universal God Self. That day Benjamin became my teacher.

One day in his senior year, he asked me to look at a poster he had completed in class, a picture of a woman and a child. When I asked what the picture was, he replied, "That's me looking up to you!" He told me the reason he had made it through everything was that I was his mother. Thank you, Universe, for bringing this sweet child to me!

Benjamin completed his senior year of high school, and in September I helped him move into his dorm room at the School of Visual Arts in Manhattan to pursue a career in film. Sam and I put the house on the market in July, 2007 and remained there until it sold in May 2008. With Benjamin no longer living at home, the feeling in our living space changed, with the two of us doing our dance, trying to remain gentle and amicable.

Getting Out of My Head

In October 2007, Jon, another angel, came across my path. After suffering an accident that doctors predicted would make him a paraplegic for the rest of his life, he experienced his own personal miracle. Refusing to believe his prognosis, Jon healed himself through the art of Qigong, a powerful Chinese system of healing and energy medicine.

I discovered Jon while reading the book, *Everyday Karma,* by Carmen Harra, who also had a weekly segment on a transformational radio show. One day I called in and had a free mini-reading on her program, where I received the same message again: "You're already healed energetically." I e-mailed Carmen to ask for Jon's phone number and then called him to schedule an appointment. At this point in my life, I trusted any person who had the integrity and capacity to heal from a life-threatening illness. Because Jon had experienced both trauma and healing, he easily won my praise and trust.

These are the words he spoke: "Your spine looks like a train wreck, especially C1, C2, C3, and C4. (cervical vertebrae of the neck and shoulder). The source of the problem is in the medulla oblongata. You suffered an injury to your brain when you were around 5 years old, which most likely caused the hand problem." While he also saw problems with my lumbar vertebrae and the adrenal glands, he told me I would heal.

Jon emphasized the role of intention in healing, as well as the need to believe in oneself. As I lay on the floor in my bedroom (my healing space), I felt the energy flow through me from head to toe. Afterward my body hurt as a result of his work, which put my body back in balance.

Over the next four months I received healing energy from a man who lived 300 miles away. Like others before him, Jon said, "You'll heal completely, and you'll bring healing to others."

The information I was currently receiving confused me, and my mind tried to put it all together. There were two distinct parts: First, on the physical level, when I hit my head at age 5, that action probably caused the onset of the neurological disease. Scientifically that would make sense. Second, on the psychospiritual level, which addresses feeling of alienation and separation, I asked myself, "What about past lives and karma? Are there past-life connections that contributed to my illness? Or should I focus on feeling grateful for the opportunity to heal and to bring the gift of healing to others?"

One day I wrote in my journal, *"I will be a healer like Jon someday and use my heart center, my openheartedness, to heal others. I know it will all come together for me when the time is right."* Again, I thanked the universe for another angel who was blessing my life. I realized that I could no longer hold onto anger or suffering when people I attracted into my life demonstrated how to live a higher life, filled with hope and healing energy.

The confusion surrounding the biological and the spiritual components of my disease continued to disturb me, so I addressed the issue with my dear friend Joanne, who was a healer herself. We spoke about my desire to connect the dots between the physical and the spiritual, and she offered wonderful feedback.

"The stress was already in your system from early life and from past lives, making your biology vulnerable to physical assault," she said. "Another child might have sustained a blow to the back of the head and been fine, but because of your vulnerability, you had a brain injury that manifested itself as it did."

At the beginning of our next session, Jon asked me what I wanted to do in my life. He suggested that I keep the door open to all opportunities, even ones I hadn't considered. After the session he asked me a great question: "What are you going to do to open the door? Let the universe know you want to serve others, and it will happen. Just open the door, and stop trying to figure everything out rationally. In other words, get out of your head." I allowed Jon's words to penetrate me, but I felt lost and unsure of myself. What did Jon mean when he said, "Just open the door?"

To clear my mind, I went for a walk with my dogs later that day. As I walked down the tree-lined street, I looked up to the sky, asking the universe for some clarity about what Jon had said. My eyes filled with tears when I realized that all I wanted to do was bring my healing experience to others. I had been waiting for my hands to be totally healed and return to normal before stepping out of the safety of my present life. Unconsciously, I was in resistance because there was no need to wait for anything. The issue wasn't about my hands, but the fullness of heart that I wanted to share with others based on the healing of my soul. I was facing old issues of self-acceptance and self-worth.

Later I wrote in my journal: *"I'm not seeking a cure, which is physical, but healing, which is soul-centered. People heal when they feel safe, listened to, and loved for who they are. I can do that! I will offer others the courage and strength that I gave myself. I never wanted to feel so alone, and nobody should have to feel that way."*

The next time we spoke, Jon said, "Don't wait; healing others will help you heal. I don't see you returning to the field of occupational therapy, but doing your own thing." His statement reminded me of what Marcus had said a few months earlier: "You won't work with your hands; you'll heal others with your heart."

I told Jon that I wanted to bring my story, my wisdom, my open heart, and myself to the children who were in discomfort or crisis. I was beginning to formulate a plan that involved working with families, with parents and their children, to open communication and foster understanding. "I have only one question for you." Jon responded. "Why aren't you out there doing it? The truth is that you wear your heart on your sleeve, which is an asset for the work you'll be doing. You have emotional issues to clear first, and then the physical will heal."

A Beacon of Light

In November, 2006 I had a reading with Carol, a seer from Northern Virginia. At the time I called her, I had no idea how important she would be in my life. My sister had just had a reading with her, and the information she received was amazingly accurate. So I said to myself, "Why not? What's another reading!"

Like other seers, Carol told me that I should get ready for my life to change. "You're in the midst of releasing sadness and saying goodbye to your old life," she said. "You're also beginning to understand the truth of who you are. Everything you do in this lifetime will be aligned with the deepest compassion, which you'll express in the world."

As I listened to Carol's reading and her explanation of certain periods in my life, the picture became clearer. Carol pointed out how I held onto early patterns of learning, especially between the ages of 10 and 14, which was a sad time when I didn't feel good enough.

"A driving energy moved through you," she said, "but it wasn't yours. You got hooked into someone else's tragedy and pain, either an older sibling or strong male figure. You looked up to this person and took on the pain.

"You'll begin to shift when you realize this was misguided compassion," she said, continuing to channel information. "Your sadness comes from holding onto it, but it's no longer yours to hold. When you were 4 and 5 years old, you had an innocence of heart, a gentleness of spirit that protected you until you were 7. It then left you, not to be alone in the harshness of the world, but to be on your own to encounter learning experiences for your soul's growth. Some were pleasing, while others were definitely severe.

"You'll liberate yourself when you see and feel the truth of who you are. Something will click, and you'll know that you need to walk out of your life and stop fighting against what you think you should do and start doing what's truly in your heart. You'll have a deep level of awareness strongly aligned with your sense of purpose. You've been fighting to find your purpose for a long time, and what's coming up will set you on that light-filled path. The energetics from the past are gone, and you're stepping into an open state of readiness where you'll merge deeply, intuitively and with sure-footedness into a high state of being, in which master teacher energy will flow through you. Your life path and purpose are one and the same. Who you are is what you do!

"You have some distortion in your energy field that needs to clear first," she continued. I asked Carol whether she saw me healing, and she gave me a response that was consistent with others I had received. "Yes, but really it's a non-issue that's leaving you," she answered. "You're going to return to 100 percent health, better than you've ever known. Just focus on the Self."

When I asked what she saw me doing, she replied, "You'll be teaching, doing a lot of public speaking, channeling high-frequency energy into your energy field. Your physical vessel is being purified for this task, which will involve telling your story as part of inspiring others to heal themselves."

In retrospect, the connections Carol made to specific times in my life, between ages 4 and 7 and between 10 and 14, made perfect sense. During those years, which were significant times in my life, my soul already knew the journey that lay ahead of me, which involved the stages of surviving, healing, and thriving. But to reach a state of physical and spiritual well-being, I had to rewrite my story by dropping attachment to the old and moving into a deeper sense of purpose. Everyone who crossed my path continued to confirm that I was disease-free and ready to share my journey of healing with others.

I now believed that the disease wasn't what the doctors had said it was. The messages were clear: As I heal the soul, I heal the phenomenon that is within me that caused my hands to be unsettled and to shut down.

Despite the steady flow of confirmations and affirmations from healers and psychics, I found myself continuing to deal with deep-seated issues of abandonment and fear. I continued to yearn for my sister's and my mother's love. But slowly I recognized that opening to inner sources of love and acceptance was more important than receiving others' approval. As I stayed in my truth, my authentic self, I learned to allow others to be who they were and not judge how they responded to me.

As I struggled to release Sam from my heart, I yearned to find my soul mate, so I wouldn't have to complete this journey alone. Still prone to self-doubt and the deep ache of not loving myself enough, I sought feedback from those outside myself to confirm that I was on the right path.

Sam and I filed for divorce in May, 2007. Our divorce became final in January, 2008.

Clarity, Wisdom, and Grace

During the next visit to my sister's house, I went to her chiropractor, who was also an intuitive. Rick took one look at me and said, "There's only one place I need to touch, and that's your first cervical vertebra. Your physical problem is in the medulla."

He put me in a contraption and jerked my neck so hard that I thought I would throw up and pass out. I felt a wave of heat go through my body, and I started to cry. Rick told me to lie down for 30 minutes. As my head spun, he said, "This was your crucifixion. You were cut off from Source: that's why your body went limp, and your hands crimped inward." He paused and added, "You were disempowered and not nourished by your parents."

As Rick spoke, I heard Val from my shamanic healings; I heard Maria, Alice and Jon. Everyone was absolutely clear about the source of my disease—everyone.

On December 15, 2006, I noticed I could hold my fork with a perfect grip. I used my left hand, even though I was technically a right-handed person, but I held the fork perfectly. I noticed that my fingers looked a little straighter, and I could hold the pen between my right thumb and index finger, having gained slight movement in my right thumb at the first joint. I was overwhelmed with joy as I said, "Thank you, God." A wave of excitement ran through me every time I noticed that my physical functioning had improved even in the slightest way. These minor miracles confirmed that I was on the right path. When I looked at my hands and noticed these changes, I knew undeniably I was doing everything right.

These moments also helped me surrender to the sadness I felt over the end of my marriage. Sam and I had a grace period to repair our broken dreams. The time we lived together while waiting for our house to be sold helped us heal our relationship karma. Although separated, we learned how to live together and how to be gentle and gracious with each other. Indeed, we stepped into our Higher Selves, a state of expanded consciousness in which one is not driven by fear, anger, and resentment, but by compassion, love and inner peace. It was a gentle moment that felt great.

During this time, a Rabbi from Elat Chayyim recommended that I look into Trans-Generational Healing and Family Constellation work with a healer named John. Family Constellation is a healing modality that includes energy work, psychotherapeutic process, soul work and ancestral work. Within the context of Family Constellation work, one enters the realm of the soul. Through ancestral and soul work, the individual enters into a healing process that can touch many generations, past and future. Over the course of a year, I attended four three-day workshops. I was drawn to the work because of my love for families and my strong belief that they must be involved in the healing and treatment of the child. What I received from the workshops was beyond words.

Prior to my first workshop I read John's first two books, *The Healing of Individuals: Families and Nations Trans-generational Healing and Family Constellations* and *The Language of the Soul: Healing With Words of Truth,* which brought to the surface many new insights in regard to my mother, my deceased father, my husbands, and my relationship to my hands.

After the workshops I had a better understanding of the dynamics that played out in all my intimate relationships. I realized through this work that the loss associated with Sam, Matthew or even Jessica had its origins in old wounds linked to the loss of Buddy and my mother. After the first weekend I wrote in my journal: *"I need to energetically release the pain—not understand it but release it. I must release the pain and hurt I absorbed from Mom. I must release the hurt over Buddy's not being there to love and hold me. And I need to release the pain Matthew caused by not loving me as I needed to be loved. I simply have to release it all."*

I attended three more Family Constellation weekends with John, and through these experiences I realized that energy healing really works. For example, when John chose me to join someone else's family constellation, through energy and not thought, I was guided exactly where to stand in the circle. I was quite aware that this energy wasn't mine; rather, it was the energy of the person I was role-playing. I had never before experienced this sensation. I was convinced that the power was in our energy field and our vibration.

During soul work John guided me into those areas that needed healing and my body responded energetically to his promptings. Once John grasped the extent to which I was held imprisoned by my family's energy and the depth of the tension this caused me, he helped me release it energetically.

In addition to John, I was guided to David, who did work in vibrational medicine in Colorado. Vibrational medicine brings together techniques from microbiology and alternative medicine. David's premise is that everything vibrates. By matching the vibration of the pathogen or the *miasm* (the weaknesses of our bodies inherited from the illness of our ancestors that appear in electrical form in our DNA) with the vibrational formulas he designs (a form of electricity put in a bottle of water), practitioners help eliminate the pathogen or disease. Because of my unquenchable curiosity and deep desire to heal, I called his office in Colorado to set up a phone interview.

When I spoke with him, David stated that the problem with my hands would be eliminated. That was all I needed to hear. I filled out the lengthy Energy Field Analysis and sent him my photo (he does a holographic reading of the body). Four weeks later I received the results, along with a list of vibrational formulas he prescribed for me. He labeled my disease Spinal Muscular Atrophy (which was the medical differential) and made a specific cerebellum remedy to eradicate any lingering vibration. He wrote a personal note in which he stated that I should expect to see steady reversal of the condition. I'll never forget the smile on my face when I read his note. He explained that I had miasms for lymphoma (both my biological parents had it), scleroderma (relating to contractions in the tendons), and the adrenal glands.

As I read David's analysis, I asked myself, "Do I need another intervention?" Was it ridiculous to add one more to my growing list of healings? Clearly, I had engaged a steady stream of healers since I met Maria. When I got quiet, my inner voice said, "Go forward; you need to do this." Despite my enthusiasm, I had discernment, and I certainly didn't accept every healer's offering. I simply knew which healer was meant to be in my life, and I trusted my intuition, driven by the desire to expedite my healing process. So I followed David's program, which consisted of taking drops from a bottle three times a day—pretty simple for the gain I received. I observed slow, steady changes in my hands and in my overall energy. I attributed my progress, in part, to this healing process.

Thus I continued to have readings because they validated that I was on the right path and that my healing would continue. They also gave me the encouragement I needed when the emotions of daily living became overwhelming. Throughout it all, part of me still needed external support.

As my healing proceeded, I became involved with Carol Fitzpatrick's community in Fredericksburg, Virginia. After my initial reading, I participated in telesessions over the summer, and in September, 2007 I decided to attend an Intuitive Workshop held by Carol in her home. The workshop provided an opportunity to develop and strengthen our intuitive abilities through guided exercises. We spent the day engaged in activities that allowed our intuition to flow. During one exercise, for example, we each found a partner and looked deep into each other's eyes, sharing what came through from our heart, our intuition. I asked my partner whether I could hold her hands because I could feel the energy flowing from my heart into my hands as I connected to Spirit. I realized that my hands were a vessel for healing! I was amazed to feel the depth of connection, the flow of energy between us, and the clarity of our intuitive knowledge. I loved the environment and knew that I had found something special.

At one point during the day, I was paired with Carol. My immediate response was, "Oh, my God, how am I going to do this?" Even though the other readings I had given all day were quite accurate, I was still nervous. I looked into Carol's eyes and shared the vision I saw based on information I received intuitively. When I had finished, she said, "What you received in your vision you couldn't have known through ordinary means. That was great."

I had heard from many others that I had intuitive abilities, but that was their perception, not mine. My experience that day helped me tap into my own intuitive abilities and inner wisdom. I cherished my awakening abilities with heart-felt appreciation and vowed to develop the skills I needed to enhance my gift. What pure grace to be around other empathic, intuitive healers! I had found the next step on my spiritual journey.

Revisiting Boston

In early October I drove to Boston to visit my daughter and my hand surgeon. I hadn't visited Mark in quite some time, but now I was ready. I had postponed my annual visit because my hands were changing, and I wanted him to see me when my fingers were absolutely straight. I knew this would be a monumental moment for me.

As I sat in the examining room waiting for Mark, I felt excited and even a bit anxious. When he came in, we chatted for a few minutes, and then I proudly held out my hands and said, "Look at this!" He examined my hands and said, "It's a miracle! Keep doing whatever you've been doing. This is truly a miracle."

Mark commented that my joints looked better, and he didn't see any reason why my hands wouldn't continue to improve. He was awestruck by how straight my fingers were. When he tested me with the dynamometer (a tool used to measure muscle strength), my right hand went from zero to six pounds, and my left hand from six to eight pounds. Encouraged by my progress, he believed I would continue to restore muscle strength.

"I always believed that the mind, body, and emotions were connected," he said. "And by the look of things, you've emptied out lots of emotional baggage you were carrying. I've never witnessed such a dramatic turnaround, and I simply can't explain it. I'm so happy for you!"

I hugged Mark and promised to return in a few years. As I closed the door behind me, a flood of emotions surfaced. This hospital where I had experienced so much pain and so much fear was now behind me forever. As decades of physical and psychological suffering flashed before my eyes, I said goodbye to the Laura who was filled with disease and who needed medical intervention to survive. Energetically I felt different: I no longer belonged there. The diseased Laura's energy fit in well with the hospital vibe, but that person was no more; I had transformed into a completely different person. As I drove away, I cried for the miracle that had taken place in my life. Having Mark witness my transformation was indeed a special moment for me.

Dr. Mark Belsky, who was my hero and my angel, had come into my life when I needed someone willing to reach outside the box. For 26 years he treated all of me—heart, body, and soul—with compassion, gentleness and grace. How blessed I felt on that day. Clearly, more than my hands were opening up, ready to receive.

Opening Up

As a result of my extensive inner work, I was ready to explore further intuitive and healing approaches. Not only was I curious what the universe had in store for me, but I wanted to develop my gift as an intuitive. As this became my mission, I continued to attend Carol's Intuitive Workshops every three months in Virginia, as well as attending Intuitive and Healers Workshops where I lived. Both communities encouraged me to stay on my path.

As I boldly stepped forward, I became interested in hands-on healing and energetic table work. I was awestruck by the psychic information and energetic release that came from a reading or a healing. On this journey to the heart of the soul, I was finding my true self. These incredible experiences were awakening and enlivening my inner core. What started as a quest to heal my hands became an opportunity to awaken my heart. I had healed enough to step out and become the healer I truly was.

During one of my retreats at Elat Chayyim, I met a man named Steve who lived in California. Professionally, he was a cantor who performs Bar/Bat Mitzvahs for special-needs children. Steve had an uncanny ability to draw others to him because of his spiritual nature. As a cantor, he had a magical voice that came from the depth of his soul. Our connection grew from the personal experiences we had working with children, most of them autistic. Because we saw them through the same lens of unconditional love, our relationship deepened. We spent hours on the phone sharing our beliefs and visions of a better environment for these children to learn and grow in. I was fascinated by Steve's ability to bring the children out of their cocoons while treating each of them as a whole person, not just a broken child carrying the diagnosis of autistic.

Because of my own journey and spiritual growth, I had already begun to see children through the eyes of the soul. He was a cantor and I was a clinician. Although we came from different professional backgrounds, our hearts were aligned with the same mission. This connection eventually brought me to California, but not immediately. I had other work to do first.

CHAPTER 15

Moving Forward and Surrendering

THE UNIVERSE KNOWS WHEN YOU are ready to move forward on your path. If there is any interference you will be stopped dead in your tracks until your soul is ready to ascend to the next level. This doesn't necessarily coincide with what you may want or desire.

Sam and I were anxious about selling the house because the market in early 2008 was extremely slow. One morning in early March, I woke up with a deep intuitive sense that I was done with New York. It was that simple: I was done. The feeling, which was so much bigger than me personally, was pushing me to move on. I wasn't in control anymore; something greater than me, my Higher Self, was guiding me to my next destination.

By early 2008 I had started to receive messages from my Higher Self that guided me in my decision-making. By attending all those intuitive workshops and developing my intuitive abilities, I was learning how to honor my own knowing and relying less on someone else's intuitive reading. Now, as I listened to messages originating from within myself, I knew that I would eventually relocate to California. But first I had to move to Virginia.

After he completed his first year of college, Benjamin decided that he and his friend Mike would spend the summer in Los Angeles to get into the "thick of film." My friend Steve offered Benjamin and Mike a room in his home in exchange for taking care of his dog. Suddenly I had no one to be responsible for, and I could start my new life with my children's blessing.

Whereas before I was always trying to control my life, now I was ready to surrender and get out of my way. I had learned to trust that the universe would provide exactly what I needed to walk on my path. In late March I wrote in my journal: *"I've stepped out of the old paradigm, the old way of relating based on fear and the need for security. I'm ready to leap into my new life. I see myself jumping off a cliff into a beautiful body of sparkling water, totally immersed in the joy of being refreshed by the coolness and spaciousness that a body of water brings. I've arrived on the other side, and now I need to get going. There is nothing to wait for. I'm ready to assist others along the path, to help them go through transformation while offering them gentleness and grace."*

Let It Flow

Carol taught us that life would be easy once we let go and believed the universe would guide us. I now saw clearly that spirit had been guiding me all along my path. I certainly had been listening over the years, but I never fully had the confidence to totally trust and let go because I simply didn't love myself enough. I had heard these words from every spiritual person I had met. Now I was ready to let go of the life I had known without allowing old fears to interfere. I felt a sense of freedom, and once I set myself free, other people around me benefited from that grace. When a soul is freed, it automatically begins helping others.

The real shift began when I surrendered and became present for Sam. He approached me one day and said, "I'm going to have back surgery, and I'm taking the house off the market temporarily." I was shocked; I knew I was ready to move on and had already made plans to move to Virginia. My immediate reaction was, "He can't do this to me."

I couldn't imagine postponing my move. I felt as if I was being stabbed in the back. But Sam was determined to go ahead with his plan. He also informed me that his girlfriend would stay at our house for the first few days to take care of him. I was relieved that I would be in Virginia and grateful she would be gone before I returned.

I was enraged and stormed off to my room, where I cried and asked Spirit, "What am I supposed to learn from this situation? What's the lesson in this?" As I opened myself up to Spirit and asked for God's help, I realized that I had an opportunity to release all the struggle and strife that we inflicted on each other. By expressing my Higher Self in this situation, I could put aside my needs, release resentment and serve Sam in his crisis.

I e-mailed Sam and told him that I was available in whatever way he might need me to help him recover from his impending back surgery. "Although we're divorced," I wrote, "we've shared much over the past 15 years, and I'm here for you now."

I felt wonderful, overflowing with gratitude and gentleness for the man who had been there for me so many times in the past. I believe that this reversal of care giving roles had to happen for us to gracefully move forward. After the operation, when Sam came home from the hospital, we shared a wonderful healing space together, both emotionally and physically. We used this critical period to heal our relationship karma.

It came as no surprise, therefore, that within a two-week period we received a bid on our house. At last we were ready to let go and move on. We couldn't have done that, however, before releasing the stale energy to which we were clinging. The sale of the house proceeded without interruption, and we set a temporary closing date for the end of May. Now it was time to start packing. I knew exactly what I wanted to do, and the universe was making it easy, having eliminated all roadblocks. As everything fell into place, I started to pack my belongings.

"What do I need to bring on my new journey?" I asked myself. Leaving my home and everything I knew in order to start a new life was something I had never done before, certainly not alone. Before launching into this unprecedented experience, I spent weeks weeding through boxes of memories, deciding what was worth saving and what I could finally discard. In a burst of freedom and release, I emptied out everything that wasn't pertinent in my life. I finally threw away letters I had kept from Michael, my first boyfriend. I couldn't figure out why I needed them anymore. I was no longer that person and had no desire to bring the past forward. How wonderful to let go of the past and to move unburdened into the present. I packed up my belongings and put them in a storage unit down the street. Since I was staying at my sister's house during my time of transition, I brought only the essentials I needed.

Saying Good-bye

I was leaving my home, my friends, and, most of all, my dogs. To live at my sister's house, I had to give away my two beautiful dogs that I'd had for 10 years. It broke my heart to leave them behind, and I was grateful that Jessica agreed to take the dogs on a temporary basis, until I had a better idea of my plans. Leaving my dogs was extremely difficult, but somehow I found the courage and strength to leave them. I truly loved my dogs because I had received so much nurturing from them. But deep inside I heard the message that I needed to free myself of all restrictions. To be free didn't mean schlepping two mini-poodles everywhere I went. Even though I knew this intellectually, streams of tears flowed down my face as I wondered how I could part from them. I drove three hours to Jessica's home in Boston with the dogs at my side, convinced that to cope with their loss, I had to see this as a temporary situation. When I drove back to New York the next day, I cried in the car. Through my tears I asked myself, "How can I leave them? They're the only attachment I have left." That's when I got it: I can't be attached to anything or anyone on this journey.

Even though I knew the journey would be extremely trying at times, I believed completely in what I was doing. It took a year for me to truly understand the ride I was on.

Sam and I worked together harmoniously the day the movers arrived. After we had taken our belongings to our respective storage units, I returned to the house to say good-bye. I went upstairs to the master bedroom, and while looking out the window, past the trees and the lake, I thanked the universe for blessing me with the opportunity to use my creative talents in designing this beautiful living space. I took a shower, got dressed and headed over to my friend Joanne's house, where I stayed for the remainder of my time in New York. I drove away feeling freedom and joy, and never looked back. "You're not homeless," I said to myself. "You're home-free." My time in the house was complete. Ready to embark on my new path, I sang as I drove away.

I lived with Joanne throughout June, finished some part-time work I had contracted for, and then drove to Virginia to begin the next leg of my spiritual journey.

PART III

HERE I AM: STEPPING UP TO THE PLATE

Transmuting pain into joy is the greatest gift you can bestow upon yourself

CHAPTER 16

Living the Miracle in Virginia

WE ARE GIVEN THE OPPORTUNITY to live from our heart's desire when we open to the unknown, the magic of what may be waiting for us just around the corner. When we believe we are always guided to be in our highest and best self, life becomes simpler.

I arrived at my sister's in late June. I had met a number of people during the weekends I attended Carol Fitzpatrick's workshops, so when I arrived, I had a community of friends. I soon reconnected with a woman named Valerie, whom I had met the previous March at an Intuitive Workshop. Valerie and I offered each other the gift of unconditional love and healing, and we knew that our friendship would sustain us in our spiritual journey. We had an instant trust and openness, a commitment to serve each other in the highest possible way in the bonds of sisterhood that words alone can't express. I realized that our friendship offered a grand opportunity to expand my spiritual nature and to develop the skills needed to become a more complete healer.

Keith, another member of the community, also became a key person in my life. Keith, whom I saw as my soul brother, had a studio, East Meets West, where he practiced the art of medical qigong and led qigong, Tia chi and other classes based on Eastern spiritual practices. The studio was just blocks away from my sister's house, so I would visit him almost daily. We engaged in deep talks, questioning and exploring the world we lived in and the world within. In my exploration I found a support network that encouraged my healing, internal growth and expansion. Thrilled to the core, I opened myself fully to love, friendship and teachings.

I immersed myself fully in Living the Miracle, Carol Fitzpatrick's community of like-minded people. The core community, which developed a rapport that was soul deep, consisted of approximately 26 people. As a member of the community, I attended monthly activations (small group configurations and individual healings, focused on opening the heart for personal and global transformation), intuitive workshops and weekend retreats.

My sister and I both joined the same spiritual community, something we had never done before. The community provided an opening for us to heal the childhood wounds imposed on us by our nuclear family. With the unconditional love and support of our community, she and I could express our authentic selves without the distortions of our upbringing. Without roles or rules to follow, we were free to live our truth.

Going Straight to the Source

My friends and I often met to do hands-on healing and intuitive sessions with each other. As my consciousness expanded, I learned how to become a vessel for healing others and myself. I began to trust that my hands were a vehicle for healing. I had heard this message in many readings, and I opened myself to receive the truth of this insight with complete acceptance. I began to see visions and to share with others the messages I received to assist them on their journeys. During my intuitive work I became aware of increased body sensations, which confirmed that my intuitions were accurate. In healing sessions with people, I connected energetically with the inner child that remained hidden and afraid to reveal itself. During these sessions my hands, which were linked to my heart, were guided by the energy to the third chakra, the center of self-worth and personal power located in the solar plexus, where the inner child resides. Through this work I was discovering my soul purpose; I was grateful for this clarity, as I was beginning to know and trust my abilities.

On July 25, 2008, I wrote in my journal: *"I have been experiencing remarkable shifts as I open myself to my new community. I feel as if my channeling ability has opened wider, and I am deriving stability and tremendous joy in my connection to Source. I experience life with great freedom. I have no external constraints, the chains are broken, and I am a free bird, flying gracefully through the sky. I have accepted who and what I am. The joy I am receiving and bringing to my community of like-minded people is filling my heart and soul, and I am overflowing. Although soaring through the sky, I remain grounded and stable."*

I spent the next seven months attending workshops while meeting new healers and intuitives. One day Stephanie, a member of the community, suggested that I read about "the new children," those diagnosed with Attention Deficit Hyperactivity Disorder (ADHD) Attention deficit Disorder (ADD), as well as those labeled autistic. These children carry a high vibration and are not necessarily children in need of cures. As an occupational therapist, I knew these children well. I had worked extensively with children having this diagnosis for whom medication was the chosen way to remedy the malady. In fact, my own two children were diagnosed with ADHD.

The message was clear in all my psychic readings: I will work with high-frequency children whose special gifts are frequently at odds with our culture. Since this is my life's work, I jumped at the chance to read some books Stephanie recommended, especially *The Indigo Children: The New Kids Have Arrived,* which affirmed my own beliefs. As I read this eye-opening book, I had an "aha" of recognition that my son was an indigo child, not an ADHD child, as he was formally misdiagnosed by the medical world. When I called Benjamin to share this with him, we together went through the list of qualities that indigo children share, surprised at how many applied to him.

Essentially, indigo children carry a higher vibration than other children, and have difficulty fitting into the world as it's currently structured. They are warriors of light, here to transform the world into a peacefully energetic place. They come equipped with deep, intuitive wisdom, but because our culture doesn't recognize it, and has few means to draw out their innate knowledge, the medical profession and educators label them as problem children. What an eye opener this was for me personally!

Now I understood why my friend wanted me to become familiar with this revolutionary way of perceiving these children. Actually, I had begun to see them through a different lens years earlier. During my last two years as a practicing occupational therapist, I had shifted away from the medical model to a more expansive, spiritual way of dealing with these children and their families. Once again everything fell into place.

As the summer continued, I felt California calling to me. I wanted to visit my son and spend time with my new friend Steve. Benjamin had decided to take a year off from college to work on a documentary involving Steve and the special-needs children he worked with. I decided to go to California at the end of September.

More Connections

As I looked through the books that my friend Stephanie had loaned me, I came across *Indigo Celebration,* by Lee Carroll and Jan Tober. I opened it and came to a chapter written by Rabbi Wayne Dosick entitled, "Rabbinic Insights," which was about the spiritual healing of indigos that involved parents in the process. I read each line in tears, deeply touched by his message. He was writing about the work that I would one day be doing. "I must meet this man," I said to myself. "He understands."

I knew of Rabbi Dosick through my affiliation with Jewish Renewal, and I owned a few of his books. I looked him up on the Internet and found that he lived in Southern California. It's amazing how the universe works! I quickly contacted him and set up an appointment to visit him during my trip. Just that brief connection brought such excitement to my soul. Coincidences like this one fascinated me, although I knew that what we call coincidence is the universe's way of lining everything up perfectly. Soon I would be moving to California—the whole thing felt divinely orchestrated—but for now I was enjoying life in Virginia, where loving, healing friends surrounded me.

I continued exploring, talking and learning about indigo children. My friend Keith and I engaged in lengthy discussions, especially since his son, Evan, carried the higher frequency of these new children. At the time, Evan was experiencing difficulty at school because of the misalignment between traditional teaching methods and the way his deeper nature needed to be taught. School personnel wanted to label him ADD, but luckily he had a spiritually knowledgeable father who didn't accept that incorrect diagnosis.

Spending time with Evan, this spiritually aware child, gave me a wonderful opportunity to share my new self with him. I showered him with joy, grace and openhearted acceptance. I felt blessed to be present in his life and to offer him unconditional acceptance.

One day I witnessed Evan at an Intuitive Workshop at Carol's, where he was attentive, fully present and fully engaged without any evidence of ADD. He had none of this dysfunctional behavior because he felt safe, accepted and included by the community just as he was, in all his authenticity as a spirited soul. He was fully seen, fully heard, fully present.

Why wouldn't he express his true nature under those circumstances? He felt the energy of inclusion and self-acceptance, and he flowed with it. When he isn't permitted to be his authentic self at school, his energy flow becomes restricted, contained, boxed up. He then shifts his behavior to meet the needs of the structured environment. He loses both his attention span and his enthusiasm, and his body responds by what's called ADD behavior. At this point, Evan becomes a "problem child." If, on the other hand, he felt the vibrational connection at school as he did with this group of healers, his behavior would be entirely different. At the workshop, the group was amazed at how deeply intuitive and connected to Source Evan was. He gave intuitive readings to those present, demonstrating a depth of knowing that was consistent with a master healer. When given the opportunity to be authentic, any child (or adult, for that matter) will express with ease and grace. I felt so honored to be a witness to this process.

Everything I was learning confirmed that I was on the right path. My old life in New York had fallen away, and I didn't miss any part of it. Carol had predicted more than two years earlier that I would exit that life, which is exactly what I did. My new life brought me reflection, joy and unimagined opportunities to step beyond my inherited life scripts and to be fully present as my authentic self.

Sharing the Story

For years I had felt the urge to write my story. When I first attempted to write in 2006, I found it extremely difficult. I tried writing about what happened to me, struggling to understand my decades-long exploration of disease and healing. At first I felt as if I were writing a paper for school, a diary arranged in chronological order, of all I had endured. As I continued my first tentative beginnings, readers and psychics kept encouraging me to tell my story for the sake of people in search of healing. Spiritual readers often asked me, "When are you going to start writing?" Some would tell me, "After this book, two more will follow."

I struggled to motivate myself to write when I was living in New York. In Virginia the difficulty continued, but I had spurts in which I began doing automatic writing (bringing in Spirit to assist me in writing). I would write in my journal, and when something important needed to be recorded verbally, I tuned in and spoke the message into my digital recorder. Encouraged by my friends, I used this process frequently in my writing. Here is a channeled message that I recorded in my journal on September 9, 2008,

"You need to write every chance you can get because the words need to come out now on paper. You will meet people who will understand exactly what you need to do, and they will support you totally and completely. Your story will be

the proof behind the healing. This authenticity will set you apart from others, and people will listen to you. Your authenticity comes from personal experience, and that's what people need. You will help many others with your openheartedness and your depth of pure joy and acceptance. Now is the time and you know it. You're ready now to do the work."

By the time I had been in Virginia for three months, I was already a different person than the woman who walked away from her life in New York. I felt incredible gratitude for everyone who had helped me.

At the end of September, I decided to visit my son in Southern California. My friend Valerie dropped me off at the airport, and as I was taking my luggage out of the car, someone came over to ask me if I wanted assistance. "Yes, thank you," I said. I checked in my suitcase, and immediately stopped to purchase a luggage roller for the heavy shoulder bag I was carrying. In all my years of travel, I had never asked for help. When I was with my husbands, they would always help out, but here I was alone, and I had to do it myself.

As I was carrying my large shoulder bag that morning, I was physically hurting. As a result, I worked myself into a stressful state over my anticipation of the suffering I would once again have to endure carrying my bag around. I then did something I had never done before: I recognized that I had a choice. I could choose to wallow in my pain, feeling disabled and inadequate, or I could choose not to. This time I chose to empower myself by accepting the situation without judgment and by following a course of action that made me feel healthy.

When I realized what I had worked through, I cried. I knew at that moment I had experienced a major shift in complete self-acceptance. I also realized that the unconditional love and support I had received from my new community was helping me let go of all my old, disempowering patterns. In a note to myself, I wrote, *"When you detach from the pain and suffering, you become a vehicle for healing. Let go of the pain and find the joy."*

Opportunities Arise

During my visit I attended High Holiday services with Cantor Steve, as well as a special-needs service for children and families. This opportunity enabled me to see how Steve related to children with his spirited music and dance. During the services I met Alec, a 13-year-old boy, who would be traveling with Steve, Benjamin and myself to a conference in Omaha, Nebraska, in late October. Steve had been invited to present his work providing B'nai Mitzvah training to the special-needs child. Benjamin videotaped Steve's presentation, which later became a documentary entitled *A Vision of Wholeness*. Steve invited me to join them because of my interest in the work and my love for the children. The experience gave me the opportunity to relate to this child from my heart and spirit, not just from a clinical perspective.

The trip, which was amazing for all of us, confirmed our belief that children flourished in an environment that offers safety, acceptance and unconditional love. I witnessed Alec, a child with autism, open up and playfully express himself without the need to challenge, confront or throw a tantrum. He was fully and completely present during the three days we spent together. He was quite different from the boy I had met at services a month earlier, who remained in his seat rocking back and forth while ruminating over his hot chocolate. I was grateful that Benjamin invited me to participate in the documentary. This eye-opening experience enabled me to share both my clinical expertise and spiritual knowledge.

During my visit to California I met with Rabbi Dosick. We spent the afternoon sharing our common love for Elat Chayyim and our connection to some wonderful teachers, including David Cooper. As our conversation flowed, he shared with me his work with the indigo children, and I shared with him my story and my deep intuitive sense that I was going to relocate to California. During that joyful afternoon his wife, Ellen Kaufman Dosick, told me about her work as a facilitator of Soul Memory Discovery.

The following week I returned to have a session with her. Soul Memory Discovery is a healing tool that accesses and releases memories that no longer serve us. The memories are lodged in our body cells and our soul from this lifetime and past ones. During a session the facilitator channels information received from guides and from the angelic realm. With Ellen I spent three hours grieving the release of memories I continued to hold in cellular memory. I will never forget the words that Ellen channeled: "You gave your mother your muscles and your spine, and you still weren't good enough." This message really hit home. This and other messages were not new, but this time I had the opportunity to help remove the painful memories that remained in my body. I had an intense session and walked away with joy and a deep sense of calmness. After the session I knew that I wanted to study Soul Memory Discovery, which deeply resonated with me. I also knew Wayne and Ellen would be key players in my ongoing growth and healing. Everything was lining up. I saw clearly that I would live in California in order to deepen my trust and receptivity of Spirit. It was that simple.

Loving Yourself Enough To Be Free to Love Another

The lessons we have to repeat over and over again until we get it, really get it! Even in my expansiveness, I got caught up in illusion and desire. Now that I was single, I wanted a man to sweep me off my feet. As much as I felt brave and independent, I didn't want to spend my life alone. I yearned to meet a beloved partner. I hoped that every man I met would be the one. My readings consistently reassured me that I would find a soulful partner, one who would share the spiritual path with me. I heard this prediction ad nauseam. Even though I was a relationship person, I convinced myself that this was my time to be alone, to find myself and to continue healing. Still, on occasion I would lie in bed in anguish because *he* hadn't shown up yet. Although I knew I had a mission and believed in myself, I was also restless and impatient to have a loving relationship that would keep me from worrying about anything. Why couldn't life unfold smoothly? Why couldn't I move from one relationship to another after my divorce so I wouldn't have to experience the fear and anxiety of being alone?

Every time I met a new man, I would get a reading. Readers told me several times that this man or that man was the one, and I believed them, although in my gut I knew it couldn't be true. I told myself, "If this man changed and expressed the qualities of his Higher Self, he could be the one." Obviously, I was playing games to lessen my fear and to secure my safety. Hadn't I gained enough strength in my emotional and physical healing not to be so needy? In divorcing Sam, hadn't I learned to love myself enough?

In reality, I was fooling myself in many ways. I convinced myself that things would shift, yet in the depth of my heart, I knew I had more healing to do before my beloved would appear. Thus, when I found a new man, I stepped into a relationship that was similar to the ones I had left behind, hanging on to the old familiar refrain that "anything is better than nothing." It took me awhile to understand what my beloved teachers and healers had been telling me all along: I had to love myself enough before my beloved would come to me.

I'll never forget the day I finally got it. Standing on the balcony of a friend's apartment, I said to myself, "This man can't be my beloved because he's way too detached for me. I love myself too much to be with someone who is emotionally unavailable."

On that day in October, 2008, I set myself free from the need for anyone else to help me on my journey. I was beginning to own my self-worth. I would never settle for less than the best. Because I trusted the universe, I knew that when the time was right, my beloved would appear. I had finished looking, yearning, begging for someone to take care of me. I was fully competent to take care of myself as I pursued my life path.

A Pool of Bliss

I returned to Virginia at the beginning of November. Two weeks later I attended my second "Living the Miracle" retreat. During the three-day retreat, I experienced something I had never experienced before: an out-of-body experience. After a day and a half of releasing and activating my energy internally, I received an intense, hands-on-healing from two of my friends. When the session was complete, I sat up and realized that I wasn't grounded. I told Christine that my eyes felt weird, and she suggested that I sit for a moment. She then made a gesture for my sister to take me to a chair and have me drink some water. She did this, but within a few minutes I felt myself getting even woozier. Then I blacked out. I couldn't see anything. I heard panic in my sister's voice as she called loudly for help. I heard the voices of my friends, who crowded around me to see what had happened. I also heard someone say, "She doesn't have a heartbeat," after which she yelled for Carol.

Carol came over and started to blow her breath directly onto my neck as if she was breathing life back into me. Wondering what was going on, I felt a warm sensation throughout my body, as if I was floating in a pool of water. I was as happy as I could be, immersed in a pool of bliss. I felt no pain, no concern, nothing at all as my friends anxiously tried to arouse me from my state. I came to for a few minutes and told everyone that I was in bliss. When I came back to the present moment, I tried to explain how peaceful I was. Then I left again. My eyes rolled back into my head, and I went somewhere far away, accompanied by the worried voices of my friends. This experience lasted for an hour and a half, during which I was escorted outside the retreat room, so the program could continue while I rested in the lobby.

As I sat there floating in and out of this reality, I made eye contact with three different people. One woman, Nancy, asked me gently to come back. Having been there herself she understood why I wanted to stay in the bliss of the out-of-body experience. Although I was grateful for her understanding words, they weren't enough to pull me back to earth. The second person who asked me to come back was my sister, who told me with great urgency that she loved me. I felt the fear in her voice when she said, "What am I going to tell Mom and Dad if you don't come back?" Repeatedly, she kept insisting, almost demanding, that I open my eyes and stay present.

I sat inside my blissful bubble and said to myself, "I'm not coming back just because you're asking me. I'm happy exactly where I am." I understood her concern and everyone else's. There I was, floating in and out of my blissful state, and it appeared to everyone that I was making the choice of death over life. Of course, I had no idea where I was or what I was doing; I only knew it felt great.

The third person who spoke to me was my soul brother, Keith. He called my name and asked me to come back. He told me how much he loved me and how I needed to stay present, in order to work with the children. I momentarily came back long enough to make eye contact with him, then I left again. When Keith asked me to look at him, I did, and physically held onto him for dear life.

Keith then channeled his son, Evan, who said to me, "Miss Laura, look at me. I need you. I want to go out for pizza with you. I want you to come play with me." I looked at Evan, wanting to connect to his purity of heart. I wanted to stay, but again I floated away.

At one point Keith and Mark, Carol's partner and husband, walked me up and down the hall, hoping that if I stood up, I would stay present. At that time feelings of fear arose in me. I had "disappeared" for quite some time, and I felt anxious that maybe my soul wanted to transition. Of all the times to exit life, this time didn't make any sense, because I was in such joy, surrounded by my loving community, enjoying every second of the deep healing work we were engaged in.

I had just returned from California with clarity of heart and mind. "Why now?" I asked myself. "Why now?" It didn't make sense to me. "What's happening?" I wondered. "And why can't I return." I was getting scared.

Finally, Carol suggested that I listen to the music that Sam, one of our community members, was playing. With Carol in front of me and Mark behind me, with his hands on my shoulders, I sat on the floor, holding grounding stones to anchor my energy. Sandwiched between the two of them, I tried to stay present, even though I felt the pull to leave. When I heard Sam sing, I knew it was time to return. I couldn't make out the lyrics of the song, but I resonated with the purity of his voice that evening. "If I weren't here," I told myself, "I wouldn't be able to hear him sing." Suddenly, I wanted to hear him sing with my whole being.

Within moments I felt a warm sensation flow through my body. My eyes opened widely, and Mark felt my life force return. I was a bit confused and disoriented, but I was back.

When Carol spoke to me later that evening, she said, "There's something you need to learn about the children you'll be working with, and that's why you had this experience." At that moment, I didn't understand what she meant. The next day she explained to the group that my out-of-body experience offered me choices—whether to stay and do my work, or leave and work from the other side. My soul gave me the opportunity to make this choice; it took me a while to sort through and digest my options.

Three days later, as I sat at a Starbuck's with Keith, the reason for my out-of-the-body experience became clear. I saw the connection between my visceral response and the choice before me. I understood the input of the loving people who spoke to me when I was in expanded awareness, their pleas for me to return and their tone of voice. I recalled feeling comforted by Nancy, who understood and acknowledged where I was at that moment, having had her own out-of-body-experience. Her tone was gentle and loving, while my sister, who spoke from fear and confusion, demanded that I come back. I knew she loved me and was concerned about our parents, but her demands felt motivated more by self-concern than by selfless love. As for Keith, he related to me with love and friendship, with energy so different that it brought up sadness in me that I couldn't be present with him.

Most importantly, my connection to the children emerged from the experience. I had an "aha" moment and understood what Carol meant when she referred to the children I would be working with. I told Keith how this experience directly related to the children I had treated in the past and more recently to the child who had accompanied us to Omaha.

"When we're understood and encouraged," I said, "we feel loved and safe. We know on an energetic level that we're accepted for who we are. When we're given the freedom to be our true self, we will be less guarded, more spontaneous and joyful."

Nancy's understanding gave me permission to be myself. Keith's tenderness and concern made me feel appreciated; I wanted to be held by him because he was safe and accepting. My sister's behavior was consistent with parents, clinicians, doctors, and teachers who want children to conform to their expectations and to forego being who they really are.

The outside world demands that everyone conform and fit in. Like myself, children respond by saying, "No, I'm not coming out." In my experience I found it safer to remain inside and hidden rather than come out and pretend to be something I wasn't. All children do this to some extent, but the ones who are locked inside have even more difficulty with self-expression.

Looking back on my experience, I realized the critical moment occurred when I recognized the source of my bliss. I wanted to stay inside because it felt blissful. I didn't have to react to anyone if I didn't care to, or fulfill other people's demands and expectations. I could simply stay in the pool of bliss.

After I finished my coffee with Keith I went home to absorb all that we discussed. I lay on my bed in complete stillness, recapturing what had happened to me. I'm not sure whether the following message was partially channeled or not. However, I had my digital recorder on to capture the words that came through:

"When I left my body, I was in a pool of water that was pure bliss. It was magnificent, calm, and loving, and I felt comfortable, at my ease in a state of being without separation or dualities. In this blissful place I heard people all around me saying, 'Come back. Stay with me. Don't leave because we need you here. Laura, look at me, listen, you have to stay.' They made so many demands, yet the voice in my head said, 'Leave me alone, I like it here. I'm calm here and nobody is bothering me.' All I heard on the outside were pleas to return. When I came back momentarily, I felt uncomfortable and immediately returned to the

pool of bliss with which I felt a sense of oneness. I went in and out several times as I tried to listen to everyone. I focused my eyes to see them each time, but my eyes slipped back into my head. I struggled to stay outside, but within minutes I returned to the quiet within."

I saw clearly that the children on the autistic spectrum stay in their own world for a reason. Why would they come out into a world of sensory overload and bombardment when it's peaceful inside? There's no reason to come out when they feel a blissful oneness by remaining within. When I was out of body, just like these children, I was bombarded by well-meaning friends and loved ones. There were so many hands on me, so many voices, that I preferred staying in the peaceful comfort of my altered state.

When children are bombarded with sensory overload, it's hard for them to integrate the sensations they're feeling. Parents, educators, doctors, and specialists become consumed with curing them instead of seeing them. The key is to connect with them through their eyes, to acknowledge their being, and to discover what brings them bliss on earth. The key to each child is different, so as responsible adults we need to be open to uncover what brings each child into his or her own bliss. We have to be sensitive and caring enough to learn what opens a child's heart and makes them stay present. In this way, they don't need to leave their bodies and go inside to find peace. We need to ask, "What will keep them present in this world?"

I want to look into these children's eyes, acknowledge their beauty, and watch them open to me because they see me right back. To free them from their prisons of isolation, we have to help them find their bliss, their passion here on earth. While we all have a pool of bliss, not all of us are lucky enough to consciously contact it and release it in everyday life. That's what these children connect to when they withdraw into themselves. Parents, clinicians and educators believe they know what these children need to fit into the normal world, when, in fact, they have their own bliss but have no way to release it in the outer world. We must find a way to support children in accessing their amazing gifts and sharing them with the world.

To begin with, we need to hear them. Our world can be as much fun to play in as their world. The key to unlocking their imprisoned energy is to join them in their world by looking into their eyes, seeing them and bringing their joy forward. It's beyond medication, therapy or food; it's clearly seeing children and where their pool of bliss is within.

After the retreat I knew my mission, and was excited about relocating to California. After my session of Soul Memory Discovery, I wanted to become a facilitator. The course began six weeks later, and Ellen graciously offered to find a place for me to live during the three months of training. Everything fell into place once again, and I allowed it to happen.

By the end of the year, I had a place to stay, just miles from Wayne and Ellen's, and I was ready to become a facilitator in Soul Memory Discovery. I sensed that the experience would enhance my ability to go deep into the inner child while exploring past-life experiences, bridging the present and the past. Living in Southern California would enable me to be close to my son and to pursue a working relationship with my friend Steve. I looked forward to this adventure. My community in Virginia encouraged me to follow my intuitive knowing. Even my family and friends in New York were supportive. I was clearly on a roll, attracting nothing but amazing experiences. Intuitively, following my inner and outer guidance, I knew I was ready to take the next big step. I attended the last "Living the Miracle" group activation on January 11, 2009, with some sadness, knowing I would be saying good-bye for now.

During a meditation I said quietly to myself, "I'm not leaving my community; I'm going to do my work." It was my time to move forward. Carol hugged me good-bye and said, "You're ready to start your grand adventure." It comforted me to know that I would return in early April to attend the third "Living the Miracle" retreat.

CHAPTER 17

California Dreaming

ON JANUARY 20, 2009, I boarded a plane for Los Angeles carrying two suitcases and a computer. I was traveling light on what happened to be Inauguration Day.

When I arrived in L.A., I spent two days with my son Ben, who had invited me to participate in a documentary film on autism that he and Steve were making. He wanted my participation because of my background as an occupational therapist and my special way of seeing the children. I was a bit intimidated at first and thought, "What do I know?"

To relieve my doubt, Ben said, "Just speak your truth about how you see the children." I gave him a curious look as he attached the microphone to my sweater. "Okay," I told myself, "I can do this." I looked at Ben and said with trepidation, "What am I going to say?"

Reassuringly me gently, Ben said, "Just be yourself."

I took a deep breath, closed my eyes for a moment and words began to flow. I found myself speaking with compassion and a surprising sense of authority. Afterward, I realized that Ben had given me this grand opportunity to "step up to the plate." When he replayed the video, I saw myself in a new light. I was touched by my gentleness and my heartfelt conviction about how I perceive the children, which allowed me to bridge my clinical expertise and my spiritual understanding. I laughed and commented to Ben and Steve, "You would think I'm an expert and that I know something." They both looked at me in dismay and said, "You do!" I realized then that Ben had given me quite a gift. I had taken a big step forward, and there was no turning back. Feeling empowered, I had started to bring my gentle, intuitive wisdom into the world.

I arrived in the San Diego area a few days later and met the woman whom I would be living with. I knew within minutes of meeting Ellyn that we would get along well, and I was ecstatic. The house, which was one mile from the ocean, immediately felt like home.

The facilitator's class in Soul Memory Discovery (SMD) began two days after I arrived. I drove to the Dosick home early Saturday morning, excited to begin my training. Twelve of us were taking the class. We would meet one week a month for the next three months. I knew within the first three hours that I had made the right decision. I fell in love with the process and the people I was studying with. I was clearly on the right path because the spiritual technique I was learning, with all the inherent components for clearing people of their unhealthy patterns of thought and behaviors, resonated deeply in my soul. Somehow it all came so easily, as if I was relearning knowledge I had already known.

The course gave me a tremendous opportunity to continue my learning while challenging me spiritually in every way. As I read the words from the manual, I could feel myself merging with the vibration of each healing message. I went deep into past-life patterns that continued to bind me energetically to my family members, bringing these relationships into the light of healing. The clarity and wisdom that emerged was profound. The puzzle pieces came together as I explored deeply what was being held in the cells of my body, ready to be released and set free. I also felt an ease and grace as I practiced with my peers. SMD gave me tools to embark on a whole new life, and I was filled with anticipation and excitement wherever I went, whether walking on the beach or shopping. I moved with a newfound lightness, repeating joyously, "Here I am! Here I am!" I was a different person in California than I was in New York. As I continued opening to each new experience, I learned to free myself from attachment, as well as to surrender and let go of expectations without pushing and controlling things excessively.

Not having my own home helped lessen my need of material belongings. All I needed was what I had around me. I would be leaving Ellyn's home in three months, and I didn't know where my next stop would be, but somehow I could live with that uncertainty. Indeed, this attitude was an approach to living that I had never known before.

When I wasn't in my SMD training, I enjoyed meeting people and acclimating to my new life. Fortunately, I attracted gentle people who assisted me along my journey. I walked the beach, attended classes and workshops, and spent lots of time alone, being contemplative and learning what it means to love myself enough. I experienced firsthand how to ride the emotional roller coaster as one lets go of one way of life to embrace another. I was feeling my way through life. I accepted confusion and loneliness, fear and joy—whatever life brought me each day.

During this time of intense learning, I explored my needs and desires as I redefined myself and my way of working in the world. My new work had to have a spiritual component, something lacking in the clinical occupational therapy I had done in the past. I spent a great deal of time writing, jotting down thoughts as they came to me. I wanted to write my life story, but the time wasn't right. I continued asking the universe for guidance, for messages to make my path clearer. During this period, as I focused on living in the moment, I continued longing for a beloved. While I didn't want to live alone, I knew exactly why that was the perfect setup for my growth. My work had to come first, and a relationship would interfere with that.

As I learned the art of non-attachment, I observed how certain characters in my life script appeared to offer lessons for my continued learning. For example, I felt completely unseen by a man I had befriended. Through some energetic healing work, I realized that he was a soul mate who had shown up to help me resolve a core issue left over from a past life. Knowing this, I let go of my sadness and felt grateful for the opportunity to release an attachment. Everything turned around when I shifted the way I perceived things. More importantly, I realized from this relationship that I would never again pursue a relationship in which I wasn't fully seen. As I wrote in my journal, *"I will be seen for exactly who I am. My entire book will be dedicated to all the children who were never seen."*

In that moment of illumination, I was ready to begin writing.

A Trip Back East

I returned to Virginia in late March to attend a "Living the Miracle" retreat. I had just finished training as a facilitator in Soul Memory Discovery, and I was eager to share this healing modality with my friends. Even though I had met new friends in California, I missed my friends back East. The lines of communication had remained open, no matter where we physically resided. We spoke to each other almost daily, offering encouragement and empowering each other to stick to our inner knowing and to see ourselves as pioneers. We were always present for one another; no one ever felt alone. This connection clearly made the journey easier for each of us.

After my extended visit to the East Coast, I made the decision to permanently relocate to Encinitas, a suburb of San Diego. It was time to completely claim California as my home. I visited my community in Virginia and then returned to my hometown in New York. I found a moving company to transport the belongings I had put into storage a year ago. As the end of a chapter approached, my life in New York was really over.

Before I left California, I found an apartment to which I would return to write my book. In the three months I had been in Encinitas, I had established a wonderful relationship with the woman I stayed with. I also had a community of friends through Jewish Renewal, and through the class in Soul Memory Discovery.

As I stepped onto the airplane bound for Dulles Airport, I was a changed person who felt fully alive. Valerie greeted me at the airport, and we held each other tightly. I had been gone for three months, and it felt great to be reunited with my soul sister. Being in Virginia, however, felt strange, as if I didn't belong there anymore.

Two days later we set off for our three-day retreat at Yogaville. I was excited to see everyone, and we spent our days doing activations, hands-on healing, and intuitive readings. We laughed, played and enjoyed the closeness that naturally arises when people are spiritually bonded. I loved our retreats, since I always felt safe to be fully open and completely honored by fellow participants. In our community I was always fully seen, heard and present. I felt blessed to sustain my allegiance to this group of openhearted, compassionate souls who lived 3,000 miles away.

I stayed on the East Coast until May 20, 2009. In that time I did 10 sessions of Soul Memory Discovery, organized my belongings to be shipped out west, had lunch with my ex-husband Sam, and said good-bye to my friends.

I found the trip to New York significant on many levels. For one thing, it was the end of New York as my home. I was really leaving this time, severing all my attachments. In a way, it was cathartic no longer having a New York address. In addition, I had to let go of my physicians and the support system I relied on for more than 20 years. Because I had to cut a lot of ties and reestablish myself in a new place, I felt both overwhelmed and excited. Reality began to hit home when I realized that I was no longer vacationing, but actually moving 3,000 miles away as a result of following my inner guidance. Once again, the experience felt much bigger than me. I felt a tinge of anxiety as I drove from New York to New Jersey to spend a night at my parents' house before returning to Virginia.

Heal Yourself /Empower your Child

As you heal yourself, you empower your child.
As you empower your child, you heal yourself.

I had a difficult time at my parents' house. I felt sad as a result of my mother's emotional detachment. There was no joy in their home, no lightheartedness. The memories of living in that home brought up feelings of restriction, and the next morning, when I said good-bye and got into my car, I broke into tears. I grieved for myself as a child and young adult who lived in a home where I felt energetically misaligned and disempowered. I tried to stay centered and grounded as I drove along the familiar roads with tears in my eyes. I asked my guides to help me understand what I needed to learn in this situation. When I turned on my tape recorder, I suddenly made a deep connection to Spirit. "Here I AM," I said over and over. "Here I AM." I began chanting these words in English and Hebrew, with deep conviction.

I recognized how my mother had to keep me disempowered to empower herself. She herself had never claimed her own power. How can a child feel empowered when the parent clearly is not? Obviously, a disempowered parent can't raise an empowered child. It became apparent (no pun intended) to me that the child within the adult (parent) who had never been seen or heard couldn't see or hear his or her own child.

I believe that these parents are gifted with children who rock them to the core, enticing them to wake up and step out of their disempowered state and to claim the life they deserve. With this realization my grief transformed into gratitude as I realized how much I had learned from the experience with my mother. And, of course, I had another confirmation that my work was unfolding.

When I arrived at Valerie's house, she was in the middle of an explosive conflict with her 17-year-old son. This blowup felt familiar to me, since I had gone through similar experiences with my daughter. I couldn't help notice the coincidence, the divine timing of this eruption, since I had just spent five hours processing the same issue of parental control and the child's disempowerment.

A perfect opportunity once again had landed in my lap. I shared my thoughts with Valerie and her ex-husband, who both asked me for guidance. I told them about the teachings I had received at the Hyde School that helped me disengage from Jessica and her abusive behavior. I told my dearest friend that if she didn't love herself enough, she couldn't stand up to someone's else's wrath. I cried along with her as she recognized how her own disempowerment had gotten in her way and how it had affected her son.

We had a long, arduous, yet miraculous week exploring her wounded inner child. Equipped with knowledge and tools to empower herself, she could now set her son free to find his power. My soul sister was brave enough to step into the lion's den, to confront her fear and to set herself free.

I also spent time with Andrew, Valerie's younger son, and offered him the opportunity to express and release his feelings and fears. Knowing how siblings influence each other, I asked him how an older brother who was constantly acting out and being disruptive affected him. He replied, "That's all I've ever known."

While Andrew and Zach are both high-vibrational indigo children, energetically they're quite different, just as my two children are. Zach is a warrior, and Andrew is an angel, yet both have amazing gifts to share with the world. Fortunately, Valerie, who is a gifted intuitive, has the children who will help her heal. Like Valerie, if we can recognize the opportunity to heal that parenting offers, we not only can grow psychologically and spiritually, but also guide our children to fulfill their highest potential. Our children offer us many gifts, and if we're fortunate enough, we'll receive them gratefully. Parenting is a full circle of self-love and acceptance that transforms us and the relationship we have with our children.

Reconnection

While I was in Virginia, I had healings and readings from Wanda and Marcus, two important people I had seen a few times prior to my trip west. Keith had suggested back in October that I work with Wanda, a special lady who had healed herself from her own disease. Keith believed that she could help me heal my hands to a greater degree than I already had.

Because of her caring, compassionate nature, Wanda was certainly at the top of my list of healers. During the session she said, "Your healing is going deeper, and molecular reconstruction is occurring." As she continued channeling energy, I felt my thumbs move into a flexed position, a sensation I've had before. This time the surge of energy was almost painful. "You're in the right place," she continued, speaking with a loving heart, "and the door will open for you. You'll teach people how to heal themselves."

I was so drawn to see Marcus that I couldn't get on a plane and leave Virginia without seeing him. Besides having a reading, I wanted him to experience the new me. I also wanted to thank him for his kindness, encouragement and wisdom. The session was wonderful. He saw a clear path ahead of me of disease-free living and of healing work through speaking and writing. "You're well on your way," he said. "I applaud the great changes you've gone through. You've freed yourself from your restrictive life, and you have the courage to trust unconditionally that the universe is always guiding you."

Now I was ready to make my way back west, determined to celebrate my 54th birthday in a new land. I'm not sure why I chose to leave my friends at that time, but I felt energetically that it was important to be in California to start my new year. I said my good-byes, invited everyone to visit sunny California, and boarded a plane on May 20, 2009. My furniture was scheduled to catch up with me in mid-June. In the meantime, I stayed at Ellyn's again, this time for three weeks, before moving into my new apartment in Encinitas.

CHAPTER 18

Showing Up

Be the person you want to attract.

I'VE LEARNED THAT THE ONLY road to healing is to follow your heart. The path may not always appear clear, but it will always lead you to your next step.

Glad to be back, I celebrated my 54th birthday with Ellyn. Excited about moving into my new apartment, I spent hours purchasing little items to make the space uniquely personal. I had not lived alone in an apartment for more than 20 years. In the midst of busy activity, I was suddenly seized by a state of fear, which I attributed to all the changes I was going through. I had to change my legal address, my driver's license, along with my medical and auto insurance. I even had to change my legal name back to Mayer from my married name. I had completed the required continuing education credits, so I could apply for a license to practice occupational therapy in California if I chose to do so.

As a resident of California, I had relinquished my former residency in New York. Still adjusting to the change, I had to take things one day at a time. I allowed myself to rest while I grieved the loss of my old life.

Essentially, I took time out and did nothing, becoming quieter, more inward and attuned to the new life that was emerging.

By late July my interest in writing reemerged, and I began spending time each day at my computer, prodding myself to work. Without knowing exactly what the next step was, I trusted that everything would fall into place as I reached out to connect with new people and situations. In retrospect, I was trying too hard to figure out what my next step was. Each day I reached out in prayer and asked the universe for support and guidance. I even asked for an editor to help me begin the awesome process of writing my story.

I continued working through issues of dependence and self-sufficiency, loneliness and empowerment. These issues never seemed to go away, and I had to dig deeper through the layers of my mind to eventually find inner peace. Like an archeologist on a dig, I discovered and released energies that bound me to the past. Because I had the gift of unstructured time, I experienced breakthroughs, "aha" moments, almost every day.

During this time of many emotions, I never felt balanced for more than a day or two. I would swing emotionally from the joy of independence to the pain of self-doubt. Even though I had made many friends, I still felt alone. Something was missing, but I couldn't quite pinpoint it.

Physically, I felt great. My hands were opening and softening every day. I found myself doing new tasks, or doing them with more grace than the week before. My friends, who noticed the difference, watched in amazement. I continued to observe changes in my fingers and hands each day as I enjoyed life in my new home. When I returned to Ellyn's, she remarked that my hands appeared straighter than when I arrived in January. At a concert of Indian Kirtan music, I noticed that I was clapping full hand on hand, touching the pads of my fingers together as I had never done before. As I clapped, I could feel the softness of my fingers, the ease with which they were dancing along, with no pain, stress or discomfort. I could clap without taking breaks. This was a new experience for me. I embraced it joyously.

Still, while my physical healing was in full swing, emotionally I was on a mini roller coaster ride. I often spent days in my apartment without getting dressed. I wrote in my journal and spoke to my friends back East, receiving support and encouragement. I missed them dearly and was thrilled when Valerie said she was coming to visit at the end of August. I met a new friend, Melissa, at an Indian chanting concert one evening, and we became each other's sounding board, spending hours together exploring the meaning of life.

On August 10, 2009 my path became crystal clear, and I wrote in my journal, "The healing is bringing me my work." If I continued my healing process of clearing and releasing, the rest would all fall into place. I realized that I still held onto an illusion, an old belief that I couldn't take care of myself. Once I acknowledged this, I released it into the universe and announced, "I can take care of myself, and I don't need to be dependent on anyone. I'm perfectly capable of caring for myself in all ways." A few days later I had another "aha" moment. As I wrote in my journal, *"I never felt worthy enough to be taken care of. My new affirmation is 'I am worthy."*

But no matter how hard I worked on myself or how much healing I did, old fears continued to surface from the unconscious, taking me deeper and deeper into my core.

Just as I was writing in earnest, my computer began to act temperamental, and I knew I needed a computer that was reliable. I debated whether to purchase a small, lightweight Mac, one I could take with me when I traveled, or to repair the one I had. I had visions of carrying a white computer with me everywhere. When I went to the computer store to find out about repairing the one I had, I told the technician that I needed my computer back as soon as possible because I was a writer!

These words, which flew out of my mouth, startled me. I had never said or thought that before. I actually looked around in awe and thought with bewilderment, "Did I say that?" Without a doubt, I had to claim myself as a writer. Miraculously, two weeks later a friend of mine, a writer himself, introduced me to Ron, his editor. There I was, declaring myself a writer, and within a few weeks I had an editor! All I could say was, "Thank you, God. Thank you, God. Thank you, God." The universe had heard my plea and had responded.

Until I met my editor, the process of writing was extremely exhausting. I was practicing soul retrieval, trying to transfer my inner discoveries onto paper, and I was tired. It was grueling work releasing the distortions that I had taken on and learning to honor my inner spirit. Despite its difficulty, I remained open to the process, knowing that my total commitment to self-knowledge would free me from my history and bring peace to my soul. I had no doubt about that, so I listened. As gifted healers and my own spirit revealed to me, I must believe in the unbelievable, trust in the unknown, and reach beyond my conditioned past. In California, where I was alone and growing in faith, I would heal for real.

The universe continued to line everything up for me in perfect, divine order. Here's what happened when I first met Ron at a Borders Book Store where my friend Alan introduced us. When I arrived, Ron and Alan were engaged in conversation about Alan's manuscript. I sat down and joined them. Ron intuitively sensed my essence and said, "You're a heart-oriented mystic just like us." We spoke at length about my journey, my mission, my need to write my book. Ron, who co-authored *From Age-ing to Sage-ing with Rabbi Zalman Schacter-Sholomi*, said he would take my manuscript home and get back to me in a few days. I was flying! I felt a kinship with Ron, who had the wisdom of a sage and the gentleness of a kind teacher. I had just met my next *Rebbe*, (beloved teacher), someone to guide me spiritually, not just cross the t's and dot the i's of my manuscript. When I left him that day, I once again felt blessed that the universe was taking care of me.

Two days later I received a call from Ron saying that my writing had potential, but that it needed a lot of work. He asked whether I had the courage to see the project through to completion. "Absolutely," I answered. "It's why I'm alive." Ron coached me to feel the events of my life, not just describe them. He urged me to go deeply into the energetics of even the most painful experiences I had endured. He advised me to be as honest as possible while being completely vulnerable with the reader. "Of course, I'll do it," I said simply. "I live from my heart, I couldn't do it any other way." He then handed me an outline and said," Go for it." What a gift to have such a spirited soul encourage me to speak my authentic truth and share my being as never before. It was time to share my story from my perspective. Ron's gift of presence gave me a vehicle for self-expression, self-worth and integrity that I could share with others. I accepted the challenge with all my heart and soul.

The Excavation

Valerie arrived two days later. What a glorious moment when she stepped off the curb at the airport and ran into my arms! We had both transformed and we had much to share. Each day I woke up early and I read to Valerie what I had written the night before. She encouraged me to "go deep" (throwing back to me my favorite line), and I cried as I touched upon the sadness and isolation I felt in my early years. She also encouraged me to tell the truth as seen through my eyes. Isn't that what soul sisters do for each other? My healing became her healing. We went back and forth, opening each other's heart and soul with gentle inquiries. Like at an archeological dig, we were both stepping into places that had been covered up for decades. In this way, my story got birthed into being.

A week later I drove Valerie to the airport, and she returned to her life in Virginia. We both grew tremendously from our California experience, and my friend left knowing that through love and grit she had served as a midwife to my book.

Writing became my full-time job. I spent hours every day sitting in sacred space with pen and paper in hand. As I sat on the floor, my back resting against the couch, I felt an ease and grace when I used a pen rather than computer keys. The physical act of holding pen in hand gave me an opportunity to feel proprioceptively and kinesthetically.

Writing chronologically, I asked Spirit to be present as I closed my eyes and fell into a particular time period. Writing from my depths, I felt energy flowing through my body, far removed from my mind and ego. I frequently cried as I relived feelings of loneliness, pain and discomfort. In this way, I recaptured my history, writing as a determined 54-year-old woman fighting to reclaim her life. Throughout the process, I invited the pain of my inner child without merging with her. My inner child needed me to tell her story, not relive the pain and suffering, which were long gone. The purpose was to heal myself, so I could help heal others. Witnessing the story rather than identifying with it was liberating, in part because I no longer held onto anger. Without anger, I felt the rawness of the pain without interpreting it as "bad," as something that shouldn't have happened to me. It was analogous to when the doctor put needles into my hands when I didn't have the muscle mass, so the needle went straight to the nerve, an extremely painful experience.

Ron met with me regularly to monitor my progress in encountering the past and to coach me through this demanding process. We met at the Borders Bookstore, where I shared the latest revelation of my inner work that was finding its way into my writing. In the beginning I often cried unashamedly, releasing floods of emotion as I grappled with the residue of my past that had arisen in the present moment. Through it all, Ron encouraged me to let go, to release the pain, to empty myself fully. "Let your heart break open," he said," "and be vulnerable every step of the way." When I questioned my course of action, or when I was filled with confusion and sadness, he encouraged me to get comfortable with the uncomfortable, to embrace the dark. I knew that the way out of pain was through it, yet I found myself wanting to hibernate and stay in "my cave." Ron reminded me that confronting sorrow releases a lot of creative energy and that every tear I shed returned me to my authentic self.

Through his kind heart and wisdom, Ron, my Rebbe, encouraged me to persevere when I floundered a bit; he reminded me of my tenacity and determination. Writing liberated and transformed me, and I gradually watched myself reach the other side. Through writing

I honored my triumphs, acknowledged my determination and will, and accepted my life with forgiveness and gratitude. I fell in love with the woman who had the courage and soulful presence to reclaim her true nature. In the end, I had transcended the pain.

CHAPTER 19

Journey into Wholeness

"It is in the becoming whole within yourself that you may offer your greatest gifts to others."
—Gregg Braden

WE NEVER REALLY BELIEVE WE are as great as we are. How wonderful when we can recognize the person that we truly are, and accept ourselves in all our glory and our weakness. It is only then that we become whole.

Writing my story has healed me tremendously. It has taught me how to reconcile the past, move forward, and celebrate life. As my writing evolved, I was surprised by all the hardship I has endured and all the transformation I had gone through. It's one thing to live your life; it's an entirely different thing to relive it. I surprised myself as I wrote word after word about the enormity of pain and discomfort that my life evoked. I found it emotionally draining reading episode after episode of the actual events. I also acknowledged my victories and triumphs, which proved that I was truly a spiritual warrior, driven by the determination to have a new life as a soul-infused being.

As I reread my own words, I honored the person I was writing about, who had the integrity to move forward, no matter what challenges were put in her path. I learned to champion myself in a nonattached way that felt wonderful.

The trick was to openheartedly connect with past pain without revisiting the suffering that gave rise to anger and resentment. Openness to the pain without creating an identity around it as a suffering "me" led to genuine catharsis.

As I revisited the details of my life, I found myself releasing wave after wave of pain. Filled with emotion and compassion, I wished to hold the little girl, the teenager, and the young woman I was writing about. I fully entered my story yet remained unattached, healing everyone and everything I wrote about.

Much like a person who goes through life review after death, I saw each person and situation through compassionate eyes, not through the eyes of someone diseased and disconnected. I beheld all my experiences with gentleness and grace, seeing each person objectively, not how he or she impacted my life. I recognized that each person's journey was separate from mine. As I empowered myself, I empowered others, bearing witness to the pain experienced by all.

The journey led me to embrace change instead of resisting it through fear. My eyes opened to the beauty and joy that surrounded me. Like a child whose innocence has been restored, I looked forward to whatever life had in store for me. Life never ceased to amaze me. I woke up each day with a sense of calmness and serenity that I had not known before. Through this journey I had freed myself to live my life with awe, in gratitude and joy.

Hand Changes

The awareness that I can do something new every day brings me such joy! Since my landing in California, I have experienced profound changes in my ability to use my hands. These changes are monumental for me.

I began to reflect upon my hand changes over the past five years. I asked myself, "What can you do today that you couldn't do in the past?" The answer came quickly. I can pick up tiny items with two fingers, push the button down on my camera, and hold the camera with one hand. I'm independently able to wiggle my fingers or use them independent of one another. I can hold a coffee cup, glasses and dishes with one hand. I stopped needing both hands to do a task. I no longer struggle with change in tollbooths or fumble when opening doors. I am no longer afraid for my safety, or worried about manipulating my seatbelt.

More examples: I can type for hours without feeling pain in my fingers, arms and shoulders. I can hold my key with the proper grip, pick up small objects from the floor, hold my pen with my index and thumb. I can tie my running shoes, strings and ribbons easily. I can manipulate objects in my hands with more coordination and ease. For instance, I can hold my fork in my right hand, crack an egg one-handed, cut with scissors and open the small lock on the doorknob. Best of all, I can play the drum because my fingers are now fully extended. I have more energy to do all the activities that I enjoy and that make me feel healthy, such as yoga, walking, dancing, hiking.

Most of all, I no longer live in fear or flare up in anger that I can't do something.

Yes, I still have difficulty doing some things, mostly because my thumb is fused and doesn't bend at the joints, interfering with hand positioning. On this score, I continue to be in the healing process. My fingers will continue to heal, totally and completely. I will ask Dr. Mark Belsky for pictures of my hands because I feel it's important for others to see the physical transformation that has taken place over the past five years. As I promised myself, these pictures must be in my book, so others can witness the change and be inspired in their own lives.

CHAPTER 20

Moving Forward Professionally/Making the Invisible Visible.

WHEN WE HEAL, EVERYONE WE come in contact with benefits from our healing process. In seeing through a softer lens, I was able to make a difference from the inside out, from the place where the source of life begins.

In September, 2006, years before writing my story, I had contracted with a private healthcare agency and started to treat three children, ages four through five. All three children showed developmental delay in fine and gross motor skills as well as difficulties in the area of sensory integration. I wanted the opportunity to work meaningfully without jeopardizing my healing process. Something in me knew I was ready to step out. I wanted to be of service, and occupational therapy was what I knew and what I was good at. However, I wasn't strong enough, or healed enough to resume a full caseload. My work was so "hands on" that it would exhaust me if I expended too much energy. I constantly had to remind myself that I was in the process of healing; I wasn't finished yet. I had to devote the next few years to healing, which was my primary work. Thus I needed to be patient, which normally wasn't a virtue of mine. When I reentered the profession, I said goodbye to 10 years of believing I would never practice in the field of occupational therapy again.

This time I saw through different eyes: Now I believed in healing, not cure. I didn't believe in relying on shortcuts or quick fixes, but in coming from the heart, opening up to the children as they are. I was committed to helping families and children be fully seen and heard while being fully present. Without a doubt, I was returning to the practice of occupational therapy differently from the way I had practiced it the first 22 years of my professional life.

I scheduled one session a week in their homes and one in their pre-school program. I wanted to be inside the family, having always believed that family involvement was imperative as part of the children's treatment and healing process. My heart's desire was to work with the family, not just the child, following my new methodology of *Seeing Through the Eyes of the Child*. In working with these three children and their families, I offered them my blessing, as well as my skill as a practitioner.

In each case I went straight to the heart of the situation. If the child doesn't feel loved unconditionally, healing from the inside won't happen. My work now involved healing children's hearts, seeing them exactly as they were. No one is invisible; everyone has a right to be seen and loved for being a unique individual. Although parents often make their children feel invisible, in reality they never are; they *feel* that way, however, because they don't fit in. Lacking the tools to deal with their children's differences, parents don't know how to love them effectively, with unconditional self-acceptance.

We live in a world that discriminates against anything that's different, an attitude that puts a tremendous burden on children to be normal. This attitude, which makes loving our children extremely difficult, leads to an even deeper problem. The way parents react to children's nuances, quirkiness and behavior affects the parents themselves, who are at a loss to help their children who don't fit the norm. So they begin looking for remedies and cures. "What can I do to cure my child?" they ask themselves. "What medication, therapy, or doctor can fix the problem?"

The problem is exacerbated by the notion that children need to be fixed. Parents fear that problem children won't fit in to our society and be normal like everyone else. This fear drives their parenting. I'm not making a judgment based on right or wrong; I'm simply describing how things are. Parents, who are understandably scared, are guilt-ridden and fearful that maybe they did something wrong in their parenting. In this way, they internalize the "problem." To undo this misperception, they need to release their own judgments. Well-meaning parents will do anything for their children except the one essential thing: looking within to release their fears, guilt, anguish and shattered dreams. More often than not, parents spend their time and money transporting their children to whomever promises a miracle cure, which is always easier than investigating their role in the family dynamic.

When I work with children from this new perspective, I speak with parents, coming from my heart with all the compassionate insight I've gained from my personal healing journey. I speak to them with softness and compassion, accepting them as I accept their children. I encourage parents to see their children not through adult eyes, but through the eyes of their children, to understand what it feels like to be them. True, children often have difficulty with sensory integration, including attention skills and fine motor, visual motor and organizational skills. They also have difficulty writing, following directions, and doing many other activities. Usually, children treated by an occupational therapist have heightened sensitivities and are quicker to emote than others. In spite of these differences, they all have one thing in common: They know they are different, and their parents know this, too. Because their children feel different, parents are overcome with concerns about the future. "Will my child outgrow this?" they ask. "Will my child be normal?"

My sole (soul) purpose is to assist parents in relating to their children with love and grace, to understand from the heart, not just the head. I feel honored when parents share their deepest fears with me, such as guilt, shame or anguish. They usually question whether the problem is their fault. Would their child be different if the parents had done something different? Sooner?

I help to dispel all this mental, self-imposed anguish, freeing parents to be available for their children's healing. I speak to them as the woman who has engaged in the healing process herself, not as a professional occupational therapist.

When I speak heart to heart, soul-to-soul, both children and parents respond. Parents quickly engage their children differently. The emphasis shifts from whether Johnny can throw a ball as well as the other teammates to whether Johnny is having fun, feeling part of his community, and feeling proud of who he is, not who they expect him to be.

Children want to be seen and heard. They don't want to feel that they're not good enough, nor do they want to be invisible. We must see all children for who they really are. Even when I did clinical occupational therapy, I did it with a different mindset. I wanted to make children feel part of their milieu, with parents and siblings participating in the activity. Therapy became a family event, not just an isolating experience in which Johnny was shuffled off to another room to receive a "session."

A mother named Linda once shared with me how terrible she felt about her child. If she had known better, she said, she would have asked for help sooner. She was flooded with guilt. I allowed her to express her feelings and release all the built-up tension inside her. As she cried, I held her, reassuring her she had done nothing wrong. She did what she knew to do. By giving her a few tools and techniques to evaluate her son's behavior, I helped her see through the eyes of a therapist, so she could work with him when I wasn't there.

This approach teaches us to see children differently, and we begin by healing the child within. The child carries the fear and shame imposed by our culture and upbringing. We carry the wounded inner child with us and inflict our fear and shame on our children. To break the cycle, we must heal and empower ourselves and then, in turn, empower our children. I say this with the deepest conviction, having witnessed the truth of it with my own children.

CHAPTER 21

Becoming Visible

The More We Honor and Respect Ourselves, The More We Honor and Respect Our Children

IN LOVING OURSELVES WE DEMONSTRATE to our children what honor and integrity is all about. Children learn from what they see, not what we say. There is no greater gift to bestow upon our children.

The theme of my life and this book is about making every child visible. As a parent, I recognize how my two children challenged my life, helping me wake up to see the world differently. I had the choice to view parenting as a blessing or a curse. My experience was mixed.

At first, I viewed parenting with Jessica as a curse because I lacked awareness of how to cope. Basically, I was struggling in my own life just to survive. As I entered upon a healing path and came to wholeness, I then could allow Jessica to heal herself. In retrospect, it's clear that Jessica needed to act out as part of her own learning and healing process. This stressful period provided her the opportunity to heal the grief, disappointment, fear and self-doubt of her own wounded inner child. Jessica had to individuate and separate from her father and me to discover her authentic self and live life with dignity and grace.

In the past five years Jessica has transformed her life. Through our own individual healing processes, we have complemented and supported each other every step of the way. By opening and letting go, I opened the door for her to find personal freedom. I'm grateful for all the lessons she provided along the way.

I applaud Jessica's strength, tenacity and courage to find her own path to freedom. She helped me learn the art of letting go and standing up for myself by mirroring my own disempowerment and disease. Jessica was doing what she needed to do to survive. She, too, is a real warrior, and I am blessed to have her as my daughter.

By the time Benjamin decided to step out of the box, I was already well into my own healing and realized how I had been blessed all along. I had two children who guided me in differentiating between what was really important—loving unconditionally—and what were simply old, dysfunctional belief patterns.

I made the choice to leave my own unhealthy conditioning and step out of the box. Once I made the choice, I had an easier time in all areas of my life, even with my children. When Benjamin decided not to return to college after his first year, it would have been hypocritical of me to insist that he stay in school when, in truth, I believed he should follow his heart.

How could I have thought differently? A year before I had followed my own heart, leaving my husband, home and the life I had known. I had no security in that decision other than the prompting of my soul. Of course, I was concerned and worried about Ben's choice. As a college graduate, I knew the importance of getting a good, solid education. But I had to look beyond that, beyond my needs and desires, in order to see things through his eyes and with his vision.

I had already learned through my experience with Jessica that I needed to get out of the way and let her live her own life. I had to let go and allow my children to live their lives as they wanted to, not as I desired. Children need to be loved and honored for who they are. They're not here to live our dreams, but to live their own, even when they make no sense to us as parents.

What I'm suggesting isn't an easy task for most parents, including myself. It's been almost two years since my son decided not to return to college. He has spent that time finding his way, engaging in activities that feed his soul. He's currently the editor of a skateboarding magazine, *Poweredge*, and has completed a documentary on autistic children, *Vision of Wholeness,* as well as a full length documentary about skateboarding, entitled, *We Are Skateboarders*—works that have brought him recognition at film festivals and other venues.

Ben made this decision with his heart, not his mind, turning down an easy life for living his passion. Ben was a fortunate child, who had a trust fund that paid for his college expenses and lifestyle. All he had to do was live as a typical college student and go through life as prescribed. But he couldn't follow that preset path because he would have denied his dreams, his passion, by remaining in school, safely caged in other people's dreams for him.

Ben believed in his core that there's a difference between just living and being radiantly alive. He has chosen to be alive, not live within the confines of old-paradigm thinking. He has experienced difficult times, severe loneliness, and disenchantment with the world and its rigid thinking. Some days have been extremely tough for him, while others have been filled with pure joy. In either case, he has been living his dream, knowing that because he is following his soul's destiny, he can live no other way. Like my courageous son, that same spiritual intelligence has been guiding me. How, then, can I deprive my son of his freedom? I may have more life experience than he does, but I can't superimpose my personal beliefs onto him. The realization that Ben can trust his own inner wisdom to guide him has brought peace to my soul.

Today Ben continues to "do his thing," writing for the magazine, skateboarding and sharing his light with others who honor his unique gifts and vision of the world. After enduring trials and tribulations, Jessica has turned her life around by becoming grounded and focused. Witnessing her growth has been an indescribable gift. In the five years since she left the family home, she pursued her studies and learned the intricacies of surviving and thriving, transforming herself into a kind, openhearted and compassionate woman. Today, we're extremely close, enjoying and respecting each other in ways that would have been impossible four years ago. I feel such joy that Jessica and I have transformed our past relationship into one filled with tenderness, ease and grace.

Jessica has graduated from college and plans on going to graduate school, where she'll study to become a social worker. Her healing journey has inspired her to become a healer herself, giving back to others the gifts she has received. Her intuitiveness and natural healing energy will be an inspiration for others. What joy it brings to share spiritual conversation, insights and depth with my amazing daughter. She has emerged as a light being, graced with an abundance of innate wisdom and a deep knowing of how to relate to others, and she does this with a spirit of joy and warmth.

By not interfering with my children's lives, I've enabled them to rise to their highest potential. Of course, as their mother I provided guidance to them when they requested it, without being attached to the outcome. I learned to love them unconditionally and without judgment. In this process, the more I learned about myself, the more they settled, and over the past few years, the three of us have grown up together. Today, both my children live their lives deeply. Guided by spirit in their actions, they have learned to trust their inner voices.

I've accepted that what was important for me when I grew up isn't important to some of today's children. They're another breed, carrying a different vibration altogether. Because what they need is to be seen and heard for who they are, we must not make them feel invisible because of our shortsightedness. Parents must give their children the freedom and joy to explore the universe in which they live. As parents and adults learn to go within, clean out the cobwebs and reveal their hidden secrets, they'll inevitably see their children more clearly. To be a clear reflection of the truth for their children, parents need to ask themselves, "Who am I at the core of my heart and soul? Do I allow my children to shine in all their glory?" If the answer is unclear, you're still hiding behind someone else's expectations and desires.

To create an enlightened culture, we must encourage the invisible child to become visible. We must give each of them the freedom to live in authenticity. Are you living your authentic life? Have you said to yourself, "This is who I am in all my honor, dignity, and grace?" No matter what others might say, you can have the courage, confidence and awareness to live with unparalleled freedom and complete authenticity.

AFTERWORD:
THE JOURNEY CONTINUES

THERE IS NO SURPRISE THAT the pain I felt in my heart manifested in a physical disease. As my heart healed from the pain of isolation and abandonment, my hands healed, and I slowly regained the strength I had lost years before. Forty years later, I am blessed with the capacity, both physically and spiritually, to hold the key that unlocked my *invisible child* and live the life I deserve.

Every day my journey continues to bring forth more healing and new opportunities. When people and events in my life trigger old fears, I know that the universe is providing me with opportunities to continue my healing. On those days that I temporarily forget that I'm on the right path, I look at my hands and feel the softness in my heart for a reminder that I've transformed my life from survival and disease into joy and wellness. Sometimes I lie in bed and cry, "Why God, why another lesson?" Other times I feel such joy and oneness with the world around me that I'm totally overwhelmed and amazed by my ongoing physical and psychological healing.

Today I'm grateful for all the healing I have gone through and the discoveries I've made over the past 11 years. While people and events in my life will always trigger something from my past, I've chosen to see each and every event as a teaching opportunity.

As I write this in the spring of 2010, I see clearly the vast amount of healing I've accomplished. Writing this book was a monumental undertaking in my healing process. The healing of my heart and soul continues to be an ongoing process as new people and revelations surface. When people enter my life who trigger old patterns, I instantly sense that little girl within me, the invisible child, resurfacing. Instead of reacting in unconscious ways, I recognize old patterns, own them and let them go. Healing for me happens on a cellular level. When I understood that my relationships and self-concept were limiting and unhealthy, I was guided to healers who helped me transcend my past and move into healthier life patterns. Instead of living to survive, I survived and learned how to live, and in the process I accepted that healing is different than being cured. I also learned to be a co-creator of my own destiny by getting quiet and listening to the still, small voice within. In this way, I appreciate life's richness as I continue to open myself to its larger dimension. In the process, I've learned to embrace my own unique destiny.

As I was writing, I found it fascinating that events in my life were paralleling events in the book. It was as if I was recapitulating my life, bringing the past into the present moment to completely release old ways of reacting. For example, while I was writing about my early hospitalizations and treatment for a lifelong debilitating disease, I was hearing in present time from my new physician that I needed to have a swine flu shot to prevent becoming paralyzed due to my illness. I walked out of his office filled with tears and fears, but quickly processed these old reactions by remembering that I no longer was a diseased person. Similar issues regarding isolation, loneliness, inadequacy and relationships with men all resurfaced for me to witness. If I was writing about it, it reappeared in real life. This time I felt it and released it. Writing my life story has been an amazing healing experience.

Living in California was a gift from the universe that enabled me to become fully visible. Being alone for the first time in many years, I had to see myself without holding on to comforting illusions, the hope that someday a special someone would magically appear to rescue me and make my life better. I spent years in that illusion. Being unattached to a partner enabled me to be fully present to myself without distractions. It opened the door to self-discovery by eliminating all hiding places that kept me from writing my story. I was upfront and naked, an open book, so to speak. Writing my story made me visible to myself. Now I'm free to be fully seen, fully heard and fully present. I am visible.

I'm grateful to have shared my story with you. I've always believed that if I could heal, anyone could heal. If I've empowered one person to have the courage to have enough self-love to heal, then the story was worth every tear that fell from my eyes. Here I AM!

In June 2010, with my heart, mind and soul open to receive, I was guided to return to the East Coast to be with my parents who have been seriously ill for some time, my mother with a late stage cancer and my father with a rare lung disease. I made a vow to myself that I would be fully present for them in their time of need. I stand here now with love in my heart and open hands to assist them in any way I can as they continue to battle their dis-eases. My mother, in return, has opened her heart to me in way I never thought possible. We have begun a new dance, one based on love, appreciation and the full acceptance of the other.

The day I made the decision to self-publish, in 2011, I felt a gnawing ache in my belly, realizing my parents would soon read my story. My heart knew the timing was right. Later that night it became l clear that I had some residual fear of what their reaction would be. I was being faced with another choice point.

The next day when I went to visit my mother in the hospital, I shared my decision to move ahead with the book. She was excited and asked when she could read it. I sat there with a few tears in my eyes and said, "I do not think you will like it.' She replied, "Why, is it a mommy dearest?" I said, "No, it's not, but it's my truth and my truth might be hurtful to you. I am not angry. I could not have written the story if I was filled with anger."

I said this as she lay in her hospital bed receiving chemotherapy. I knew when she asked me to read the book that I had to make a choice. The choice for me was to stay in my integrity and honor, release all fear and let go of the outcome. I shared the premise of the book and my belief that there's an energetic core to all dis-ease. She listened as I express myself, without judgment.

As I kissed her goodbye I said, "Please read my book in your higher self." She replied, "I will." I walked away knowing that was the last remnant of being invisible. I was ready to completely show up.

As I write these final words, I know the Universe has given us a tremendous gift—an opportunity to rewrite the script and show up differently. With gratitude in my heart I offered, "Mom, I am here for you and I will remain here as long as you need me. I give you my word."

Indeed, this healing journey has taken me from heartbreak to bliss.

"Life is a vibrating possibility up to the last millisecond." —Carl Johan Calleman

EXERCISES

I HAVE INCLUDED TWO EXERCISES that I believe will assist you on your journey. I recognize that my path included many outside interventions from gifted healers and readers over the course of the past five years. I appreciate that everyone may not have the finances to support such an endeavor. For me, because I was in crisis, I felt I had no other choice. I was fortunate enough to support this process through my alimony and disability income.

May these exercises below be tools for transformation without incurring any financial expense for you. I have done quite a lot of work, and it brings me great pleasure to share my learning with you.

Exercise 1: Writing as a Therapeutic Tool to Heal the Wounds of the Inner Child

Heal Yourself—Empower Your Child
Empower your Child—Heal Yourself

To heal for real, you must heal the child within. Acknowledge the pain and trauma that the inner child holds by giving her permission to release all energetic connection to past trauma and abuse of any nature. By releasing old baggage and struggle, you can free yourself of any shame or grief that, unknown to you, still resides at the core of your being.

When your inner child is healed you'll see the world through new eyes of empowerment, freedom and compassion.

Your child will feel whole in herself, fully capable of creating from a new level of self. She will create a life of freedom and inner peace by listening and following internal guidance for support and affirmation.

Today's children require adults who live with honesty and integrity and who truly honor themselves by being authentic. These children arrive in the world already grounded in this knowing. If, as adults, we don't relate to them with this same depth of being, we separate ourselves from them, and the disconnection between adults and children begins. Most of us experienced this disconnection in our own childhood. We felt it as a deep sadness and yearning to belong, to be acknowledged and loved for our essential selves. When we as parents heal ourselves, we heal our children at the same time, thus providing a safer, more loving environment for the beings we birth into this world.

Close your eyes. Go within and remember a time as a child when you felt a sense of disease, disconnection, separation from the source of your being.

Enter that feeling. Energetically BE it, feeling what it was like when you first experienced it. Feel the sensations that arise and the yearnings that come forth. If tears well up, allow them to flow. Feel the truth rise up from inside you. FEEL, FEEL, FEEL with every cell in your body. Then write down your feelings with a tactile, kinesthetic sense, writing from the hidden depths of your being. Write with a total disregard for spelling and grammar; instead, let your feelings flow, releasing the energy of that inner presence that has accompanied you for years, even though you were unaware of it. Welcoming it will heal you on a cellular level, as well as psychologically and spiritually. You'll be free to be YOU, the YOU that radiates joy and aliveness. Know that you've returned to your authentic self. Repeat this exercise for each occurrence in your life that you wish to release energetically. Now introduce the new you to your inner child and watch her thrive as she grows up with the gift of empowerment you've given her, the gift you'll pass on to the next generation. Congratulations!

Exercise 2: Seeing Through the Eyes of the Child

You can chose to do this exercise with your inner child or with the child you gave birth too. This exercise gives you the opportunity to see how your child sees the world. Close your eyes, recall a situation that has an emotional charge, and see yourself as the child who's experiencing it. Now climb inside your child and look through her eyes. What do you see? How does the world look through this perspective? Does it feel different? How?

Now write what you see and feel from your heart, not from your head. Because this is an exercise grounded in feeling, it's important to keep intellectual understanding at bay. If you want to visualize a particular event, feel free to do so, especially if visualizing helps to evoke feelings. For instance, remember the last time you had a dispute with your child or a reaction to something he or she did or said. You can also visualize a time or place, such as dinnertime or a softball game. Stay in your feelings and be ready for amazing insights to surface as you view the world through the eyes of the child.

ACKNOWLEDGMENTS

WITH MY DEEPEST GRATITUDE I thank everyone who encouraged me to speak up and share my miraculous story so that others will trust that they too have the power to completely transform their lives.

To the angels, healers and teachers that appeared in my life to make this miraculous journey possible. Without your gentle support and intuitive guidance I might never have had the courage to heal.

A special acknowledgement to the three angels that appeared in the medical world: Drs. Mark R. Belsky, Steven H. Horowitz and Seymour Gendelman. Thank you for your medical expertise and your spiritual wisdom and grace. I am grateful beyond words.

I want to thank my friends who have been a witness to this amazing transformation. Thank you for your ongoing encouragement, faith and the untiring support you have offered me throughout this process. I appreciate the hours you each spent reviewing my manuscript, providing me with invaluable feedback. With heartfelt gratitude, thank you—Valerie Sargent, Keith Harrington, Laura Beth Straight, Gail Rulhman, Lucy Cartwright, Melissa Rubin, Liz Borman, Deborah Nelson, Paul Morris, Naomi Diamond and Mark Collins. My special thanks go to my dear friend Carole Hodges, not only for her support but for photographing the author and cover pictures.

To my editors, Ron Miller, Stephanie Gunning, Ellen Kleiner and Robert Mayer, thank you for believing in my work and for your professional skills, encouragement and constructive feedback. Each of you played a significant role in the development of this project. More importantly, I thank you for honoring me and seeing the bigger picture.

And lastly, to my beautiful children, Jessica and Benjamin, for your unconditional love and support. Thank you for sharing this journey and choosing me to be your mother. You are the two bright lights in my life, and for that I am blessed.

ABOUT THE AUTHOR

LAURA MAYER, Founder of Soul Dancing Healing Practice, is a spiritual transformation counselor and a licensed occupational therapist (OT). She received her undergraduate and graduate degrees in occupational therapy from New York University. Later, becoming a certified facilitator in Soul Memory Discovery and Indigo Spiritual Healing, Laura opened a private practice that now includes energetic healing (using her hands as a guide), as well as simply intuiting and holding space for others to transform their lives as she has done. Her work with children and the inner children of adults is based on the dramatic self-healing experience that is at the center of *Unlocking the Invisible Child*.

Laura's professional career spans three decades as a licensed OT in psychiatry and pediatrics, and more recently as an energetic healer engaging children, parents and other adults to look deep inside and heal for real—from the pain lying dormant at their core. Her clinical experience includes serving as director of the occupational therapy departments at Silver Hill Foundation and Stony Lodge Psychiatric Hospital, supervisor at Tufts-New England Medical Center's outpatient psychiatric hospital, as a school-based occupational therapist, and as the owner of a private OT practice in New York. Based on her courage to "step outside the medical box" and heal herself from a highly debilitating and life-threatening condition through energetic and intuitive guidance, she is a living example of possibility, and provides the impetus for others to heal. Laura has the gift of seeing every situation from many sides—patient, clinician, child, mother, the wounded, the healed and the wounded healer. She currently resides in Tenafly, New Jersey.

For further information on her healing practice, workshops and speaking engagements, visit her website at www.dancingheart dancinghands.com

CPSIA information can be obtained at www.ICGtesting.com
Printed in the USA
BVOW03s0917160114

342030BV00001B/3/P

9 781452 541907